Dictionary of Polling

DICTIONARY OF POLLING

The Language of Contemporary Opinion Research

Michael L. Young

GREENWOOD PRESS

New York • Westport, Connecticut • London

Library of Congress Cataloging-in-Publication Data

Young, Michael L.
    Dictionary of polling : the language of contemporary opinion
research / Michael L. Young.
        p.   cm.
    Includes bibliographical references and index.
    ISBN 0-313-27598-X (alk. paper)
    1. Public opinion polls—Dictionaries.   I. Title.
HM261.Y684   1992
303.3'8'03—dc20   91-24198

British Library Cataloguing in Publication Data is available.

Library of Congress Catalog Card Number: 91-24198
ISBN: 0-313-27598-X

First published in 1992

Greenwood Press, 88 Post Road West, Westport, CT 06881
An imprint of Greenwood Publishing Group, Inc.

Printed in the United States of America

The paper used in this book complies with the
Permanent Paper Standard issued by the National
Information Standards Organization (Z39.48-1984).

10 9 8 7 6 5 4 3 2 1

For my grandparents, Mary Louise and Roy

Contents

Preface

Dictionary of Polling defines the most important terms in contemporary public opinion research. These are the approximately four hundred words that mark out the field of polling--the words necessary to command before one can claim literacy in the field. These words can fairly be described as the language of polling.

This book has been written with two primary audiences in mind: the people who produce polls, that is, pollsters; and the people who use polls. For pollsters and other professionals working in the survey research field, this book is designed to be used as a ready reference source. For poll users--journalists, political professionals, elected officials, and federal, state, and local officials are among this second audience--this book provides a guide to practice and usage in the field.

Approximately four terms were considered for inclusion for every term finally included. Two main criteria were used to determine which terms would be chosen: (1) a minimum of five citations in books or journals was required before listing a given entry; (2) most highly technical or specialized terms were excluded, on the grounds that they would not be relevant for most readers. In practice, excluding highly technical terms meant that the more esoteric sampling terms and infrequently encountered statistical terms do not appear in *Dictionary of Polling*.

A final word about organization: the text is designed to be used in two main ways. First, the alphabetical format facilitates direct reference to the approximately four hundred entries. A reader looking for the term "response rate," for example, would simply turn to the Rs. Most main terms also include extensive cross listings to other terms in the book so a reader can follow terms through a reference chain of related terms.

A second way to use this book involves the index at the back of the book. The index enables readers to track major themes or ideas discussed in the main entries. A reader may turn to any topic listed in the index and then follow that topic through all the polling terms related to it.

Acknowledgments

I am indebted to my colleagues, friends, and students for the generous support and helpful advice received while writing the *Dictionary of Polling*. There are several people who I wish to thank individually.

Margaret DeGrange, my "home editor" and typist par excellence, who aided me enormously in pulling together the manuscript, detecting my innumerable errors, and somehow magically turning it all into "the book."

Anita Alleman and Louise Morgan, friends and Penn State secretaries, who kept track of me while I was keeping track of the book.

Dr. Robert Bresler, Penn State Harrisburg colleague, friend, and Head, Division of Public Affairs, who provided support and encouragement through the project.

Dr. Christopher McKenna, a Penn State Harrisburg colleague offered many valuable ideas and suggestions which have found their way onto these pages.

Penn State Harrisburg's Associate Dean of Research, Dr. Howard Sachs, supported an early version of the project.

Berwood Yost, Director of Penn State's Survey Research Center and polling colleague, read major sections of the manuscript and supplied many useful constructive ideas.

Mildred Vassan, Political Science Editor at Greenwood Press, had the prescience to "acquire" the book. Mim was immensely helpful in suggesting format changes and other editorial improvements.

Penny Sippel, Production Editor at Greenwood, had the practiced skill to pilot it through all the esoterica of production, and the endless patience to deal with the glitches and hitches that came up along the way.

Lastly, I wish to thank the scholars and practitioners of polling whose intellectual legacy inspired this book. Only before you become a book author can you hold the naive idea that authors "write" books. Perhaps authors write down books, but the books themselves are written by the author's intellectual benefactors. To this book's intellectual benefactors, the community of polling and public opinion research, I thank you.

Dictionary of Polling

Introduction

The literature of modern polling falls into two main categories:

1. The Methodological Literature--the larger of the two main categories, includes:

    general reference
    interviewing
    sampling
    question writing

2. The Context Literature--the second main category, includes:

    history of polling
    theories of polling
    political polling
    critiques of polling
    poll evaluation
    media and polling

This introductory section discusses first the methodological literature, then second the context literature, with particular emphasis on the leading books and articles in each topic area.

THE METHODOLOGICAL LITERATURE OF POLLING

General Reference

Polling methodology has been enriched with many good general reference overviews of the field. Among these are many older books, such as Pauline Young's *Scientific Social Surveys and Research* (1949) and Mildred Parten's *Surveys, Polls and Samples* (1966), both still widely used. Another older general reference is C. Y. Glock's *Survey Research in the Social Sciences* (1967), which considers in separate chapters the uses of survey research in each of five academic areas: sociology, psychology, anthropology, economics, and political science. Also not to be overlooked among older books is C. A. Mosher and G. Kalton's *Survey Methods in Social Investigation* (1972), a balanced, competently written, and generally useful text that handles exceptionally well the topics of sampling and response errors. Probably still the leading general reference on methodology is Earl Babbie's *Survey Research Methods* (1973), which integrates theoretical and applied issues especially well. Also widely used is Charles H. Backstrom and Gerald Hursh-Cesar's *Survey Research* (1981), a source particularly strong on sampling, interviewing, and survey analysis.

The 1980s produced two handbook-style general references: Peter Rossi and colleagues' *Handbook of Survey Research* (1983) and Charles Turner and Elizabeth Martin's *Surveying Subjective Phenomena* (1984). Rossi's *Handbook* features many leading writers in the field in separate essays on their methodological specialization. Martin's book covers methodological topics extensively. Both volumes include exhaustive indexes.

One other book, Don Dillman's *Mail and Telephone Surveys* (1978), also deserves listing as a major general reference. It is the leading source for the design and implementation of mail surveys.

Interviewing

Interviewing is a polling method with roots in several social science disciplines, including sociology and psychology. Many of the general reference sources cited above, such as Babbie, along with Backstrom and Hursh-Cesar, put substantial emphasis on interviewing. Among single subject sources, *The Interviewer's Manual* (1976) is still the most widely used reference on interviewing. Produced and published by the Survey Research Center of the University of Michigan's Institute for Social Research, it has been used to train thousands of interviewers across the United States.

One of the best overviews of the interviewing process is Arthur Kornhauser and Paul B. Sheatsley, "Questionnaire Construction and Interview Procedure" (1976), a short but balanced distillation of interviewer techniques. Also worthwhile is Lewis A. Dexter's *Elite and Specialized Interviewing* (1970). Dexter includes a large, partially annotated bibliography with a good mix of general articles and monographs on the elite interview. Two older sources are still prominent: one is Raymond Gorden's *Interviewing: Strategy, Techniques, and Tactics* (1969)--very good for its scope and balance; another is Robert Kahn and Charles Cannell's *The Dynamics of Interviewing*, (1967)--a very readable yet scholarly theory of interviewing that uses concrete applications and examples.

Sampling

The development of sampling theory made modern probability polls feasible. As with interviewing, many good sampling sources are found in general reference category books. Rossi and colleagues *Handbook of Survey Research* (1983) is one example; another is Charles Roll and Albert Cantril's *Polls: Their Use and Misuse in Politics* (1972), which includes perhaps the single most lucid discussion extant of applied political sampling.

The classic sampling reference is still Leslie Kish's *Survey Sampling* (1965), a sometimes difficult, but thorough, treatment of sampling theory and practice. Two other older works are still widely cited: Donald P. Warwick and Charles A. Lininger, *The Sample Survey* (1975), a good broad-scope treatment; and William Cochran's *Sampling Techniques* (1978), which is somewhat more abstruse and theoretical. Maurice H. Hansen, William N. Hurwitz, and William G. Meadow's *Sample Survey Methods and Theory* (1953), almost forty years old, is considered a classic. This book has an especially crisp discussion of cluster sampling.

Among more recent books on sampling, Seymour Sudman's *Applied Sampling* (1978) is very good-- short on esoterica and long on practice. *Applied Sampling* is particularly useful because it is written with a sensitivity to two practical constraints faced by many researchers: limited resources and limited knowledge of sampling. Two other useful texts are Krewski and colleagues *Current Topics in Survey Sampling* (1981) and Des Raj's *The Design of Sample Surveys* (1972). For concise, clearly written sampling material, Isidon Chein's "An Introduction to Sampling" (1976) is probably the best source.

Question Writing

Pollsters now generally acknowledge question wording to be the most critical variable in determining the accuracy of polls. A poll is unsound and unreliable far more often because of poor questions than because of such things as sampling error or interviewing technique. Stanley Payne's classic *The Art of Asking Questions* (1965) is still the single best guide to question wording. Also good is Patricia Labaw's more recent *Advanced Questionnaire Design* (1981), which stresses techniques for producing clear, valid questions. Two standard general texts on questions and questionnaires are Howard Schuman and Stanley Presser's *Questions and Answers in Attitude Surveys* (1981), and A. N. Oppenheim's *Questionnaire Design and Attitude Measurement* (1966). Paul Sheatsley's "Questionnaire Construction and Item Writing" (1983) is well written, concise, and thorough.   John Robinson and Robert Meadow's *Polls Apart* (1983) offers solid scholarship on the influence of question on poll accuracy and reliability.   Still widely used is Robinson's *Measures of Political Attitudes (1968)*, which contains individual questions and elaborate scales, used on polls done for the University of Michigan's Institute for Social Research.

THE CONTEXT LITERATURE OF POLLING

History of Polling

Brief histories of polling appear in many standard public opinion texts, such as Bernard Hennessey's *Public Opinion* (1985); Harwood L. Childs's *Public Opinion: Nature, Formation, and Role* (1965); and V. O. Key's *Public Opinion and American Democracy* (1967).   A comprehensive review of the straw polling era (roughly 1820 to 1930 in the United States) is Claude Robinson's *Straw Votes* (1932), while George Gallup, Sr. deals with many historical issues in *The Sophisticated Poll Watchers Guide* (1972).   More systematic is L.John Martin's "The Genealogy of Public Opinion Polling" (1984), which tracks the pedigree of modern polling from its historic roots in ancient Greece, and its intellectual roots in philosophy, mathematics, and economics.   Peter Rossi and his colleagues' *Handbook of Survey Research* (1983) provides a good, albeit brief, account of survey history from its antecedents in census taking, straw polling, and quota sampling.   Jean Converse's *Survey Research in the United States: Roots and Emergence* (1987) is one of surprisingly few broad-scope treatments of modern polling.   The best short account of U.S. polling history is still Melvin Field's "Opinion Polling in the USA" (1983), a chronology of the milestones of polling since 1932.   Similar historical accounts in Robert Worcester's *Public Opinion Polling* (1983) cover polling history in several countries, including England, France, and Germany.

Theories of Polling

While there are no comprehensive theories of polling; there are two popular theories unique to polling and survey research.   The most prominent of these is Elizabeth Noelle-Neumann's "spiral of silence" hypothesis, described in *The Spiral of Silence* (1984).   The book describes a general theory to explain how majority opinion forms and becomes predominant.   A second important theory about polling is the "pluralistic ignorance" hypothesis.   Pluralistic ignorance holds that most people are usually ignorant of real public opinion on any given issue.   Consequently, majority opinion is regularly mistaken for minority opinion, and vice versa--see, for example, Hubert O'Gorman's "White and Black Perceptions of Racial Values" (1979).

Polling practice itself is influenced by a number of theoretical perspectives. Sampling, for example, is based on an elaborate set of mathematical and statistical assumptions, referred to generally as probability theory. Similarly, interviewing is underlaid by several theories of social interaction and social exchange (Dillman, 1978; Gorden, 1969). The nature of public opinion itself has been theorized about endlessly; see, for example, V. O. Key's *Public Opinion and American Democracy* (1967), and Walter Lippman's *Public Opinion* (1965).

Political Polling

Political uses first thrust polls into prominence, and politics and polls continue to be closely associated in the public mind. It is not surprising, then, that a generous number of books and articles address political polling. Leading examples include: Larry Sabato, *The Rise of the Political Consultant* (1981), which describes the role of pollsters as political consultants; Barbara Salmore and Stephen Salmore's *Candidates, Parties, and Campaigns (1985)*, which deals with polling in the context of political campaign management; and Charles Roll and Albert Cantril's *Polls: Their Use and Misuse in Politics* (1972), which provides probably the single best account of the role of polls in political life. Several other books deal with polling as an aspect of politics. Representative examples are Edward Schwartzman's *Political Campaign Craftsmanship* (1988), and Herbert Asher's *Polling and the Public* (1988).

Among leading articles dealing with political polling is Mark Levy's "Polling and the Presidential Election" (1984). Margaret Conway's "The Use of Polls in Congressional, State, and Local Elections" (1984) is a rare review of the growing role of polls in state and local politics.

Critiques of Polling

Polling and pollsters attract skepticism and criticism from many quarters. By far the most frequent complaints about polls concern methodology. In its most generalized form, the methodological critique holds that polls are subject to so many technical errors that they are not reliable indicators of public opinion--that is, polls are not to be trusted. The foremost exponent of this view is Michael Wheeler, whose *Lies, Damn Lies and Statistics* (1976) has become an enduring polemic of both polls and pollsters. More restrained, but equally damning, is John Robinson and Robert Meadows's *Polls Apart*, which makes the scholarly argument against relying heavily on polls to make public policy.

Polls are also criticized on nonmethodological grounds. Popular with nonmethodological critics are charges that polls are unethical and manipulative. In her *The Survey Method* (1982), Catherine Marsh is an aggressive proponent for this point of view. Somewhat more restrained is Leo Bogart's *Silent Politics* (1985), which argues that polls can be (and have been) used to mislead public opinion and produce unsound public policy. Also in this vein is a widely read article by Seymour Martin Lipset, "The Wavering Polls" (1976), which argues that polls are usually too crudely done to measure the real subtleties of public opinion--much less to set public policy. The best summary of the major critiques polling is Mervin Field's "Political Opinion Polling in the USA" (1983).

Poll Evaluation

A related stream of the polling literature deals with the evaluation of polls: are they accurate, are they well done, and so on. The most thorough source here is G. Cleveland Wilhoit and David H. Weaver's *Newsroom Guide to Polls and Surveys* (1980), published for reporters confronting technical polling information. Shorter but very useful is Warren Mitofsky and Martin Plissner's "A Reporter's Guide to Published Polls" (1980), which provides lucid explanations of tricky concepts such as statistical significance, weighting, and "likely voters." Also good on evaluation of polls is Burns Roper's "Are Polls Accurate?" (1984), which explains why poll accuracy is rarely a yes-or-no issue. Polls, says Roper, are more or less accurate--the more or less depending on the poll's topic and respondents' familiarity with it.

Media and Polling

No other aspect of polling has received more attention than the relationship of the mass media to the polls. The best-known book describing the use of surveys in news reporting is still Philip Meyer's *Precision Journalism* (1973). Arnold Ismach's "Polling as a News Gathering Tool" (1984) is a good overview of the polling carried out by the print and electronic media.

Articles have figured prominently in this literature, especially those speculating about polls' effect on the media and vice versa. Charles Atkins and James Gaudino's "The Impact of Polling on the Mass Media" (1984) is important for explaining why polls are so popular with the media; Burns Roper's counter article "The Media and the Polls: A Boxscore" (1980) describes the effects media attention has had on polling itself.

A special emphasis of the media/polling relationship has been exit polling-- by far the most controversial aspect of public polling. All the major networks now perform exit polls; the practice began with CBS in 1967. But exit polls still generate fire on two grounds: first, critics say, they reduce voter turnout by disclosing election outcomes before polls close; second, charge critics, exit polls are methodologically flawed in several ways because of special sampling and interviewing demands associated with them.

Mark Levy's "The Methodology and Performance of Election Day Polls" (1983) is the most concise and thorough description of exit poll operations and procedures. Seymour Sudman's "Do Exit Polls Influence Voting Behavior?" (1986) carefully examines the evidence pro and con. Both journalists and pollsters champion exit polling, but they do not always agree on the specifics. Journalist Richard Salant, for example, in "Projections and Exit Polls" (1985), states that polls are news--and that reporting news as early as possible is the "North Star" of journalism. But pollster Burns Roper, in "Early Election Calls: The Larger Danger" (1985), does not go along with this view. Roper argues that journalists have a right to do exit polling, and that exit polls do not influence election outcomes. But, he says, journalists and pollsters, right as they may be, are foolish to use exit polls to forecast elections, because their public images suffer from doing so.

POSTSCRIPT: THE INFLUENTIALS

Relatively few books and articles have had a disproportionately large influence on modern polling. Some of these influential works became important because of their timeliness, others because of their topic, and in one or two cases, because of the stature of the author. The following list is the author's, and no broad consensus is claimed for it. The books and articles cited are not necessarily great literature, but collectively they represent the accumulated knowledge of modern polling.

Books

Babbie, *Survey Research Methods* (1973)
Dillman, *Mail and Telephone Surveys* (1978)
Gallup, *The Sophisticated Poll Watcher's Guide* (1972)
Kish, *Survey Sampling* (1965)
Lippman, *Public Opinion* (1965)
Payne, *The Art of Asking Questions* (1965)
Robinson, *Straw Votes* (1932)
Roll and Cantril, *Polls: Their Use and Misuse in Politics* (1972)
Survey Research Center, *Interviewer's Manual* (1976)
Wheeler, *Lies, Damn Lies and Statistics* (1976)

Articles

Converse, "The Nature of Belief Systems in Mass Publics" (1969)
Gallup, "The Quintamensional Plan of Question Design" (1947)

Lazarsfeld, "The Art of Asking Why: Three Principles Underlying the Formulation of Questionnaires" (1954)
Lipset, "The Wavering Polls" (1976)
Noelle-Neumann, "The Spiral of Silence: A Theory of Public Opinion" (1974)
Paletz, "Polls in the Media: Content, Credibility and Consequences" (1980)
Perry, "Certain Problems in Election Survey Methodology" (1979)
Sudman, "Do Exit Polls Influence Voting Behavior?" (1986)
Tufte and Sun, "Are There Bellwether Electoral Districts?" (1975)
Waksberg, "Sampling Methods for Random Digit Dialing" (1978)

A

AAPOR   The oldest and largest of the professional polling associations. AAPOR is the American Association of Public Opinion Research.   It was founded in 1940 and now has about 1,400 members.   AAPOR is made up of individuals rather than organizations.   Its membership includes both academics and practitioners--who poll for business, politicians, government, and the mass media (AAPOR, 1988, 1989: Directory of Members).

"AAPORIANS" hold an annual conference in the spring of each year. These meetings feature panel presentations of scholarly papers; and lively plenary sessions which focus on a current issue in public opinion research. AAPOR is probably best known for two things: the publication of *Public Opinion Quarterly*, and the AAPOR *Code of Ethics*.

Public Opinion Quarterly is acknowledged as the leading scholarly journal on polls and polling.   Its fall issue each year contains a summary of the proceedings of the AAPOR annual conference. The AAPOR *Code of Ethics* was adopted in 1968.   The actual code (incorporated as Article IX of the association's bylaws) has three separate sections (American Association for Public Opinion Research, 1988).   Section Three, regarding disclosure, is the most specific. It requires that all facts necessary to interpret polls intelligently be disclosed. These include five key items: sponsor identity, question wording, sample characteristics, interviewing techniques used and the dates interviews were conducted (AAPOR Code of Professional Ethics and Practices), (AAPOR, 1988:ii-iv).

AAPOR is one of three professional associations formed to promote and improve polling.   The other two are the National Council on Public Polls (NCPP), founded in 1968, and the Council of American Survey Research Organizations (CASRO), founded in 1975. AAPOR has the broadest base of the three.   NCPP members are mostly larger polling organizations, and CASRO includes members who do a substantial amount of market research (Turner and

Martin, 1984:61-66). *See also* CASRO; DISCLOSURE; NCPP; *PUBLIC OPINION QUARTERLY.*

ABC-*WASHINGTON POST* POLL   *See* MEDIA POLLS.

ACCIDENTAL SAMPLE   *See* CONVENIENCE SAMPLE.

ACQUIESCENCE BIAS   *See* RESPONSE SET.

ADD-A-DIGIT DIALING   A popular technique for constructing a random digit dialing (RDD) sampling frame. Add-a-digit dialing (ADD) addresses one of the most vexing problems associated with random digit dialing: up to 80 percent of randomly dialed calls are made to nonworking numbers (Tull and Hawkins, 1980:127).

There are two main versions of ADD. One of these, known as "Plus One," has two steps. First, an actual telephone number is randomly selected from a telephone directory. Then a number between zero and nine is substituted for the last digit of the directory number. For example, if the number 566-7323 were selected from the directory, the actual number called would be 566-7324 (3 plus 1 =4). The other version of ADD also randomly selects a number from a telephone directory. But instead of adding plus one, a random number generator is used to replace the last two digits of the directory number (Frey, 1983:67-68).

ADD has some methodological flaws. The main one is that it may violate equal probability of selection rules, because some telephone numbers are not listed in the directory. ADD's strength, however, is that it begins with actual numbers occurring in a published directory. This means that ADD produces a high proportion of working numbers. Thus it is more efficient than some other methods, and is particularly efficient when telephone companies assign telephone numbers in large contiguous banks, for example 5,000 through 5,999 (Landon and Banks, 1977:232-241). *See also* RANDOM DIGIT DIALING (RDD).

ADIs   The acronym for Areas of Dominant Influence, a standard system designed by Arbitron to track and measure television audiences. ADIs are based on geography. There are about 212 ADIs across the country. Every county (over 4,000) is assigned to one and only one "dominant" area of influence (Beville, 1981:267). A given county may receive signals from television stations in several markets. But each county is assigned to an exclusive ADI on the basis of measured viewing. The ADI that registers the viewers within a county is that county's ADI (Nieburg 1984:202).

Arbitron's business competition, the A. C. Nielsen Company, operates a system known as DMAs--Designated Market Areas. There are about 220 DMAs across the country. A given county is assigned to a DMA when 5,000 or more of that county's audience watch a given transmitting center. ADIs and DMAs resemble each other. In fact, the two systems often include identical counties. ADI was developed by Arbitron in 1956; Nielsen's DMAs followed quickly. Both systems are now widely used by advertisers, media planners, time buyers, and others (Sabato, 1981:182-185). One unmistakable mark of the influence of ADIs and DMAs is their use beyond television. Today, even newspaper and radio audience ratings are reported by ADIs. *See also*   PEOPLE METER; SPONSOR.

ADVOCACY POLL   Any survey conducted to advance a point of view, or further a partisan objective. Advocacy polls are controversial (Bogart, 1985: 1-13). There are two main concerns about advocacy polls. One is that advocacy research cannot be objective, since its purpose is the promotion of some point of view. In particular, critics charge that advocacy poll question wording almost always reflects the sponsor's bias. The other major criticism of advocacy polling is that it leads to selective reporting of poll results-- contravening the ethical codes of all major polling organizations, which require full disclosure when polls are published.

Charles Turner and Elizabeth Martin (1984:84-86) use the practices of Union Carbide to illustrate the danger of advocacy polling. In the 1980-81 period, that company pursued specific policy goals by commissioning surveys, then selectively reporting only the results favorable to their point of view. To Turner and Martin, the growth of advocacy polling means that "abuses of this type may become an increasing problem in the future."

Not everyone condemns advocacy polling. Supporters defend it as both legitimate and useful. One widely quoted article by Henry O'Neill actually argues that advocacy research is in the public interest:

> This is a large, diverse country trying to function in a
> democratic manner. Advocacy and public policy issue
> research play an important role in this process since research

provides a representative point of view unlike that obtained in
any other way. (Cantril, 1980:178-179)

Arguments like O'Neill's--linking advocacy polling to the furtherance of the
democratic process--do have some merit. Using poll data to support or oppose
a particular proposal raises little serious objection by itself. But advocacy
polling will doubtless continue to be controversial. The survey tool is too
widely accepted not to be pressed, at least occasionally, into service for special
interests or political purposes. And when that happens, it will trigger those
perennial research issues of fairness, bias, and real-world objectivity (Crespi,
1989:40-42).

AGGREGATE DATA   Data such as voting statistics, economic indicators,
and census data. The defining characteristic of aggregate data is exclusion of
information on individuals. For example, election statistics might show party
voting strength by state, county, and precinct levels--but no data about
individual voters.

Aggregate data is widely available and inexpensive. Most of it is collected
and published by the government. It does not pose a confidentiality problem,
because individuals cannot be identified. And aggregate data usually permits
trend analysis from one time period to another (Warwick and Lininger, 1975).

There are some drawbacks to using aggregate data. Accuracy can be a
concern. Census data, for example, apparently undercounts certain groups,
including blacks and Hispanics. Another limitation is timeliness. Much
aggregate data lags months or even years behind the event. Probably the most
serious constraint, however, has to do with the descriptive nature of aggregate
data: it summarizes what happened, but gives no information about why
(Agranoff, 1976:116-117). This inability to answer why can lead to the so-
called aggregative or ecological fallacy; this is the logical error of inferring
information about individuals from summary level data. For example, voting
statistics may show that Republican and Democratic candidates in a certain state
have been receiving stable proportions of the vote for the past ten years. But
this may conceal extreme volatility at the individual level, as voters swing from
one party to the other or as classes of voters shift one way while other classes
shift another. Aggregate data, then, is macro data; it cannot detect micro
change because it does not measure at the individual level (Selltiz, Wrightsman
and Cook, 1976:439-440). *See also* ECOLOGICAL FALLACY.

AGREE-DISAGREE   A question format in which a statement is read and
respondents are then asked if they agree or disagree. For example: "The most

important problem facing the country today is the deficit. Do you agree or disagree?"

More involved, but also more useful are agree-disagree questions that employ a 5-point "Likert scale" to measure intensity of agreement. The example above might be redesigned as follows:

The most important problem in the country today is the deficit. Do you:

STRONGLY AGREE	SOMEWHAT AGREE	AGREE	SOMEWHAT DISAGREE	STRONGLY DISAGREE

Some writers have argued that agree-disagree questions are overused in polls. Another common criticism is that they are poorly crafted. Fowler (1984:31), for example, observes that "asking two or three questions at once" is a very common problem with the agree-disagree format. And Robinson and Meadows (1983:115) conclude that "pollsters would be better off with balanced alternative items than with agree-disagree items." Despite the criticisms, however, agree-disagree questions remain popular. They are simple to construct, allow multiple questions to be asked quickly, and facilitate analysis and reporting. *See also* LIKERT SCALE.

AIDED RECALL   A technique used by interviewers to help respondents answer questions about the past. Aided recall involves some sort of prompting or cues given as part of the question. For example, the interviewer might ask what television programs the respondent watched last week, then read a list of scheduled programs. Or the interviewer might ask what brands of soap the respondent has seen advertised lately, then provide a list of competing brands (Mosher and Kalton, 1972:279,331).

Unaided recall refers to questions that do not prompt in any way. Simply asking people what programs they watched last week is unaided recall; so would be asking about brands of soap seen advertised, without mentioning specific brands. One writer compares the difference between aided and unaided recall to the difference between multiple choice and essay examination questions (Tull and Hawkins, 1980:260). Each technique has strengths as well as drawbacks. Surveys that use unaided recall probably undercount events that occurred some time ago--or were not considered very important when they happened. Aided recall does generally provide more detailed information, but it increases the likelihood of a serious memory bias known as "telescoping"--reporting something as happening recently (last week, last month, etc.) that actually occurred in an earlier interval (Bradburn, 1983:309). *See also* BOUNDED RECALL; TELESCOPING.

ANONYMITY   *See* CONFIDENTIALITY.

APPROVAL RATING   The most frequently asked poll question. Approval rating questions ask respondents how well an incumbent is performing. Gallup and Harris phrase the questions somewhat differently. Gallup says: "Do you approve or disapprove of the way (the incumbent) is handling his job as president?" Harris uses: "How would you rate the job (the incumbent) has been doing as president--excellent, pretty good, only fair, or poor?"

Approval ratings for presidents going back to Franklin Delano Roosevelt show strikingly similar patterns. Gergen and Schambra have summed up the Record:

> From 1945 on, Gallup pollsters have asked people how they think the President is doing his job. The ...approval curves...for all presidents from Truman to Ford tell the same story. Each president begins with great popularity; the trend from there is gently downward with occasional short-lived sharp ups and downs. Finally, toward the end of his term, barring death or resignation, the approval curve turns up slightly: he wasn't so bad after all. (Gergen and Schambra, 1979:64)

Presidential approval ratings are best known, but approval ratings are also used for other incumbents, such as governors, senators and mayors. As job performance indicators, they follow three predictable trends:

1. They fluctuate considerably over time. Harry Truman, for example, ranged from a high of 87 percent approval to a low of 23 percent.
2. Economic conditions profoundly influence approval. A 1 percent rise in unemployment or inflation pulls down presidential approval ratings about 3 percent.
3. Approval ratings decline gradually long term, but short term they shoot up or down sharply in response to passing events or crises. (M. L. Young, 1987:90)

Approval ratings command attention, but there is controversy about what they mean. On the one hand, their political significance is undisputed--high approval ratings enhance an incumbent's power. In fact, as Barry Sussman of the *Washington Post* puts it, approval ratings are themselves a source of partisan power.

> There is no denying that a high approval rating alone has been seen as a potent political weapon by the Washington establishment and political

observers elsewhere.   People equate a high rating with raw power.
(Sussman, 1985:37)

But while approval ratings confer political power, they may not be that
good at gauging actual political support. Pollsters and others have questioned
their measurement validity, pointing out that they are erratic and ephemeral--
sometimes fluctuating wildly with passing events. An even more serious charge
is that approval ratings do not predict voting behavior very well.   Some
incumbents may have high approval ratings, but eventually lose a bid for
reelection, while other incumbents have low approval ratings, but then go on to
win reelection.

Approval ratings confer political power, but cannot always measure the
public support upon which power rests. This apparent paradox is explained the
same way as so many other inconsistencies in polling: the political
establishment pays attention to approval ratings, but the public does not. *See
also* MOST IMPORTANT PROBLEM QUESTION; NAME RECOGNITION
QUESTION.

AREA SAMPLE   *See* MULTISTAGE SAMPLING.

ATOMISTIC FALLACY   *See* ECOLOGICAL FALLACY.

ATTENTIVE PUBLIC   People who follow public affairs regularly and who
hold informed views about current issues.   The attentive public makes up
perhaps 20 percent of the adult population.

The term was coined by Gabriel Almond in his book *The American People
and Foreign Policy*.   The attentive public has been operationally defined in
several ways.   Among the criteria are score on knowledge questions, attained
educational level, and extent of political activity (Almond, 1950: Ch. 7).
Respondent reports of "following the news" or "reading newspapers" are the
single most common variable used to define membership in the attentive public.

Kenneth D. Adler has studied the attentive public concept using survey data
from United States Information Agency Polls. He offers three conclusions: (1)
opinion differs among members of the attentive publics--sometimes sharply--
from opinion held by the general public; (2) the opinions of attentives predict
policy trends better than the opinions of the general public; and, (3) attentives
are not necessarily the best educated members of society.   In fact, attentives

resemble the general public much more than do the best educated people (Adler, 1984:143-154).

The notion of an attentive public has some practical implications for polling. It allows identification of the opinions that "really count." On this point there is little doubt: all the empirical evidence suggests that the attentive public does much more than just know more about current issues. Attentives also have enormous influence on what policy makers do about those issues (Devine, 1970: 41-92; Erickson, Luttbeg, and Tedin, 1988: 280-285). *See also* PHANTOM PUBLIC; PUBLIC OPINION.

ATTITUDES   The deeper feelings and fundamental beliefs that underlie opinions. Attitudes are fixed perspectives--the channel markers that predispose individual opinion.

Methodologists make a sharp distinction between attitudes and opinions:

> We distinguish opinion from attitude in that opinion is focused and expressed. Questions about *opinions* try to learn what people think or feel at a particular point in time about a particular subject. Their thoughts and feelings are, however, the fruits of an underlying, deeply ingrained, attitude system. Questions about *attitudes*, then, tap the respondent's basic personality orientation acquired through years of experience. (Backstrom and Hursh-Cesar, 1981:125)

So opinion is "focused and expressed" in terms of a specific issue or problem--while attitudes are broader, more deeply held, and part of the "basic personality" of a respondent. These distinctions between opinion and attitude are useful, but not always easy to maintain. The typical poll mixes opinion and attitude questions freely. Indeed, whether a question is measuring opinion or tapping attitudes depends more on how the answers are analyzed then on what answers are given:

> For example, a person's opinion on legalization of marijuana may reflect that person's attitude toward societal change, and a person's opinion on the President's performance may reflect that person's attitude toward the political parties. (Weisberg and Bowen, 1977:4)

Some writers differentiate between political polls, which measure opinion, and academic surveys, which tap attitudes. There is some merit in the distinction, since political polls do focus on describing opinions while academic surveys try to explain them. But there are many exceptions to this. Moreover, political polls have increasingly become subject to rigorous analysis and elaborate interpretation (Hennessey, 1985: Ch. 18). One other point about attitudes and opinions: the survey research literature is filled with loose and inconsistent usage in this area. The two terms, attitude and opinion, are often used interchangeably, even in scholarly writing. *See also* NONOPINIONS; PUBLIC OPINION; SURVEYS VS. POLLS.

AUDIMETER *See* PEOPLE METER.

B

BACKGROUNDING   Researching a topic or issue before drafting a questionnaire. Backgrounding provides baseline information about a particular problem area, what resources are available, and what issues are unresolved (Backstrom and Hursh-Cesar, 1981:27-28).

Survey researchers use three important sources of background information. One is the questions developed by other survey organizations working in the same area. Using or adapting earlier questions is considered good practice in opinion research. It allows different surveys to be compared and it promotes improvement in survey methods (Crespi, 1989:97-98).

Another source of backgrounding information is the literature--the books, articles, monographs, reports, government documents and other records that deal with the subject of interest. A third backgrounding source is the expert. This may be a subject matter specialist, or it may be a pollster who has previously done research in the area. Backgrounding builds new research upon the accumulated findings of earlier research. In even more practical terms, it saves researchers from duplicating work already done. *See also* INSTRUMENT.

BACK TRANSLATION   A sophisticated technique for translating poll questions from one language to another--for example, from English to Spanish. Back translation aims for linguistic equivalency-- finding words in the second language that have the same meaning as the words used in the first language. The back translation procedure requires the skills of three bilingual translators. Translator one works from language A to language B; then translator two works from language B back to A; then translator three works from language A back to B, removing discrepancies in meaning that crop up during successive translations (Warwick and Lininger, 1975:166).

An AIDS survey that oversamples Hispanics illustrates the four steps in a back translation:

1. The questionnaire is designed and written in English, then translated to Spanish.
2. A back translation from Spanish to English is completed, comparing both English versions for inconsistencies.
3. The second English version is back translated into Spanish, comparing both Spanish versions for inconsistencies.
4. The instrument is pretested in both English and Spanish versions, revisions are made and field interviews begin in both languages.

Back translation was originally developed to facilitate cross-cultural studies. But today the technique is also used where two languages are widely spoken within a survey population, as is the case with Spanish in the U.S. and French in Canada. Simpler translations of poll questions, however, are still the norm-- such as employing a bilingual to translate from the original language. The time and effort associated with back translation limit its use.

BANDWAGON EFFECT   The power that polls supposedly have to influence voters. The bandwagon effect is the widely held belief that voters change their opinions after being exposed to polls (Roll and Cantril, 1972:25-33).

There are two main versions of the bandwagon effect. Version one is the so-called direct bandwagon effects. Version two describes the so-called indirect effects of polls (Field, 1983:211).

Direct bandwagon effects supposedly operate to encourage voters who support the candidate leading in the poll, and to discourage voters who support those trailing in the poll. A losing candidate's voters, for example, might not vote at all. And undecided voters might flock to the winning candidate. Indirect bandwagon effects supposedly operate not on voters but on campaign workers, active supporters, financial contributors, and even the media. A leading candidate's supporters might work even harder to maintain their lead, or money and endorsements might all go to the candidate who looks like a winner.

The bandwagon effect is controversial among both pollsters and academics. Evidence for and against is mostly anecdotal. So far no one has demonstrated a systematic, direct effect of polls on voters. And there are good theoretical grounds to doubt that the general public is directly influenced by polls. The issue of the indirect effects of polls on voters is more unsettled. Some writers believe that indirect effects from polls do occur. George Gallup, Sr., for example, has talked about the influence of polls on "the three Ms." The three Ms are money, media, and morale--all critical resources to a campaign.

Encouraging polls that show a candidate doing well draw media attention, attract contributors, and raise worker morale.   But discouraging polls showing a candidate doing poorly have the opposite effect--contributions dry up, media coverage is reduced, and campaign workers are dispirited (Gallup, 1972:222-227).   Other writers are skeptical that candidates lose the ability to raise money or attract endorsements simply because they are behind in the polls.   More likely, polls simply reflect the trailing candidates lack of appeal--the same lack of appeal that makes money scarce and endorsements infrequent.   *See also* POLL/MEDIA CYCLE; THE THREE M'S.

BAROMETRIC POLLING   *See*   BELLWETHERS.

BASELINE POLL   *See*   BENCHMARK POLL.

BELLWETHERS   Local voting jurisdictions looked to for early readings of how a state or national election will turn out.   Bellwethers may be precincts, wards, counties, or whole states.   An area is designated a bellwether because it is demographically similar to some larger area--or because its voting patterns historically reflect the voting patterns of the larger area (Young, 1987:82).

Steven J. Rosenstone, who has written extensively about political forecasting, describes three types of bellwethers:

1.   "All or nothing districts," designated bellwethers because they voted for the winner in several past elections.
2.   "Barometric districts," designated bellwethers because they have mirrored the national share of votes between winner and loser.
3.   "Swingometric districts," designated bellwethers because they follow the swings or shifts in party voting from one election to another.   (Rosenstone, 1983:21-24)

Across the United States, seven states and about twenty counties are looked upon as traditional bellwethers.   The states include California, Illinois, Indiana, Iowa, Minnesota, New Mexico, and New York.   Among the prominent bellwether counties are: New Castle, Delaware; Harrison, Indiana; Palo Alto, Iowa; Clark, Nevada; Lake, Ohio; Crook, Oregon; Okanogan, Washington; and Putnam, West Virginia.

Belief in the predictive capacity of bellwethers persists--even in the era of probability polling and "scientific" public opinion research. Journalists, in particular, still watch bellwethers as harbingers of electoral outcome. And sometimes these districts do produce accurate forecasts over long periods of time. Maine, for example, was the premier national bellwether until 1936-- when it was one of only two states to back Landon over Roosevelt. This gave rise to the now famous piece of sarcasm: "As Maine goes, also goes Vermont."

Scholars, as a group, are generally skeptical of bellwethers. They argue that the past accuracy of bellwethers is simply a statistical fluke, due only to good luck and the fact that there are tens of thousands of precincts, wards, and counties. The laws of probability actually predict that some of these precincts, wards, and counties will be right for several successive elections--just by chance alone. Eventually, however, these lucky bellwethers will go wrong, since it is due to chance alone that they have been right in the past (Tufte and Sun, 1975: 1-18).

A barometric bellwether is one that perfectly replicates the demographics of some state, or the nation as a whole. But it is not a reliable guide to the future. The area might have undergone significant population change between elections, making it now unrepresentative. Or it might simply fail to change while the state or nation does change. *See also* PSEUDOSURVEY; STRAW POLL.

BENCHMARK POLL   An opinion survey taken to establish a reference point or baseline for future polls. Benchmarks are planning tools, and are most commonly used in political campaigns. They last thirty minutes to an hour, employ long series of questions, involve large samples, and are extensively analyzed. Mark Levy describes benchmarks taken for presidential campaigns:

> Starting a year or more before the first straw votes, caucuses or primaries, presidential aspirants test the political waters with benchmark surveys. Typically based on hour or longer interviews conducted in the homes of 1500 to 4000 potential voters nationwide and carrying a six-figure price tag, benchmark surveys attempt to gauge a candidate's comparative strengths and weaknesses, to identify long term trends in public opinion and to discover possible campaign themes and issues. (Levy, 1984:88)

Benchmarks yield the kind of information political campaigns need to develop strategy and tactics. Some of the data collected is custom-fitted to the particular campaign. But much of it is boilerplate: electorate demographics, name recognition scores, and trial heats featuring head-to-head matchups with likely opponents (Sabato. 1981:75-81).

Benchmarks are expensive, and they must be done early. Consequently, some campaigns do not use them at all. More and more, however, politicians see benchmark polls as indispensable tools for setting strategy and devising tactics. Benchmarks also have some important functions apart from planning. Among these are demonstrating credibility to skeptical reporters and prospective supporters.

A potential drawback with benchmarks is their timeliness. Campaign are turbulent environments, subject to sudden shifts in conditions and voter sentiment. A nationally known pollster once remarked that the "half life of a poll" is about ninety-six hours--probably an exaggeration, but the point is well taken. The information value of a poll does deteriorate over time. Political polls taken in spring or early summer are usually obsolete by election day (Salmore and Salmore, 1989: 115-121). *See also* TRACKING POLLS.

BLAB WORDS   Words or phrases that convey no concrete specific meaning. Blab words are the abstract, general, often polysyllabic language sometimes used in polls: words like reform, fairness, approval, optimism, policy, and leadership. These words are used in "blab-blab" questions like "Is our foreign policy working?" or "Should the tax laws be reformed?"

The term blab word was coined by Stanley Payne in *The Art of Asking Questions* (1951:149), a now classic treatise on writing clear, concise survey questionnaires. Payne argued that blab words create unreliable information because respondents share no common sense of what they mean. Blab words have so many possible interpretations that one respondent's understanding may differ markedly from another's--or from that of the interviewer.

Methodologists refer to the different meanings people have for the same word or phrase as the frame of reference problem--essentially any confusion about where the interviewer asking questions is "coming from." Blab words always increase frame of reference confusion. Avoiding the blabs reduces the problem (Turner and Martin, 1984:251-256). *See also* GENERIC WORDS; GOOD WORDS.

BLANKS   Names or telephone numbers that turn up in a sample, but no longer exist in the population itself. Blanks, also called "deadwood," might be the name of someone who has moved or died, an address that no longer stands, or a telephone number that does not work (Hoinville and Jowell, 1978:69-71). Blanks cause no particular methodological problem. The proper procedure is simply to ignore them when they are found in the sample. For example, a simple random sample of 500 might yield 25 blanks; the working sample then is reduced to (500-25) 475.

The practical effect of blanks is that the original sample is reduced because the blanks must be thrown out. A sticky problem can occur if blanks can not be identified until after interviewers in the field have encountered them. Even then, however, blanks are rarely a major problem. Researchers simply anticipate some proportion of blanks and set the original sample size high enough to adjust for them (Sudman, 1978:59-60).

Some writers distinguish between blanks and foreign elements. Blanks are listings no longer in the population, while foreign elements are listings still in the population but not appropriate for a particular study. People no longer registered would be foreign elements for a poll of likely voters. And people recently retired would be foreign elements for a study of current wage earners (Mosher and Kalton, 1972:61-63). *See also* COMPLETION RATE; ELEMENTS; RESPONSE RATE; SAMPLING FRAME.

BOILER ROOM OPERATION   The physical location from which telephone interviewing is conducted. Boiler room operations are more clinically known as telephone banks. The term "boiler room" comes from the early practice of locating telephone canvassing operations in basements or other marginal space. Boiler room operations today are more likely to be in modern air-conditioned office buildings than hidden away below floors. Many now have sophisticated equipment, including high tech monitoring devices and computer assisted telephone interviewing systems (CATI).

The typical phone bank operation used for interviewing might have eight to twelve interviewers in a single large room. Each interviewer is equipped with a phone, a list of numbers to dial, and a questionnaire. Often the callers are enclosed within cubicles and connected to a supervisor, who is available to monitor and assist (Nieburg, 1984:115-116). Telephone banks are also popular outside the polling industry, particularly in sales organizations, which use telephone banks to solicit. Sometimes this involves the abusive practice known as "sugging" (selling under the guise of a legitimate poll). Many observers blame declining response rates in bona fide polls to sugging. Certainly deceptive boiler room operations have alienated many people who now may hesitate to be interviewed (Baxter, 1964). *See also* INTERVIEWERS; SUGGING.

BOOKING IN   A monitoring procedure that follows up on interviewing assignments. The person booking in cross-checks each completed questionnaire against the original sample. Telephone and face-to-face interviews are booked in when the interviewer hands in the completed instrument. Mail surveys are booked in when the questionnaire is returned by a respondent (Hoinville and Jowell, 1978:145,121-123).

Booking in has two major purposes. One is monitoring of survey response rates. The other is quality control. Booking in means interviewer work can be continuously evaluated and errors can be corrected. Survey organizations that do not book in are hard pressed to calculate accurate response rates--or to discover and eliminate sloppy field work by interviewers. *See also* COMPLETION RATE; HOUSE EFFECTS; RESPONSE RATE.

BOOSTER SAMPLE *See* OVERSAMPLING.

BORDER BIAS *See* TELESCOPING.

BOUNDED RECALL A technique in which interviewers remind respondents of answers given during earlier interviews. Bounded recall was developed to eliminate a methodological problem known as "telescoping." This is when respondents report something as happening, for example, last week that actually happened two weeks ago. Bounded recall is mostly used with questions about behavior. A respondent might be reminded of what they reported earlier about a purchase or use of some product. Bounding insures that reports about current behavior will not be confused with memories of earlier behavior (Bradburn, 1983:309-310).

Bounded recall can only be used with panel studies, since the interviewer must have information from previous interviews to remind respondents of their earlier answers. Moreover, bounding does not eliminate all respondent memory problems. In particular, omissions--simply forgetting that something happened at all--is still possible. Another technique, aided recall, is used when omission is the problem (Mosher and Kalton, 1972:340). *See also* AIDED RECALL; TELESCOPING.

BUMPER STICKER POLL *See* SILLY POLLS.

C

CALLBACKS   Attempts to reach a respondent who was not available earlier to be interviewed or to check on inconsistent or missing information on the questionnaire.   Callback techniques vary according to the interviewing mode being used--repeat telephone calls for telephone polls; return home visits for face-to-face interviews; and follow up mailing for mail surveys (Alreck and Settle, 1985:404).   Callbacks are time-consuming, can produce reluctant, even hostile respondents, and are often futile.   Nevertheless, they are essential.   If they are not done, the sample becomes unrepresentative, slanted toward people who are at home more often, or are easier to interview (Backstrom and Hursh-Cesar, 1981:115; Martin, 1983:701).

Virtually every poll requires some callbacks, since up to one-half of all initial attempts to interview are unsuccessful for one reason or another.   But callbacks are a technique in which more is not better.   In fact, callbacks are not efficient after the second or third call.   About 95 percent of respondents who will ever be reached have already been reached by the third call.   After that, the completion rate improves only marginally with more call backs (M. L. Young, 1987:83).   *See also*   NOT AT HOMES; RESPONDENT.

CALL-IN POLL   A type of straw poll conducted by radio and television outlets.   Call-in polls register public reaction to recent events by inviting listeners to call a designated number to record their opinion (Weisberg, Krosnick and Bowen, 1989:33).   Cable News Network (CNN) runs a feature called the news night poll that illustrates the style of call-in polls.   During the 1987 Iran-contra hearings, CNN viewers were invited to call a 900 number and record their answer to this question: "Did Oliver North tell the truth when he said President Reagan didn't know about the arms for hostages deal?"   CNN added the following disclaimer: "The news night poll is not a scientific poll but it does represent views on subjects important to our audience."

The most notorious call-in poll occurred during the 1980 presidential campaign.   ABC conducted a call-in after the Carter-Reagan debate, then announced that Reagan had "won." That story not only ran on ABC, but was picked up by some other news organizations. The network was widely criticized for releasing results without issuing any warning about the severe selection bias of this type of poll (Nieburg, 1984:63-64).

Most call-in polls are done by local TV and radio stations. Many of these are occasional, tied to some unusual or particularly compelling situation. Some stations, however, do daily "people polls," which ask listeners to call in and register their view on this or that current issue.

The newspaper/magazine version of call-in polls is the "clip and mail" poll. Readers are asked to fill out and mail in a questionnaire appearing in a newspaper or magazine. Usually these deal with one or two topics of current interest. The publication often follows up with a story or series based on the poll results.

Call-ins are criticized by pollsters and others who allege that these polls are biased, self-serving, and dishonest. The charge is not entirely fair. Like other types of straw polls, call-ins do use procedures that are likely to produce unrepresentative samples. In principle, however, there is nothing wrong with an honest straw poll that discloses its nonprobability basis (Hennessey, 1985:60-64). The problem arises when call-in polls are released without any disclaimer about their validity. Even worse are call-ins that carry misleading disclaimers implying that scientific procedures were used when they were not used (Turner and Martin, 1983:75-76,308-309).   *See also* PSEUDOSURVEY; QUBE POLL; STRAW POLLS.

CALL RECORD   A running log of the calls that have been made trying to reach designated respondents.   Call records are maintained because many interviews cannot be completed on the first call. Most, in fact, require two, three, or even more callbacks! Sometimes interviewers reach a member of the household other than the designated respondent; other times the respondent may be home, but refuses to be interviewed. A call record summarizes these earlier contacts for use when subsequent calls are made (Frey, 1983:159-161,163).

A typical call record uses a block format that fills about half of an 8-1/2" x 11" page. Down the left margin are rows to log calls. Across the top are columns to record date, time, interviewer initials, and a list of common codes-- such as REF (refusal), DISC (disconnected number), NA (no answer), BUS (business phone), and so on (Dillman, 1978:259-265). Researchers estimate that 95 percent of all respondents who can be interviewed will be reached within three calls. Accurate call records make necessary callbacks much more efficient.

They also increase the interview completion rate, and even benefit respondents by reducing the chance of an unnecessary call.   *See also*   CALLBACKS; COMPLETION RATE.

CANNED POLLS   Surveys conducted with a standard set of unvarying questions. Canned polls--also called cut-and-paste polls and off-the-rack polls-- use the same questions over and over regardless of circumstances. Some survey organizations have gained cloudy reputations for their "pulled-off-the-shelf" polls. And where the practice is employed, the notoriety is deserved (Sabato, 1981:96, 314). Good polls are always tailored to the unique conditions and specific objectives of sponsor or client.

On the other hand, however, very few polls are ever totally original. Most pollsters do use some of their own questions over and over, and some borrow or adapt questions from other surveys. There are three main justifications for reusing questions. All three tout the research benefits of doing so.

First, certain kinds of questions (such as demographic questions, and many fixed-choice questions) have been developed from the experiences of countless surveys. Consequently, they are usually better than a new question cooked up for the occasion. Second, standardized questions and scales that have been used frequently by many pollsters allow norms to be established. Pollsters using a standardized question can compare their findings with those of other studies (Sheatsley, 1983:196-198). Third, canned questions often make the design process more efficient. Freed from having to do again what has already been done well, the pollster can concentrate on novel issues that truly require original questions.   *See also*   DEMOGRAPHIC ITEMS; STANDARDIZED QUESTION.

CARAVANING   The practice of "piggybacking" questions onto a poll devoted to another subject--adding public policy questions, for example, onto market research done for a commercial product. Caravaning is rare in political polls, but common in commercial research (Backstrom and Hursh-Cesar, 1981:45). The economic basis of caravaning is obvious. By joining together, several sponsors can "do a poll" at a fraction of the cost they would incur working alone (Marsh, 1982:222-225). Omnibus polls, which have several sponsors, each asking one or more questions, illustrate the caravaning principle.

Caravaning has two main methodological drawbacks--context effects and order effects. Both problems are caused by weak transitions between parts of a questionnaire. The first methodological problem, context effects, occurs when answers given by respondents to a specific question are influenced by other questions or topics in the questionnaire when the question is asked. The second problem, order effects, occurs when respondents' answers are influenced by a previous question (Robinson and Meadow, 1982:21-22). One practical problem with caravaning is the type of questions that can be asked. Space and time constraints usually limit questions to closed types. Open end questions are infrequent. *See also* OMNIBUS POLL; PIGGYBACK POLL.

CARRIER SURVEY   *See* OMNIBUS POLL.

CASE The data collected from one respondent or taken from one questionnaire. Case relates to the notion of "unit of analysis"--what is being studied or analyzed in a poll (Babbie, 1973:190). The unit of analysis may be a person, a family, a dwelling unit, or some group. When it is a person--and that is typical in survey research--the case is the specific individual who is interviewed or completes a questionnaire. Thus case number 614 might be respondent Jim Smith, 722 Crestview Avenue, male, age 41, married, college graduate, telephone number 504-233-7612.

Total cases in a poll equals the number of individuals interviewed. As a rule, case numbers are assigned after a questionnaire is completed and before analysis begins. This allows researchers to track the case back when necessary to recheck the original data (Alreck and Settle, 1985:186). *See also* CALL RECORD; INSTRUMENT; RESPONDENT.

CASRO   Acronym for the Council of American Survey Research Organizations. CASRO is a trade association whose membership comes from companies that conduct survey research. CASRO was founded in 1975. Its charter lists three major objectives: (1) promoting members' interests in the survey research industry; (2) serving as spokesman on industry issues; and (3) establishing and improving professional survey research standards (Nieburg, 1984:259-260). In 1979, CASRO adopted a Code of Standards for Survey Research, which details responsibilities researchers have to clients, respondents, and the public (Council of American Survey Research Organizations, 1982). Prominent in the CASRO code are disclosure standards such as identity of sponsor, time of interviewing, the purpose of the survey, and "any other information that a lay-person would need to make a reasonable assessment of the reported findings" (Turner and Martin, 1984:65-66).

CASRO is one of three national associations formed to promote and improve the polling profession. The other two are AAPOR (the American Association for Public Opinion Research) and NCPP (the National Council on

Public Polls). There is overlap in membership and philosophy among all three groups. AAPOR is the broadest-based of the three; NCPP includes mostly larger polling organizations. CASRO includes members with substantial business and marketing research orientations. *See also* AAPOR; NCPP.

CATI   Acronym for computer assisted telephone interviewing. CATIs are software systems that involve the computer directly in interviewing. Computers are widely used in polling today, but the traditional applications have been in data processing and analysis--all "office" functions. CATI, however, thrusts the computer into the heart of the survey process.

> Under a CATI system, all interviewing is done at a CRT terminal where...the interviewer (keys) responses into a CRT...CATI directs the flow of each interview and instantaneously provides the interviewer with exactly the right question--one question at a time....error messages automatically appear on the screen if inappropriate responses are keyed in....at the end of the interview all respondent replies are automatically and instantaneously entered into the computer memory. (Frey, 1983:145)

Trained interviewers operate CATI systems. They dial a respondent's number then run through their menu of programmed instructions. CATI systems have impressive monitoring capabilities. They can schedule callbacks, record completions, and store detailed information from each interview. CATIs can even perform coding and editing functions (Karweit and Myers, 1983:391-392).

The first CATI system was developed by Chilton Research in 1972. Today most large research organizations have CATIs or are developing its, while smaller organizations are likely to be leasing or purchasing CATI systems. The reasons for CATI popularity are both economic and administrative. CATI systems reduce interviewing time; since interviewing accounts for about one-half of poll expenses, CATI time savings usually mean a substantial cost savings as well. The other main benefit of CATIs is reduction of interviewer error. Programmed error messages eliminate many common interviewer mistakes, while those that do occur are usually detected while the interview is in progress.

These advantages, of course, have a cost. Compared to paper and pencil surveys, CATIs are expensive to design, set up, and operate. They require a substantial capital expenditure and incur heavy administrative costs and overhead. The other major disadvantage of CATIs is the inevitable hardware failures. Downtime, and even loss of data are part of operating reality for any computer system; CATIs are no exception (Frey, 1983:148,149).

CBS-*NEW YORK TIMES* POLL   *See* NETWORK POLLS.

CENSUS   *See* SURVEY VS. POLL.

CHEATER QUESTION   A standard procedure used by pollsters to uncover fraudulent interviews.   Cheater questions--or control questions--are placed in survey questionnaires alongside legitimate survey items.   The main difference between cheaters and other questions is that the pollster can check answers to cheaters for evidence of fabrication.   N. L. Nieburg describes one approach to monitoring the authenticity of reported interviews:

> The control question (is) imbedded in the poll.   It looks like just another question, but instructs the interviewer merely to insert a certain mark on the answer form and the instruction varies on different interview sheets.   Consequently the interviewer (who is told nothing about it in advance) must read every sheet in order to mark the right item in the right way.   If the control question is incorrectly marked the polling organization knows that the interviewer faked the interviews. (Nieburg, 1984:127)

Interestingly, pollsters have been circumspect in describing their use of cheater questions-- referring vaguely to questions that trip up a "dishonest interviewer (to) betray himself in the way they are completed" (Gallup, 1972:102).

Some of the reluctance to discuss the monitoring technique comes from realistic concern about "giving the detailed idea away," as Payne evasively puts it in *Art of Asking Questions* (Payne, 1965:67).   Pollsters themselves claim that cheating is rare--most say that probably less than 5 percent of interviewers ever fudge results.   This may be realistic, but currently there is little hard evidence on the integrity of interviewers.   *See also* MISREPORTING.

CHUNKS   Geographic areas used to carry out multistage sampling.   Chunks are usually city blocks in urban areas.   In rural areas they may be bounded by physical features like creeks and mountains, or political boundaries such as township lines.   The University of Michigan's Institute for Social Research recommends chunks that contain from sixteen to forty housing units (Survey Research Center, 1976:37).

Chunks are actually a middle step in multistage sampling.   Before chunks are selected, primary sampling units (PSUs) are randomly determined. For national surveys, these are the largest metropolitan areas in the country. Within each PSU, specific "sample places" (cities, towns, rural areas, etc.) are drawn. Chunks are then selected within each sampling place. After chunks have been identified, two more steps are usually necessary before interviews can be conducted. Segments, which are parts of chunks having four to sixteen housing units, are defined. Finally, a sample of housing units is drawn from each segment (Welch and Conner, 1975:146-148).

The completely separate term chunk sample is sometimes used to refer to a haphazard or convenience sample. Chunk samples are usually people interviewed because they were available. Chunk samples have the limitations of all nonprobability sampling: they are not necessarily representative of any population other than the sample itself (Kendall and Buckland, 1983:31). *See also* MULTISTAGE SAMPLING.

CHUNK SAMPLE   *See* CHUNKS.

CLUSTER SAMPLING   A sampling technique that locates respondents in groups or batches (clusters) rather than one at a time. Cluster sampling often uses naturally occurring population groupings like schools, offices, civic organizations, and so on. The typical cluster sample is based on neighborhoods. A sample of 1,000 might include 100 cluster neighborhoods; in each of the clusters, interviewers would interview 10 respondents. Five to ten interviews per cluster is considered the ideal range--fewer than five reduces the benefits of clustering, while more than ten risks unacceptably large sampling error (Alreck and Settle, 1985:81-83).

The major appeal of cluster sampling is economics. Clustering reduces interviewing expense because interviews can be conducted within a concentrated area (neighborhood, school, factory, etc.). Clustering also allows interviewing to be done quickly. These advantages, however, incur some cost. On average, a cluster sample produces a sampling error one-third to one-half larger than other sampling methods (Warwick and Lininger, 1975:98-101).

The larger sampling error associated with clustering occurs because people bunched together tend to have similar characteristics and share common opinions. So samples based on clusters must always be larger to match the representativeness of other sampling procedures. In practice, cluster sampling is usually part of a multistage sampling design that may include five or more phases. Only in the final stage are the clusters chosen that contain the respondents who will be interviewed (Babbie, 1973:96-103, 118-128). *See also*

MULTISTAGE SAMPLING; SIMPLE RANDOM SAMPLING (SRS); STRATIFIED SAMPLING.

CODING   The systematic assignment of individual respondent answers to general answer categories.   Coding is done to open-ended questions, while precoding is done to closed-end questions.   Coding and precoding use similar procedures.   Both involve setting up answer categories, designating numbers for them (1, 2, 3, etc.), then assigning respondent answers to the appropriate number code.   There are, however, two differences.   Coding occurs after interviewing, while precoding is done before; coding requires some actual analysis of questionnaire data to establish categories, while precoding uses preset categories.   Earl Babbie elaborates:

> Open-ended items cannot be precoded; coding can occur only after the data have been collected. The categories into which responses are to be coded must be established by closely examining what the respondents actually had to say....In brief, the researcher reviews a sample of the verbal responses to an open-ended question and decides how many different kinds (categories) of responses exist.   Each category must then be defined and illustrated with a concrete example, and a numerical code attached to it. Once this coding scheme has been settled, (respondent responses) can be reviewed one at a time. (Babbie, 1982: 148)

Coding can become involved, because respondents often produce a bewildering array of answers to open questions. Say the following question was asked:

Q. What is the most important problem facing *our* nation today?
     In a reasonably large sample, dozens of different answers would be given.   The coding task is to reduce the data to a usable number of categories.   Schuman and Presser (1981:82) illustrate with actual field data.

> Respondent 001 answers "courts are too easy on criminals"; respondent 123 might answer "fear of getting mugged on the way to work"; respondent 671 answers "not enough police protection." All these answers might eventually be coded *CRIME AND VIOLENCE*.   Or respondent 019 might answer "too many people out of work."   Respondent 311 answers "increase in the cost of living."   Respondent 503 answers "high interest rates." All three

of these answers might eventually be coded *CONCERNS ABOUT THE ECONOMY.*

All coding presents a methodological dilemma: how many summary categories to use. Using too many categories risks missing important patterns in the data; but too few categories means much of the richness and texture of open answers is lost. The best coding always strikes a balance between the extremes, neither too much data nor too few categories. Some coding of open answers is essential--no one could analyze meaningfully hundreds of different answers to the same question--and coding is the only practical way to reduce survey data for computer processing. *See also* PRECODING.

COHORT STUDIES Surveys of some group or special population as it ages. Cohorts is a demographic term that refers to people who have had some common life experience at about the same time. Year of birth is the most common, but cohorts may be designated for such events as first-time voting in a presidential election, year of marriage or graduation from high school or college (Plano, Riggs, and Robin, 1982:22). Cohort studies track the same population (or cohort) for years or even decades. Different samples are drawn from the population each time data is collected.

For example, people voting for the first time in the 1992 presidential election would be the first-time voter cohort for that year. If that cohort was resurveyed every four years (1996, 2000, 2004, and so on), different samples of the 1992 first time voter group would be drawn.

Cohort studies can be used to follow the opinions and views of virtually any cohort on almost any topic. Most studies deal with health, employment, education, and changing social and political attitudes. The cohort is one of three basic survey designs known collectively as longitudinal surveys. Panel studies and trend studies are the others. The common element in longitudinal studies is time: they all collect information over long periods of time. Information collected at one point in time is cross-sectional data (Babbie, 1973:63-65). *See also* LONGITUDINAL SURVEYS; PANELS; TREND STUDIES.

COINCIDENTAL An audience research technique in which radio and television users are interviewed while they are actually listening or viewing. Interviewers call respondents at a particular time, ask if their radio or TV is on, and if so to what program and station it is tuned. Coincidental methodologies vary in complexity. The simplest requires the interviewer to determine if a radio or TV is being used, what program is on and how many people are listening. More sophisticated approaches ask additional questions--about the characteristics of listeners, the number and location of sets in the household, their operating condition, and the station to which they are tuned.

Whether simple or sophisticated, the essence of the coincidental method is timing: it must be conducted during actual listening or viewing. This increases accuracy because respondents do not have to rely on memory. Coincidentals have other advantages, too. Response rates are generally high, supervision and training are minimal, and results can be reported quickly.

There are, of course, disadvantages. Coincidentals do not reach unlisted telephones (unless random digit dialing is used), and they exclude people using TV or radio outside the home (for example in cars). Another limitation is that late night calls or early morning calls are usually not conducted (Belville, 1981:95-103). Coincidentals have been used in the United States since 1929-- apparently always with telephones. A personal interview version of the coincidental has been developed. So far, however, it has been used only outside of the United States, in places where telephones are not available (Raj, 1972:346). *See also* PEOPLE METER.

COMPLETION RATE   The proportion of prospective respondents who were actually interviewed.   Completion rates are calculated as the number of interviews completed over the number of people in the original sample (Frey, 1983:38-40; Babbie, 1982:119,120).   A simple example illustrates the calculation: say 600 of 1,200 persons in the original sample are interviewed or return questionnaires; the completion rate is 50 percent. An important caveat regarding completion rates: usage of the term is not consistent among survey researchers.   Some sources use completion rate as a synonym for "response rate," while others distinguish between the two.

When a distinction between completion rate and response rate is made, it concerns so-called ineligible respondents.   Ineligibles are people originally designated as respondents who later turned out to be ineligible for some reason, such as not being registered to vote (Mosher and Kalton, 1972:66). Completion rates and response rates account for ineligibles differently. Completion rates carry in their denominators everyone originally in the sample, even those who later turned out to be ineligible. Response rates, however, exclude from their denominators anyone who became ineligible for any reason or could not be reached. The practical effect of all this is that the completion rate will always be smaller for any given study than the response rate. The exact magnitude of difference will vary. However, a survey with a response rate of 80 percent but lots of ineligibles might have a completion rate of only 50 percent. *See also* BLANKS; NONCONTACT; RESPONSE RATE.

CONDITIONING   Changes in a respondent's attitude or opinions brought about by repeated interviews. Conditioning is a problem associated with panel studies. The effects of being periodically interviewed may remake respondents in some way so they are no longer typical of the population they represent. Conditioned respondents may become more knowledgeable, may pay more attention to what is going on around them, and may even begin to modify their behavior (Mosher and Kalton, 1972:142-143).

Methodologists identify two conditioning effects. In the first, respondents become acutely aware of the topic about which they are interviewed. Someone on a political panel may begin to read the political news, or someone on a consumer panel may begin to watch prices more carefully.   The second conditioning effect is on the stability of respondent reporting. Respondents try to become more consistent than they usually are. A respondent who is a self-described liberal might try hard to give answers that sound liberal.   Or a consumer who says he "shops price" might try to be consistent in that attitude when answering questions about new products (Warwick and Lininger, 1975:62-65).

Researchers use two techniques to counter conditioning. One of these--the most rigorous and most expensive--requires that a separate control group be interviewed at the same time that the panel is interviewed. Responses from both groups are then compared.   If there are significant differences, they are attributed to conditioning. The other approach used to deal with conditioning concentrates on keeping the panel fresh. Respondents are replaced periodically with new, randomly chosen people. Every three months, for example, 25 percent of the panel might be changed. Neither of these techniques is a perfect solution to conditioning. Both help, but conditioning is really a natural effect inherent in the process of repeated interviews with the same respondents. The best that researchers can do is detect and correct for it. It cannot be prevented (Backstrom and Hursh-Cesar, 1981:107-109). *See also* PANELS.

CONFIDENCE INTERVAL   *See* CONFIDENCE LEVEL.

CONFIDENCE LEVEL   A statistic that expresses the probability that a reported poll finding is correct. Confidence levels are conventionally set at the "95 percent level," and are typically expressed as: "These findings are subject to a sampling error of (such and such) at the 95% confidence level."   This means that there are 95 out of 100 chances the poll results are accurate.   Still another way of understanding confidence level is to read it as the probability that a poll finding comes from an unrepresentative sample. A 95 percent confidence level thus can be read as a 5 percent chance that the poll sample is not representative (Hoinville and Jowell, 1978:56-69).

Confidence interval is a term often confused with confidence level. Both terms involve sampling error, but their meanings are quite different. Confidence interval refers to the range of sampling error for poll results, while confidence level refers to the probability that the sampling error range is accurate (Mosher and Kalton, 1972:73-78). An example to illustrate the difference between confidence interval and confidence level: a national poll of American voters has a sampling error of + / -3 percent and a confidence level of 95 percent. It reports that 60 percent of the sample is opposed to more military spending. Researchers might describe this result by saying they are 95 percent sure (the confidence level) that between 57 percent and 63 percent (the confidence interval) of American voters oppose more military spending (Weisberg, Krosnick, and Bowen, 1989:195-196).

A caveat about interpreting confidence levels and confidence intervals. In principle, a reported 95 percent confidence level means that an unrepresentative sample of respondents is expected about 5 percent of the time--that is, one of twenty polls will be based on bad samples. In practice, however, pollsters use a variety of techniques to guard against even the 5 percent chance of a defective sample. *See also* SAMPLING ERROR.

CONFIDENTIALITY   Assurance given to a respondent that their answers are privileged information. Confidentiality means that responses to questions will not be attributed to a specific person. Someone's voting preference or annual income, for example, will not be revealed. Confidentiality is commonly used as a synonym for anonymity. However, there are important differences that should be maintained. Confidentiality only requires that survey answers not be attributed to a specific respondent. Anonymity requires, in addition, that there be no way that an answer could be traced to a given respondent (Frey, 1983:49-50; Babbie, 1973:350-352).

Confidentiality is both an ethical issue and an interviewing tactic. The ethical issue has to do with protecting respondents from harm that their answers might bring them. In general, the norms of survey research require pollsters to safeguard any data that might affect the welfare of a respondent. But promises of confidentiality are also made to ensure participation in surveys. Most pollsters believe this increases the response rate by reducing respondent anxiety about how results will be used (Sellitz, Wrightsman, and Cook, 1976:244-245).

It is not clear, however, what effect assurances of confidentiality have on response rates. Apparently most respondents do not expect results to be confidential (only 5 % in a 1979 Academy of Sciences study believed census data is confidential). Moreover, there is a question whether respondents care. Some studies, in fact, have concluded that promises of confidentiality from an interviewer do not increase response rates--nor does the absence of such promises seem to reduce response rates. It may well be that researchers worry much more about confidentiality than respondents do (Frey, 1983:180-185). *See also* RANDOMIZED RESPONSE TECHNIQUE (RRT); RESPONSE RATE.

CONGRESSIONAL MAIL POLL   *See* STRAW POLL.

CONTAMINATION   Someone other than a respondent answering questions. Contamination is mainly a problem with self-administered surveys such as mail polls. Different degrees of contamination exist. The most serious involves another person (a "third party") answering the questions. Less serious but more common is a respondent seeking help from family or friends to complete the questionnaire.

Contamination is generally viewed as undesirable; however, Don Dillman (1978:26) and others have argued that it might actually be helpful under some circumstances. According to them, contamination can actually improve survey results by facilitating recall. Consulting friends, talking to a spouse, or reviewing records may provide more accurate and complete information than would an independent answer. All of this is highly speculative. No one knows for sure how much contamination occurs--nor is it settled what effect contamination has on the quality of surveys (Nieburg, 1984: 128-129). *See also* SELF-ADMINISTERED SURVEY.

CONTEXT EFFECTS   *See* QUESTION ORDER EFFECTS.

CONTINUING ELECTIONS   The notion that public opinion polling constitutes a kind of continuous election--and, therefore, that polls serve the same purpose in society that frequent elections would serve. Continuing elections as a concept appeals to people who believe polls should guide public policy (Crespi, 1989:18-19). And, apparently, a lot of people do. Lyndon Johnson, for example, during his presidency proposed that the terms of U.S. House members be extended from two to four years. Johnson reasoned that polls now kept Congress so well informed of constituent opinion that more frequent elections were not needed.

But can polls actually be referendums on public policy? Many writers are skeptical, arguing that polling's real link to policy is its capacity to measure

public confidence in political leadership.   It is this aspect of polling that
constitutes a continuing election.   Harold Mendelsohn and Irving Crespi make
this point talking about presidential approval ratings:

> If...a President retains public confidence despite the fact that the
> (public) favors a specific course of action to which he is opposed, it is
> likely that he can and will ignore with impunity the survey result.
> (But)...if his confidence rating starts dropping, (opponents)...may be
> emboldened to oppose (him)...with greater vigor...It is the "continuing
> election" aspect of polls rather than their coverage of specific issues
> that results in their making government responsive to the public.
> (Mendelsohn and Crespi, 1970:49)

Three standard questions used regularly by national polls qualify as
continuing election questions. The first and probably most influential of these
is the presidential approval rating, which produces a trend line tracking public
confidence in the President. Presidents with high approval ratings can overcome
unpopular policies as long as their personal support remains high. Conversely,
unpopular presidents can fail even with widely approved policies (Gergen and
Schambra, 1979:64).

A second type of continuing election poll question is regularly asked about
confidence in the two major parties: which party, the Republicans or the
Democrats,   (a) will do a better job of handling the country's most important
problem; (b) will do a better job of maintaining peace in the world; and (c) will
do a better job of providing economic prosperity.   These gauges of party
strength usually turn out to forecast accurately the division of the vote between
the two major parties (Smith, 1985:264).

The third type of continuing election poll question is the familiar "trial
heat" question--if the election was held today and the candidates were X and Y,
who would you support? (Young, 1987:107).   Trial heats are notoriously
unreliable in early stages of campaigning. Nevertheless, an incumbent President
or other elected official is evaluated by the media and others according to trial
heat performance. *See also* APPROVAL RATING; MOST IMPORTANT
PROBLEM QUESTION; TRIAL HEATS.

CONTROL QUESTION   *See* CHEATER QUESTION.

CONTROL VARIABLE Any variable used to isolate the cause of public
opinions. Control variables--the common ones are demographic measures like
age, sex, income, education, religion, political party, and region-- explain why

respondents hold certain beliefs or report particular behavior (Backstrom and Hursh-Cesar, 1981:160-161). Here is an example:

> Say a poll reveals that 60% of all Protestants favor a certain policy but only 40% of all Catholics support the same policy. The pollster suspects it is income rather than religion that is really making the difference; so he controls for income and tests the relationship again. If the difference between Catholics and Protestants disappears when income is controlled for, the pollster might infer that it is in fact income rather than religion that explains the apparent differences between Catholics and Protestants. (Young, 1987:85)

Pollsters can control for one, two, three or more variables--one after another, or all at the same time. Controlling is done by statistically arranging respondents into groups that differ on the control variable (say, income), but are alike on all other important variables (such as gender, age, education, etc.). After controlling for income in the example above, an analyst might test income and education together, and then income, education, and gender together to see what influence these variables have on the original relationship between religion and voting choices (Babbie, 1973:286-288). *See also* ELABORATION PARADIGM.

CONVENIENCE SAMPLE   Any sample drawn because respondents are easily accessible. Convenience samples are also known as haphazard samples and accidental samples (Williamson et al, 1982:105-106). Examples of convenience samples abound in everyday life. Street-corner interviews with people who pass by are convenience samples. So are pull-out questionnaires in magazines, call-in polls conducted by radio or TV stations, or any study that relies on volunteers to answer the questions.

Convenience sampling is one of three main types of nonprobability sampling; the other two are quota sampling and judgment sampling. The advantage of all three is the efficiency with which they use respondents available to be interviewed. The drawback of all nonprobability sampling is that: there is no statistically reliable way to know how good or bad (that is, how representative) the sample is. Since the representativeness of convenience samples can not be estimated, it is always dangerous to use them to generalize about any larger population (Chein, 1976:517-520). *See also* NONPROBABILITY SAMPLE; PURPOSIVE SAMPLING; QUOTA SAMPLE.

COOKING THE DATA *See* WEIGHTING.

COOPER SNOOPERS   A derogatory reference awarded by agitated British citizens to the researchers conducting England's Wartime Social Survey. Cooper Snoopers were named after Churchill's minister of information, Duff Cooper, who oversaw the Wartime Survey. The Cooper Snoopers marked a very early British government use of polls. Their survey of rationing, diet, health practices, and housing seems to have gone smoothly. But when the Cooper Snoopers turned to studies of civilian morale, they were attacked as government spies--that is, snoopers (Marsh, 1982:33).

Controversies like this one often erupt when governments use the survey tool to collect subjective information about citizens. Somewhat paradoxically, government use of surveys to collect objective data--employment, housing, schooling, and so on--generates little resistance. Americans have not been quite as skittish as the British about government polling--for example, surveys went on uneventfully in the wartime U.S. that paralleled those done by the Cooper Snoopers (Rossi, Wright, and Anderson, 1983:5-7). But even in the United States, government use of opinion research has proceeded slowly--a great irony in view of the fact that American politicians use surveys themselves so heavily to get into and stay in government office (Crespi, 1979). *See also* SUBJECTIVE DATA.

COST ITEMS   The specific activities that make up the price of a poll. Pollsters use up to ten separate costs to calculate prices charged--activities such as interviewing, analyzing data, and drawing the sample (Sabato, 1981:75-81; Frey, 1983:29-31). These ten cost items are listed in the table below with estimates of the proportion each usually contributes to overall poll costs. The list is rank-ordered from highest cost items to lowest cost items.

<u>COSTS OF POLLING</u>

Cost Rank Order	Cost Item	% of Total Cost	Dollar Cost for a $10,000 Poll
1	Interviewing Respondents	50%	$5,000
2	Indirect Overhead/Clerical	18%	$1,800
3	Profit	10%	$1,000

COSTS OF POLLING - continued

Cost Rank Order	Cost Item	% of Total Cost	Dollar Cost for a $10,000 Poll
4	Analyzing Data/Writing and Presenting Report	5%	$ 500
5	Listing Elements in the Population	5%	$ 500
6	Editing, Coding, Data Entry, Computing	4%	$ 400
7	Printing and Binding	3%	$ 300
8	Drawing (Cutting) the Sample	2%	$ 200
9	Questionnaire Design/Pretesting	2%	$ 200
10	Reproducing the Report	1%	$ 100

Adapted from Weiss and Hatry, 1971:32-43.

Some rather dramatic comparisons emerge from ranking these ten cost items. Only three costs (interviewing, indirect overhead, and profit) account for almost 80 percent of the price of a poll--while such items as sampling, questionnaire design, and report writing are relatively inexpensive. Interviewing, in fact, is the major expense of polls. It dwarfs any other cost item, generally accounting for around 50 percent of overall costs (Young, 1989:47-49). Poll costs do vary some according to mode of interviewing employed. In general, face-to-face polls are most expensive; telephone polls cost about half as much as face-to-face polls of similar size and duration. This average, however, masks some huge differences between cost items for the two modes.

A careful study done at the University of Michigan by Groves and Kahn reported some of the following comparisons (1979: Ch. 7):

COST BY INTERVIEWING MODE

Cost Item	Cost if Done by Telephone	Cost if Done in Person
Sampling	$ 955	$ 8,547
Training	$ 2,066	$ 9,524
Travel	$ 0	$16,815
Telephone	$15,784	$ 5,980
Interviewing	$12,545	$32,278
Person Hours Per Interview	3.3	8.7
Cost Per Interview	$ 23	$ 55

Comparing telephone and face-to-face overall, telephone costs are about 45 percent of face-to-face costs, but specific cost items were very uneven. Sampling, for example, costs nine times as much for face-to-face, while face-to-face interviewing is almost three times as expensive as over the telephone. The only cost item not lower for the telephone poll is the telephone itself. In the Groves and Kahn study, phone costs were about $6,000 for face-to-face, but almost $16,000 for telephone surveys (1979: Ch. 7). *See also* INTERVIEWING; POLL COSTS; POLLING INDUSTRY.

COVER LETTER   The letter that accompanies any self-administered questionnaire. Cover letters are more formally known as letters of transmittal. Their purpose is to introduce the study and motivate respondents to participate (Isaac and Michael, 1971:92-95). There is much evidence that the quality of the cover letter directly influences the response rate, since respondents often make up their minds about participation in the study in a minute or less. There are two types of cover letters: bulk preprinted ones, and individual, personalized ones. Bulk letters have identical wording and use generic salutations such as "Dear Occupant" or "Dear Respondent." Bulk letters are the least expensive to produce, but also the least impressive to respondents. Not surprisingly, they do not produce high participation rates. Personalized cover letters, on the other hand, have salutations like "Dear Mr. Brown" or even "Dear Tom." Their texts are typed or printed, and may be custom-written. Personal cover letters flatter respondents and increase rates, but they are also more expensive than bulk mail (Alreck and Settle, 1985:207-209).

A number of cover letter practices are commended for their ability to yield a high return rate. Personalized letters draw better than bulk letters, as do letters advertising study sponsorship by an important or prestigious group. Letters signed by a well-known person do better than those signed by someone not well known. (Alreck and Settle, 1985:210).

Telephone surveys have spawned their own version of the cover letter, known as the advance letter or preletter (Frey, 1983:92-95). Advance letters are sent to notify potential respondents that they will be called, and to tell them about the survey and its purpose. Advance letters apparently increase survey response rates, sometimes dramatically. They also improve the quality of data provided by respondents (Dillman, 1978:243-245). *See also* SELF-ADMINISTERED SURVEY.

CRISSCROSS DIRECTORY   Cross-listed names, telephone numbers, and street addresses, all from a specific community or geographic area. Crisscross directories are published by private concerns for commercial use. All large and most medium-sized municipalities have them. A typical crisscross directory features three separate listings for each community: (1) an alphabetical name listing with street address and telephone number; (2) a telephone number listing with names and street addresses; and (3) a street and address listing with names and telephone numbers (Frey, 1983:71-73).

Crisscross directories are used to draw samples, and then later to locate respondents. Using the cross-listings this way allows the sample to be drawn by either telephone number or street address (Nieburg, 1984:190-193). Crisscross directories have some potential pitfalls when used for sampling purposes. Samples based solely on directory listings are risky--unless the listings are complete and up-to-date. Completeness is also important. Directories based only on published telephone numbers, for example, usually produce biased samples. So do crisscross directories that exclude certain areas of the community. *See also* RANDOM DIGIT DIALING (RDD); SAMPLING FRAME.

CROSS SECTION   Polling data collected at a single point in time. Cross sections may include large samples and lengthy questionnaires, but the respondent information all comes from the same round of interviews (Weisburg, Krosnick, and Bowen, 1989:27; Johnson and Joslyn, 1986:109-110). Polling data gathered at two or more points in time is classified as longitudinal. *See also* LONGITUDINAL SURVEYS.

CROSSTABS   A statistical procedure used to analyze polls. Crosstabs (or crosstabulations) are a basic tool common to virtually any type of survey analysis.

Crosstabulation starts with the actual numbers or "marginals" in a poll-- that is, 52% for candidate A and 48% for candidate B, or 60% favor policy x while 40% oppose it. It then examines how important groups in the electorate might differ from the totals--men, women, blacks, whites, Catholics, Protestants, affluent, poor, educated, less educated, etc. (M. L. Young, 1987:86)

Crosstabulation is conceptually uncomplicated: the notion is to take a variable such as age, income, religion, education, or political party affiliation, then compare the different categories of that variable on a single poll question (Weisberg, Krosnick, and Bowen, 1989:207-217; Babbie, 1973:242-250). Say the crosstab variable was political party affiliation and the poll question was:

Q: Do you approve or disapprove of the job President Bush is doing?

Schematically, a crosstab would look like this:

JOB APPROVAL QUESTION

	Approve of Bush	Disapprove of Bush
Democrats	Democrats who approve	Democrats who disapprove
Republicans	Republicans who approve	Republicans who disapprove
Independents	Independents who approve	Independents who disapprove
	Total Approves of Bush	Total Disapproves of Bush

An analyst could quickly compare Republicans, Democrats, and Independents on the Bush job approval question--and could also compare Democrats who approved with those who disapproved, Republicans who approved with those who did not; and Independents who approved with those who disapproved. Below is an example of a crosstab analyzing how support for a Pennsylvania Tax Reform Referendum differs by sex.

SUPPORT/OPPOSITION FOR GOVERNOR'S TAX REFORM PROPOSAL
BY SEX

	Males in Sample	Females In Sample	Row Totals
% Who Support Tax Reform	52%	56%	54%
% Who Oppose Tax Reform	26%	34%	30%
% Undecided	22%	10%	16%
Column Totals	100%	100%	100%

Quick inspection of the crosstab tells the analyst three key things: (1) Support for tax reform has a comfortable (54% to 30%) lead, but about one in six voters (16%) are still undecided; (2) Women (34%) are more strongly opposed than men (26%); (3) Men (22%) are twice as likely as women (10%) to be undecided. Simple crosstabs like these can be "hand tabbed" from raw questionnaire data. But that is becoming rare. Packaged computer programs like SAS and SPSS have made computer-generated data analysis almost universal. *See also* MARGINALS; WEIGHTING.

CURBSTONE INTERVIEWS   *See* CHEATER QUESTION.

D

DEBRIEFING A structured "gab" session between interviewers recently in the field and their project supervisors. Debriefing lets field personnel provide feedback to office staff about how things are going and changes needed. Sessions usually include a line-by-line review of the questionnaire and a discussion of any problems encountered with respondents (Groves and Kahn, 1979:43-44).

Debriefings occur at two main points during a survey. One is after a questionnaire has been pretested by interviewers. Supervisors then sit down with interviewers and review their field experiences. Questionnaire items are gone through for problems with wording, format, clarity, transitioning, and so on (Sheatsley, 1983:226). The other time debriefings occur is after an interviewer has completed a set of interviews. Charles Backstrom and Gerald Hursh-Cesar have described post-interview debriefings:

> Immediately after completing their assignments, the interviewers are debriefed by the supervisor.... Questionnaires are carefully checked to determine that they are properly completed, that the right people in the right houses were interviewed, that each questionnaire contains the correct identification numbers and case number, the respondent's name, address and phone number, plus interviewing time and date, and interviewer number.... Any work yet to be completed will be discovered now and the cleanup squad will be sent into action. (Backstrom and Hursh-Cesar, 1981:296)

Debriefings facilitate communication between interviewers and supervisors. But they also have some collateral benefits. One of these is an opportunity to evaluate interviewers and detect sloppy performance. Interviewers who report no field problems and make no suggestions may not be doing their job. Another benefit of debriefing is the opportunity it gives to supervisors and other office-based staff. Desk-bound researchers can lose their feel for the real world of the interviewing situation. Feedback from the field during debriefings counters this tendency (Worcester, 1972:91). *See also* PRETESTS.

DEFTS An abbreviation for "design effects," a concept used in sampling. DEFTS is a statistical procedure for comparing the efficiency of competing sampling designs (Groves and Kahn, 1979). It is expressed as a ratio--the ratio of the estimated sampling error from a simple random sample of a given size, to the estimated sampling error from a competing sampling design of the same size.

A DEFTS of 1.0 means that the alternative sampling procedure is exactly as efficient as would be a simple random sample (Frey, 1983:76-77). A DEFTS of 1.5, however, means that the alternative sample would have to be 50 percent larger to yield the same sampling error as a random sample. A DEFTS of .5 means that the alternative sample design could be 50 percent smaller and still yield the same sampling error as a simple random sample. The closer to zero a DEFTS score, the more attractive is a sampling design on the grounds of efficiency.

Still another way of computing DEFTS is in terms of effective sample size. Effective sample size is the size of the simple random sample used to evaluate other sampling designs.   Thus if effective sample size is 1,000 and the alternative sampling design requires 1,200, the computed DEFTS would be 1.2. The practical use of DEFTS ratios is to compare two or more different sampling techniques. Other things equal, the lowest DEFTS is the preferred design. A rule of thumb is that DEFTS decreases with stratified samples, but increases with cluster samples (Mosher and Kalton, 1972:103-105, 150, 201-202). *See also* PROBABILITY SAMPLE; SAMPLING ERROR.

DELEGATE POLLS   Surveys based on interviews with delegates to the Democratic and Republican national conventions. Delegate polls were first done systematically by CBS, which polled delegates to the 1968 Republican and Democratic conventions. Today all three networks, several large newspapers, and the wire services all have delegate polling operations.

The early delegate polls were relatively simple.   They asked about presidential and vice- presidential preferences, one or two issue questions, and basic demographics (age, gender, occupation, etc.). Modern delegate polls are far more elaborate. Barbara G. Farair, director of news surveys for the *New York Times*, described the 1984 delegate polls:

Each of the...delegates received about a dozen telephone calls from the media pollsters, some lasting as long as fifty-five minutes. The networks pursued the delegates relentlessly ...(tracking them down) at their summer homes, their relatives' dinner tables, business conferences, and their vacation spots. ...By the time they reached San Francisco and Dallas ...(the delegates) had learned to respond almost automatically to questions concerning their presidential and vice presidential choices and their views on economic, social and foreign policy issues. (*Public Opinion*, August/September 1984:43; Farah, 1984:43)

The record of the CBS delegate polls goes back to 1968. It provides fascinating comparisons of delegates over the years. Delegates have changed markedly in terms of gender, race and occupation, but have not changed much in terms of age, education, or convention experience.

CHANGING DELEGATES
1968-1980

		1968	1980
Gender	Male	85%	61%
	Female	15%	39%
Race	Black	3-1/2%	9%
	White	96-1/2%	91%
Lawyers		25%	14%
Median Age		40	46-1/2
College Grads		19%	23%
Attending First Convention		67%	86%

Adapted from Warren J. Mitofsky and Martin Plessner, "The Making of the Delegates, 1968-1980," in *Public Opinion*, October/November 1980, p.43.

Media-sponsored delegate polls are not the only game in town. A tradition of academic research stretches back to at least 1956 (Asher, 1988:236-238). The dominant theme of much of this research is the wide difference between convention delegates and the party rank and file voters. By almost any measure--

age, education, income, or gender--delegates are markedly different from the voters they represent. In the academic studies; much is made particularly of the ideological gap. For example, in 1980, almost half (46%) of Democratic delegates identified themselves as liberals, while only one in five (21%) rank-and-file Democrats called themselves liberal (Kirkpatrick, 1976). Similar ideological gaps have been measured between Republican delegates and rank-and-file Republicans. *See also* MEDIA POLLS; POST-CONVENTION POLL.

DEMOGRAPHIC ITEMS   Poll questions that ask respondents about some personal characteristic. Demographic items routinely include questions about income, education, gender, race, occupation, age, and political party. They are sometimes referred to as "face sheet variables" because they sometimes appear on the first page of interview schedules (Backstrom and Hursh-Cesar, 1981:160-176). Demographics are some of the most important questions pollsters ask. In effect, they provide the analytic categories needed to analyze poll results (Worcester, 1972:118-120).

Raw polling data might reveal that the sample splits 50-50 on one question, and perhaps 60-40 on another. These overall "marginals" are helpful, but demographic items allow analysts to go much further--to test, for example, how answers differ by gender, income, or race. A more formal way to express this idea is that demographic items are independent variables--that is, they are the probable causes of dependent variables such as voting choice, or a respondent's particular opinion. In researcher parlance, demographics explain poll findings.

Demographics have one other important use. They allow pollsters to match the sample with known population characteristics--such as proportion of male/female, or whites/blacks, or Democrats/Republicans. Sample demographics that are seriously askew from the known population are usually weighted.

The placement of demographic items within questionnaires is carefully planned--since many respondents resent answering demographic questions--particularly those about income or education. For this reason these items are typically placed toward the end of the interview schedule, and thus are asked after some trust has been established between interviewer and respondent (Nieburg, 1984:188-198). *See also* FACT QUESTIONS; MARGINALS; WEIGHTING.

DESIGNATED MARKET AREA   *See* ADIs.

DIMINISHING RETURNS A mathematical principle observed in probability sampling. Diminishing returns illustrates the logarithmic relationship--a situation in which increasing one variable has less and less effect on a second variable. This same principle is widely known in economics as the principle of diminishing marginal utility, which holds that for every good or service there is a point where increasing consumption produces little or no additional satisfaction (or utility). The basic idea of diminishing returns is straightforward: there is always some point beyond which additional inputs do not produce proportional gains in output.

Examples abound in everyday life. The student who studies twenty hours for a test rather than ten probably does not get twice as good a grade. An athlete who runs fifty training miles a week instead of twenty-five miles does not cut his race time in half; people who sleep sixteen hours rather than eight do not feel twice as rested. Applied to probability sampling, diminishing returns describes what happens to sampling error as sample size is increased (Warwick and Lininger, 1975:94).

A rule of thumb is that sample size must be quadrupled to cut error in half: a sample of 250 with a sampling error of +/- 6 would have to be increased to 1,000 to bring error down to +/- 3; a sample of 1,500 with a sampling error of +/- 2.5 would have to be increased to 6,000 to reduce sampling error to +/- 1.25 (Roll and Cantril, 1972:71-75). The practical effect of diminishing returns is that ever larger sample size is usually not an efficient use of resources. The upper limit for most samples is about 1,500. Only rarely are samples larger. Bigger samples not only yield minuscule reductions in sampling error, they may also increase exposure to various kinds of nonsampling error (Fowler, 1984:40-43). *See also* PROBABILITY SAMPLE; SAMPLING ERROR.

DIRECTORY SAMPLING Using the telephone directory to draw a random sample. Directory sampling can employ simple random methods, but more practical is some version of systematic sampling. One common practice is simply to count the number of pages in the directory, then estimate the number of telephone listings per page. Say a given directory has 500 pages, 200 names to the page for a total of 100,000 listings. A sample size of 1,000 would have to sample every 100 names, or 2 names per page (Babbie, 1973:93-94). Directory sampling is often considered a substitute for random digit dialing (RDD). In fact, however, these two procedures can be combined in various ways. For instance, a sample might first be drawn from a directory, then the last two digits of each telephone number selected are replaced with random numbers (Sudman, 1973:204-207).

Directory sampling is relatively simple to carry out. But it is widely faulted for using an incomplete sampling frame. The basic criticism is that telephone directories do not list everyone in the survey population; in fact, up to 50 percent of people with telephones are not accurately listed. Some of these are not in the directory because they request unlisted numbers (about 30% of all homes), while others are there but should not be because they have moved since the directory was published (20% of American families move annually). Still other problems with directory sampling are homes with multiple phones and phones listed in more than one directory.

The shortcomings associated with directory sampling have not discouraged its wide use. Nor is directory sampling always inappropriate. In fact, there are two particular conditions under which it is especially appropriate (Dillman, 1978:234-240). One of these is surveys for which telephone directories do include most of the population--for instance, rural areas where few numbers are unlisted and people move infrequently. The other good use of directory sampling is in those surveys for which directory sample bias is not a significant problem. Young people, poor people, and new residents are often missed when a directory is used. But if those groups are not important to survey results, excluding them from the sample is probably all right. *See also* ADD-A-DIGIT DIALING; CRISSCROSS DIRECTORY; ELEMENTS; SAMPLING FRAME.

DISCLOSURE   Information about a poll, how it was conducted, who sponsored it, and so on. Disclosure is the central theme in the ethical codes of professional groups like AAPOR, NCPP, and CASRO. It is also the core notion found in proposals to regulate polling (Fowler, 1984:135-144). Disclosure requires that all material facts about a poll be explicitly reported when a poll is publicly released. The ethical codes of AAPOR, NCPP, and CASRO, in fact, require that all information be disclosed that could influence interpretation of the poll.

Disclosure, as defined in ethical codes, usually includes eight elements of information: (1) *Poll Sponsorship*--who commissioned and paid for the poll? (2) *Question Wording*--exact wording of questions asked, (3) *Population Studies* --respondent demographics, age, sex, and so on, (4) *Sample Size*--actual number of people interviewed, (5) *Sampling Error*--for the entire sample at "confidence level" used, (6) *Subgroup Analyzed*--sampling error for subgroups analyzed separately, such as women or ethnics, (7) *Interviewing*--were interviews conducted in person, by telephone, or through the mail? (8) *Interviewing Time*-- specific date(s) on which respondents were contacted.

In theory, the major impact of disclosure is supposed to be on the working press, who become more sophisticated about polls and more qualified to make judgments about them. Readers and viewers then should be better able to evaluate published polls. There is evidence that little disclosure information is actually reported by the media. One study using newspaper clippings of poll stories from American and British newspapers suggests that readers get very little disclosure information (Turner and Martin, 1984:69-73). For example, time of interviewing was disclosed in just 50 percent of the newspaper clips studied, and method of interviewing was described in only 25 percent. Other disclosure elements fared even worse: complete question wording was given in only 18 percent; subsample information was produced in just 4 percent; nonresponse rate was noted in 2 percent, and sampling error was given in 7 percent.

A separate study examined the conformance of three elite newspapers--the Chicago Tribune, the Los Angeles Times, and the Atlanta Constitution--to the AAPOR disclosure standards. One hundred sixteen polls were reviewed from the period 1972-1979 (Miller and Hurd, 1982). Some of the AAPOR standards received very high conformity. These included sample size, reported in 85 percent of the poll stories; poll sponsorship, reported in 82 percent of the poll stories, and population description, reported in 80 percent of the poll stories. But other standards were observed much less rigorously. Interviewing method was given only 51 percent of the time, question wording was described only 49 percent of the time, and sampling error was reported only 16 percent of the time.

The same study found two other patterns in disclosure practice (Miller and Hurd, 1982:243-249). First, newspaper-sponsored polls adhere more strictly to disclosure standards than either syndicated polls like Gallup and Harris, or wire service polls like AP and UPI. This difference is particularly marked for three disclosure standards: sampling error, question wording, and mode of interviewing. Newspaper polls report these items much more regularly than do syndicated polls or wire polls. Another striking finding: election polls produce higher conformity to disclosure standards than do nonelection polls. Apparently editors take more seriously the responsibility to disclose when an election is impending. *See also* AAPOR; POLL REGULATION; SIDEBAR.

DISCOUNT POLLS Any opinion research that has lost some of its original value because it is dated. Discount polls are aging polls--worth less because they were completed weeks or months earlier. In general, all polls lose value over time. There are some exceptions to this--the main one involves academics working with "secondary data" from survey archives (Hyman, 1972). But for most polls the clock keeps running--conditions in the study environment change, and original findings are no longer reliable.

The Federal Elections Commission (FEC) has actually established an accounting rule that formalizes the declining value of polls. Under FEC rules, the full cost of a poll can be depreciated over 180 days (six months). The poll is valued at full cost from one to fifteen days old, at 50 percent of cost from 16 days old to 60 days, at 5 percent of cost from two months old to six months, and it is valueless after six months. At this point, it may be given to a federal candidate without counting against FEC contribution limits (Young, 1990:49).

The FEC depreciation schedule does not always match reality. Under some conditions, polls remain useful for a year or longer--particularly if the poll includes baseline data, which is less subject to change. On the other hand, conditions in a campaign sometimes make a poll obsolete in a matter of days. It is an old adage that the half-life of a poll late in a campaign is only forty-eight hours. This is particularly true toward the very end of political campaigns when sharp, sudden shifts in opinion are common. It is then that polls take their "deep discounts"--sometimes becoming utterly valueless for portraying current opinion or tracking candidate support (Salmore and Salmore, 1989:167-168). *See also* BENCHMARK POLL; POLL COSTS.

DK/NR Pollster shorthand for survey questions answered either "don't know" (DK) or "no response" (NR). DK/NR describes respondents who can't or won't answer a given question. The notation DK/NR itself often appears on questionnaires as an answer category. For example, the following question might offer three possible responses:

> Do you approve of current American foreign policy in Central America?
>
> Yes _____   No _____   DK/NR _____

Many researchers believe that respondents do not elect the DK/NR option as often as they should. That is probably true. Several influences operate during interviewing to reduce the incidence of don't know answers (Weisberg and Bowen, 1977:82-83). One of these factors is the respondent's desire to appear knowledgeable and informed. Rather than risk embarrassment, some people answer questions about which they know very little. A second factor which suppresses don't know answers is question wording. The biggest offenders are questions that give respondents only two answer choices, such as favor/oppose, agree/disagree, yes/no, and so on.

Giving respondents the DK/NR option on questionnaires is usually recommended on the grounds that it produces more valid answers. Respondents with no opinion on a topic can simply say so by choosing the don't know category (Marsh, 1972:134). While this is true, a DK/NR response can be misleading. Don't knows might be a respondent who can't answer because he is undecided or ignorant. But it might also be someone who simply refuses to answer even though capable of doing so. Usually these distinctions are ignored when reporting DK/NR answers (Hennessey, 1985:76-78). *See also* MISREPORTING; NONOPINIONS; RESPONSE RATE.

DOUBLE-BARRELED QUESTION   Any question that includes two separate issues without allowing a respondent to distinguish which one is being addressed. Double-barreled questions link the two issues together in such a way that neither can be responded to unambiguously (Payne, 1951:102-104). Here are two examples:

> "Do you plan to go to college and major in the social sciences?" (Clark, 1976:36)

> "Do you regularly take vitamins to avoid getting sick?" (Alreck & Settle, 1985:109)

The fatal defect in double barreled questions is that they include "both the action and the reason or motive in the same item." Consequently, the pollster cannot be sure which part of the question is being answered. In our example, the respondent might plan to go to college, but major in some field other than social science; or might take vitamins, but not to avoid illness. Such a respondent faces a dilemma in responding at all. If an answer is offered, a second question is necessary to clarify the respondent's position (Alreck and Settle, 1985:110).

The recommended technique for recognizing (and correcting) double-barreled questions: pretest to see if respondents might find one part of the question true, but another false. Breaking a double-barreled question into two questions is always possible, and usually necessary. *See also* PRETESTS.

DROPOUTS   Respondents who initially participate in one or more rounds of panel study interviewing, but later are unable or unwilling to continue. Dropping out, or more formally sample attrition, occurs for a variety of reasons. The most common is the difficulty in tracking the same respondents for two, three, four, or more successive interviews. About one in five people move over a year's time, one in ten will move within six months. Dropouts also occur because original respondents are traveling, sick, or too busy. And there are respondents who drop out because they have lost interest in the study, are bored, or are simply unwilling to continue (Backstrom and Hursh-Cesar, 1981:108).

Dropouts are predictable. In fact, panel studies plan for them by designing a sample much larger than those used in other types of surveys. Larger samples make it more likely that latter phases of interviewing will have enough surviving respondents. Even oversize samples, however, are not always sufficient. Given long enough, any panel will eventually become too small to allow meaningful analysis. The practical effect of this is that researchers must limit the duration of panel studies--or else periodically replace part of the sample with fresh respondents (Babbie, 1973:64,69). *See also* PANELS.

E

EARLY DECIDERS Prospective voters who make up their minds early about who they will support in an upcoming election. Early deciders then are little influenced by the subsequent political campaign. They have made their choice and are unlikely to change it.

At one time, early deciders made up two-thirds or more of the electorate in presidential campaigns. They are still a major chunk of voters, but fall considerably short of that level (Asher, 1988:115-118). In fact, more and more voters today are late deciders who make up their mind in the closing days of a campaign.

Declining party loyalty explains some of the decrease in early deciders. Strong Democrat or Republican leanings used to help voters make up their minds but fewer people today have those leanings. Late deciders typically lack strong partisan attachments to guide their electoral choice. Consequently, they reach their vote decision on the basis of other factors--including political advertising and news coverage, which tend to be concentrated late in a campaign (M. L. Young, 1987:186).

Early decider is a standard category pollsters use to classify voter behavior. Some other standard classifications commonly used are likely voter, ticket splitter, and undecided. All these labels efficiently summarize information derived from the poll and group respondents with others who exhibit the same political behavior (Martin, 1983:697-702). *See also* RESPONDENT.

ECOLOGICAL FALLACY The logical error of inferring a single person's opinion from polling data about groups. Ecological fallacies present serious hazards for those analyzing survey results (Sellitz, Wrightsman, and Cook, 1976:439-440).

A hung jury illustrates the conditions that can produce ecological fallacies:

> Suppose a jury is deciding a case and after much deliberation reports to the judge that it cannot as a group decide the guilt or innocence of the defendant. The jury is hung; as a group it is undecided. Although the jury is composed of twelve individuals, we can make reference to the group as a whole (this is essentially what we do when we aggregate data). We can say that the jury is undecided. Now to the important point. Can we move from our statement that the jury is undecided to say that individual jurors are undecided? Certainly not! Indeed, it may very well be that none of the twelve jurors is undecided; they are simply individually decided in different directions. The conceptual, logical point to be made here is that one cannot properly make inferences about individuals in groups on the basis of data about the group as a whole. To do so is to commit the aggregative, or ecological, fallacy. (Williamson, et al, 1982:298)

A common source of the ecological fallacy is the analysis of election returns at precinct or county levels. If, say, a Republican candidate does well in Polish electoral districts, an analyst might say, "Polish voters are more likely to support Republicans"; or if a woman candidate does better in a Jewish district, the conclusion might be, "Jews are more likely to support women." The basic issue here is one of logic: generalizations are being made about individual Pole or Jewish voters, but the data used is from entire election districts. Unless those election districts are 100 percent Polish or 100 percent Jewish, an analyst may not properly draw conclusions about individuals residing in them.

The logical counterpart to the ecological fallacy is the atomist fallacy, which is to make inferences about groups from individual level data. Suppose a researcher studied members of the Democratic National Committee (DNC) and the Republican National Committee (RNC), using a questionnaire to test a hypothesis about personality differences between the two sets of leaders. After examining this data, one would risk the atomist fallacy to generalize about either the DNC or RNC as organizations. An analyst should not, for example, conclude that DNC is more "open" as an organization because committee members score high on that trait.

Data about individuals cannot be generalized to make conclusions about groups to which those individuals belong, any more than data about groups can be used to make conclusions about individuals in those groups. To do the former is to commit the atomist fallacy, while doing the latter incurs the ecological fallacy.

EFFECTIVE SAMPLE   *See* DEFTS.

ELABORATION PARADIGM   A set of conceptually linked statistical routines designed to analyze survey data.   The elaboration paradigm was developed by Paul Lazarsfeld, the noted sociologist, and championed by Earl Babbie, among others (Babbie, 1973:Ch. 15).

Researchers conduct surveys to understand relationships between variables such as income and education, gender and voting, age and consumption patterns, and so on. When a variable (like education) is correlated with another variable (like income), researchers say the two have a relationship--positive if education and income go up or down together, negative if the two go in opposite directions.

Sometimes, however, simply observing that two variables are connected with each other is not enough. A third variable may be influencing the observed relationship in ways the pollster should understand. This is the function of the elaboration paradigm: to examine systematically a two-variable relationship by "testing" with third variables (Rosenberg, 1968:3-22).

The elaboration paradigm prescribes four tests: (1) replication; (2) specification; (3) interpretation; and (4) explanation.   For each test, the researcher begins with the original two-variable relationship, then statistically introduces a third variable (called a test variable) to see if it changes the two-variable relationship (Babbie, 1973:299-307).

First, replication means the original relationship is unchanged even after introducing the test variable. For example, say males are found to support Republicans more frequently than females; age is introduced as a test variable: men under 35; men over 35. If males under 35 are as likely as males over 35 to support Republicans, we say the original gender variable relationship was "replicated" under conditions of age.

Second, specification means the original relationship is (about) the same for some categories of the test variable, but different for others. To illustrate, again with men supporting Republicans more than women do: race is introduced as a test variable (blacks and whites); white males are found to support Republicans more frequently than white women, but black males support Republicans about as often as black women. We say the original gender variable relationship is race-specified: males support Republicans more than females, but only when the males are white.

Third interpretation means the original two-variable relationship exists because there is a third "intervening" variable causally linked to the other two. Again, the relationship between gender and support for Republicans: suppose a researcher suspects that an economic attitude and not gender is the real influence on partisan support. Perhaps people who say they are well-off tend to support Republicans more than people who say they are not. Economic well-being is introduced as a test variable, and it turns out that women who report economic well-being support Republicans equally with men. Then we would say the original gender variable relationship has been interpreted: more men than women support Republicans, but only because more men than women had a sense of economic well- being.

Fourth, explanation means the original relationship simply disappears when the test variable is used--the apparent relationship was misleading. A classic example of explanation is the positive relationship between the number of fire trucks responding to a fire and the amount of damage done. More fire trucks do respond to larger fires. But this does not mean that the greater number of trucks causes the greater damage associated with larger fires. A test variable, size of fires, would explain away the spurious relationship between number of fire trucks on the scene and increasing amounts of damage, and would point the research toward the real relationships--namely, "large fires do more damage than small ones and more fire trucks respond to large fires than to small ones" (Babbie, 1973:307).

The elaboration paradigm is straightforward in concept (albeit rigorous in application): the real relationship between any two variables can be understood by testing with a third control variable. That third variable may replicate, specify, interpret, or explain the original relationship. *See also* CONTROL VARIABLE.

ELECTION DAY POLL   *See* EXIT POLLS.

ELEMENTS   The individuals making up a sample. Elements are usually people, although they can be families, organizations, or even political subdivisions. Elements come from populations, which include all the possible people (or other units) that could end up in a sample (Williamson et al. 1982:105). Some examples of populations:

1. All persons eighteen years and older eligible to vote for president in 1992;
2. All students enrolled in a four-year college or university;
3. All women having abortions between 1980 and 1990;
4. American-born Catholics, age thirty-five or older.

Two specific types of population are distinguished for sampling purposes: target populations and survey populations (Frankel, 1983:23-24). Target populations are those elements that researchers will study if they can reach them. Survey populations, on the other hand, are the elements that actually are studied. As a general rule, survey populations fall short of target populations. There are various reasons for this. The most common is simply the practical difficulty of reaching certain kinds of people from the target population.

The term universe was once used in connection with the term population. A universe was the ideal population, the elements one would sample from if there were no obstacles. Today, that meaning has largely been taken over by the term target population. The term universe is now only infrequently used (Babbie, 1973:79). *See also* BLANKS; SAMPLING FRAME.

ELITE INTERVIEWS   Interviews with high-status individuals.   Elite interviews may be conducted with politicians, civic leaders, government officials, media personalities, or cultural figures--virtually anyone whose position or accomplishments afford unique knowledge or specialized information (Dexter, 1970).   Elite interviews are unstructured and use no set sequence of questions.   In the most common pattern, the interviewer prepares a list of general questions, then asks them in the natural flow of the unfolding conversation (Weisberg and Bowen, 1977:56,63).

Successful elite interviews might look to the untrained eye like an interesting but casual conversation between two knowledgeable people. In fact, however, this aura of naturalness comes after hours of background planning and research. Good interviewers come to the interview with a store of knowledge about the topic to be discussed, as well as biographical information on the person to be interviewed.

Preparation for elite interviews requires some procedures and techniques not unlike those used by journalists. Access itself is often the problem. Elites are busy, frugal with their time, and careful with whom they spend it. Once access is gained, interview ground rules become important. Sometimes confidentiality is a concern, other times not. Attribution, review before publication, and even duration of the interview are issues to be worked out. Tape recorders are often used in elite interviews. They produce a record of the interview which can protect both interviewer and subject from future disagreements about what was said. Elite respondents seldom object to tape recorders even when confidential material is to be discussed.

Justification for the planning and work of elite interviews rests on two main arguments. The first is simply that the respondents themselves are different-- they are highly accomplished, successful, and independent people who would resent being interviewed with a standardized set of questions. Customizing elite questions simply reflects that the person being interviewed is unique. The other argument for interviewing elite respondents differently is that they often have knowledge and information others do not have. Much elite interviewing, in fact, is exploratory. It is undertaken to gain more understanding of an issue, before more structured and traditional research can be pursued (Johnson and Joslyn, 1986:179-181). *See also*   INTERVIEWERS; INTERVIEWING; UNSTRUCTURED INTERVIEWS.

ENTERPRISERS, MORALISTS, NEW DEALERS, ET AL. The eleven categories of voters that have recently been proposed to explain public opinion and political behavior in the United States. Enterprisers, Moralists, New Dealers, and the rest, are part of a typology developed by the Gallup Organization for the Times Mirror publishing conglomerate (Times Mirror, 1987). The Times Mirror study concluded that traditional cleavages, like ideology, party identification, and demographics, no longer accurately describe the American political landscape. Today, instead, there are eleven distinct groups that differ on such measures as tolerance of opposing views, opposition to communism, and the role of government in society. The traditional two party system is not entirely ignored by the Times Mirror typology. Four of the eleven categories are Republican or lean Republican, while six groups are Democratic or lean Democratic. One group is apolitical.

REPUBLICAN TYPES

1. *Enterprisers*--one of every six likely voters; affluent, probusiness, tolerant on social issues and most concerned about economic issues; vote about 90 percent Republican.
2. *Moralists*--one of every seven likely voters; middle income, conscious of foreign policy and social issues; concerns like abortion and school prayer are critical issues; vote about 95 percent Republican.
3. *Upbeats*--one of every nine likely voters; middle-income, younger, optimistic; enthusiastic about America and its promise, and uncritical of government performance; vote about 64 percent Republican.
4. *Disaffected*--one of every fourteen likely voters; middle-income, middle-aged, financially pressured, pessimistic about the future and cynical about government; almost direct opposites to Upbeats; vote about 57 percent Republican (Times Mirror, 1987:13-17; 95-101).

DEMOCRATIC TYPES

5. *60s Democrats*--one of every nine likely voters; upper-middle-class female (62%), well-educated and socially tolerant. Identify politically with the great social issues of the 60s, the environment, civil rights, and peace; vote about 85 percent Democratic.
6. *New Dealers*--one of every seven likely voters; middle-income, older, blue collar, union families, religious; conservative on many social issues, but support most social spending; vote about 92 percent Democratic.
7. *Seculars*--one in every eleven likely voters; affluent, well

educated, well informed and tolerant on social issues; distinguished from other types particularly in lack of religious orientation; vote about 72 percent Democratic.

8. *Passive Poor*--one of every seventeen voters; low income, not highly educated, one-third black; favor social spending and tax increase; profess belief in American government and institutions; vote about 83 percent Democratic.

9. *Partisan Poor*--one of every eleven voters; low income, not highly educated, 40 percent black, urban dwellers; conservative on some issues like school prayer and the death penalty, but solidly Democratic; vote about 95 percent Democratic.

10. *Followers*--one of every twenty-five voters; under thirty, poorly educated, blue collar, little religious orientation; only slight interest in government or politics, very unpredictable politically; vote about 65 percent Democratic.

11. *Bystanders*--neither Republican or Democratic; one of every nine in the voting age population, but virtually zero percent of likely voters; young, white, single and urban; almost completely uninterested in political issues or who is elected president (Times Mirror, 1987:13-17; 19-23).

For some time, writers have been decrying the inadequacy of traditional categories to capture the nature of modern political life. Demographic and ideological classifications, and even lifestyle variables, seem inadequate. The Times Mirror typology of eleven voter types is important--because it acknowledges the complexities and vagaries of contemporary political behavior, and because it gives political analysts a powerful new tool to analyze American policies. *See also* DEMOGRAPHIC ITEMS.

EPISTOLARY OPINION RESEARCH (EOR)   Studying public opinion through letters to the editor columns. Epistolary opinion research is based on readers' letters printed in newspapers and magazines. Letter columns appear in most major newspapers, but opinion analysts have usually been skeptical that the letters reflect public opinion. The conventional wisdom has been that letters columns only reflect the editorial bias of the newspaper. Consistent with this conventional view is some evidence from older studies that letter writers overrepresent an elite stratum--specifically, they are older, more conservative, more Republican, better educated, and more affluent than average readers (Hill, 1981).

But these earlier findings may no longer hold. In fact, there is now reason to believe that letters to the editor do reflect public opinion--at least in some cases. Professor David Hill examined a national sample of ninety-two daily newspapers. He used letters about the Equal Rights Amendment (ERA) to compare actual (poll-measured) public opinion with the opinions found in letters published in the ninety-two newspapers. His findings--which strongly contradict the traditional view--were that actual public opinion on the ERA and published letter opinion were similar. About 50 percent of Americans polled supported the ERA; the same level of support was found in the published letters to the editor.

Professor Hill also polled seventy-five editors soliciting their policies governing letters to the editor. He found that about one-third publish all letters, another one-third publish representative letters to reflect broad opinion on an issue, and one-third use a variety of guidelines, including "news value" and provocativeness. Hill's findings, and accumulating anecdotal evidence, suggest that letters to the editor columns may now reflect public opinion at least on some issues (Hill, 1981:384-392). *See also* WEIRD SCIENCE.

EPSEM   Acronym for "equal probability of selection method." EPSEM embodies the basic rule for achieving a random sample: every element in the survey population must have an equal chance of ending up in the sample. A leading survey research text describes EPSEM as the basis for all probability sampling:

> A basic principle of probability sampling is the following: a sample will be representative of the population from which it is selected if all members of the population have an equal chance of being selected in the sample. Samples that have this quality are often labeled EPSEM Samples. (Babbie, 1973:78)

The EPSEM principal requires that any one person in a population must have the same chance of becoming a respondent as any other person. This means that for a survey population of 100,000, and a sample of 1,000, every member of the population must have exactly one chance in 100 of being selected (Frankel, 1983:40, 46).

Following the EPSEM principal guarantees a representative sample. On occasion, however, EPSEM is purposely flouted--and is replaced by an opposing method known as UPS, or "unequal probability of selection." UPS methods choose respondents by giving some elements of the population a higher or lower chance of being included in the sample. The most common application of the UPS principle is oversampling of some small but important population segment. In the United States, blacks and Hispanics are examples. UPS generates enough respondents that separate analysis is possible for these special population groups

(Weisberg, Krosnick, and Bowen, 1989:27). *See also* OVERSAMPLING, PROBABILITY SAMPLE.

EXIT POLLS Surveys conducted immediately after voters leave their polling place. Exit polls interview a sample of voters in carefully chosen key precincts. Interviewers approach respondents, hand them a paper "ballot" and ask them to answer twenty-five or so questions about how they voted and what they think about several major issues (Backstrom and Hursh-Cesar, 1981:300-303). Exit poll ballots (actually they are printed questionnaires) include four main kinds of questions:

1. *Issue Questions*--such as "Do you support casino gambling?" "Which one problem is the most important facing New York today?" "Do you approve or disapprove of state-run liquor stores?"
2. *Image Questions*--such as "How honest are public officials?" "Is the governor doing an excellent, good, fair or poor job?"
3. *Trial Heat Questions*--such as "If the Democrats nominate Bill Bradley and the Republicans, George Bush, who will you support?" "And what about the U.S. Senate race, who will you vote for if the candidates are Helms, the Republican, and Hunt, the Democrat?"
4. *Demographic Questions*--such as "What is your age...income...political party preference...political philosophy?"

There are four national election-day polls: *New York Times*-CBS poll, The NBC-*Wall Street Journal* poll, The ABC-*Washington Post* poll, and the *Los Angeles Times* poll (Levy, 1983:54-67). In addition, some private firms do exit polling for state and local broadcast outlets. One study of exit polls at the state level found that trial heats made up about 40 percent of exit poll questions. Next most used were demographic questions (25%), then issue questions (20%). Image questions (15%) were least used (M. L. Young, 1986:86-87).

Exit polling is controversial. Two main criticisms are leveled at them. One is that exit polls reduce turnout because voters lose motivation to come to the polls once they know the probable outcome. A related criticism is that exit poll predictions' effect on turnout can determine who wins lower-level races (Sudman, 1986:331-339). The second main criticism of exit polls is methodological. The charge is that exit polls have no claim to scientific rigor, because they are not based on strict probability sampling. They are, in effect, sophisticated straw polls (Nieburg, 1984:60-66).

Exit polls have many defenders, who make three main points. First, say defenders, there is no evidence that people vote or fail to vote because of exit polls; most likely the net effect of exit polls on voting is nil. Second, argue supporters, exit polls are protected by first amendment free speech and free press guarantees. Public interest in maintaining first amendment rights far outweighs any possible benefit to be gained from curtailing exit polling. Finally, exit poll advocates stress the contribution of exit polls to the democratic process. Not only do these surveys provide a rich flow of information about voters' opinions, they also prevent election fraud by providing an independent count of voting results (M. L. Young, 1989:296-298). *See also* POLL REGULATION; STRAW POLL.

EXPECTATIONS GAME   A high-stakes gambit played during the early stages of presidential nomination races. The expectations game is a kind of political handicapping system that measures actual election results against expected election results. The key players are the reporters covering the campaign, who play against campaign staff (Altschuler, 1982:178-180). Mary Levy describes how the game is played:

> And how are expectations set? Through an informal consensus negotiated between...the candidates and the political press....The expectations game requires considerable finesse on the part of campaign staffs, particularly the pollsters. All players hold the same cards, the eminently leakable results of the candidate's own polls or the results of media commissioned or academic surveys. If a campaign tries to set expectations too low...reporters will say staffers are deliberately bad-mouthing their candidate's chances. Set expectations too high, and according to the game...news stories will ask what went wrong. (Levy, 1984:89)

The expectations game becomes a major way that a candidate's progress is evaluated. The game is predicated on the assumption that winning and losing in the early contests by itself is not a reliable guide to future performance. If a candidate loses, but shows more strength than expected, that candidate wins the expectations game by beating the odds. Conversely, a winning candidate who achieves victory with a disappointing margin can lose the expectations game. The rewards for doing better than expected are substantial. Winning expectations produces saturation press coverage. This gives favored candidates a "bounce" that can catapult them into front-runner status almost overnight.

Momentum--"Big Mo"--is a notion related to expectations. Flat, uninspired campaigns lack momentum, campaigns once hot but now cooling are said to be losing momentum, while campaigns catching on and gaining support are said to have momentum. If a campaign has momentum, it will probably do better than expected, scoring high in the expectations game. Conversely, a campaign losing momentum will probably do worse than expected--and is likely to lose the expectations game (Asher, 1988:174-175). *See also* POLL/MEDIA CYCLE; PRIMARY POLLS.

EXPERT CHOICE SAMPLE   *See*   STRATEGIC INFORMANT SAMPLING.

EXPLANATION   *See* ELABORATION PARADIGM.

F

FACE SHEET VARIABLES *See* DEMOGRAPHIC ITEMS.

FACE-TO-FACE INTERVIEW   An interview conducted in the physical presence of the respondent. Face-to-face interviews require that respondents be located and interviewed at home, while shopping, in the office, after voting, and soon, virtually any place that people live, work, or play. The expression personal interview is often employed as a loose synonym for face-to-face, but careful usage maintains a distinction between the two terms. In personal interviews, the interviewer asks questions and records answers; both face-to-face and telephone surveys are personal interviews. But face-to-face requires physical presence, while telephone surveys rely on the interviewer's voice conducted over phone lines (Weisberg, Krosnick, and Bowen, 1989:84-92).

Face-to-face is one of three major interviewing modes used in polling. The other two are telephone surveys and mail polls. Face-to-face interviews once were the standard for survey research, preferred to telephone or mail almost without exception. This is no longer true (Dillman, 1978:6-11). Face-to-face interviews do have advantages. They are particularly good for long interviews (over thirty minutes) or for complex subjects. Rapport is stronger with face-to-face, and data quality is generally better. And they are effective in locating hard to reach populations like the elderly, poor people, and minorities.

But two major problems plague face-to-face interviews. One of these is money. Face-to-face interviews are two to three times as expensive as telephone and five to six times as expensive as mail. Many surveys are price-sensitive, resources are limited, and the least expensive interviewing mode is attractive (Backstrom and Hursh-Cesar, 1981:19-23). One rule of thumb is that the cost of a telephone poll is (currently) $1.50 per person, per minute. Face-to-face interviews cost two or three times as much, or $3.00 to $4.50 per person per minute.

The other major problem with face-to-face interviewing is declining response rates. Once face-to-face interviewing produced 85 to 90 percent response rates. Today, however, response is frequently no better (and sometimes worse) than less expensive telephone surveys. More people are working outside the home, so people are hard to find at home. Even when at home, there is growing resistance to being interviewed. Many people have security concerns, some fear deceptive sales practices, while others resent the intrusion.

The combination of high costs and declining response rates have made face-to-face interviewing much less attractive. Consequently, more and more surveys are conducted by telephone or mail. Many researchers, in fact, now believe that none of the three main interviewing modes--face-to-face, telephone, or mail--is necessarily preferable. Instead, each should be evaluated against the resources available and the research objectives of a given survey (Weisberg, 1983:336-338). *See also* INTERVIEWING; SELF-ADMINISTERED SURVEYS.

FACT QUESTIONS   Questionnaire items that ask respondents specific information--about themselves, people they know, or experiences they have had. Fact questions usually deal with socioeconomic data like age, income, education, political party affiliation, and so forth. Any question that is subject to objective verification is a fact question. Any question that relies on a respondent's subjective evaluation is a nonfact question (Turner and Martin, 1984:8-10). In practice, this means that specific "hard data" questions that deal with respondent demographics are factual in nature, while "soft data" questions about respondent opinions and attitudes are nonfactual in nature.

Asking a respondent about annual income is a fact question; asking whether that income is enough money to live on is a nonfactual question. Pollsters expect fact questions to yield more accurate and reliable information than nonfactual questions. They assume that people are more easily able to answer questions that draw on personal knowledge or experience than questions that are abstract or speculative (Roper, 1984:24-34).

There is little doubt that factual questions do provide more trustworthy information. But it is important to point out that both factual and nonfactual questions are subject to inaccuracy. Some misreporting occurs with virtually any type of question (Hennessey, 1985:92-95). One widely cited study illustrates how even factual questions are unreliably answered. After verifying respondent answers, it was discovered that 9 percent of the sample falsely claimed library cards, 5 percent inaccurately reported car ownership, and 3 percent said they owned their home whey they did not (M. L. Young, 1987:93). *See also* DEMOGRAPHIC ITEMS; HARD DATA; MISREPORTING.

FATIGUE EFFECTS   *See* QUESTION ORDER EFFECTS.

FILTER QUESTION   *See* THROWAWAYS.

FOCUS GROUPS   Small group interviews conducted to supplement survey data. Focus groups are sets of eight to twelve people, convened by a moderator (or facilitator) who encourages them to talk freely--usually about a specific issues, product, or problem. A focus group is not a cross section of the population. Instead, it is a homogeneous cluster of people who come from a particular market segment or who share demographic characteristics. For example, a focus group might be made up of college-educated women, people over sixty-five, blue-collar workers, or middle-income blacks. Participants from differing backgrounds normally do not interact well during discussion sessions (Levy, 1984:90-91).

Moderators carry out three important tasks in conducting focus groups. Early in the session, they establish rapport within the group and provide some sense of group objectives. Later, after the group has warmed up, moderators focus discussion on relevant topics. Finally, moderators sum up the group's points of agreement and disagreement. All of these moderator tasks are carried out unobtrusively--a key rule of focus group dynamics is that moderators should not bias groups by pulling them one way or another.

Focus groups have many applications. In marketing research, they have been used to evaluate advertising, test new product ideas, and explore consumer motivation (Nieburg, 1984:82-90).   In political work, they are used to supplement polls. For example, focus groups might be convened during the early stages of questionnaire design to talk about the subjects the poll will cover. This information is then used to help develop questionnaires (Weinberg, 1983:334).

The great strength of focus groups is the qualitative information they provide on the deeper attitudes, beliefs, and feelings that people hold. Group spontaneity often yields a steady stream of ideas and insights--and reveals them more fully than can usually be captured in a poll.

The main drawback to focus groups is their limited ability to produce quantitative data. What comes out may be meaningful, but it is hard to count. Groups are almost never based on probability samples, so generalizations to a larger population is risky. Even more troublesome is the self-selection inherent in focus groups. People who agree to participate in them are very likely to have some qualities that set them apart from people who decline, so the representativeness of focus groups is usually limited (Tull and Hawkins, 1980:362-363). *See also* HARD DATA; INCENTIVES.

FOOT-IN-THE-DOOR TECHNIQUE   An interviewing tactic used to induce participation in surveys. Foot-in-the-door technique employs two contacts with respondents--the first is brief and rapport-building, the second is a follow-up, during which the main interview is attempted. Foot-in-the-door can be used for either face-to-face or telephone interviews. It begins with a personal visit (or call) to the prospective respondent. The interviewer asks one or two short questions, then leaves (or hangs up). Soon thereafter, a second visit (or call) is made soliciting the respondent's cooperation for a longer interview (Frey, 1983:94-95).

Foot-in-the-door makes the assumption that respondents will cooperate with even a lengthy survey if they have first "invested" in it by answering an earlier round of questions. This is an old idea in marketing and sales, but there is no solid evidence that it works in polling. Researchers Grove and Magi Levy have tested the effects of the foot-in-the-door technique with two experimental groups. One group received a foot-in-the-door call first; the other was simply approached and asked for a thirty-minute interview. The response rates of both groups were essentially the same (80%), which suggests there may be no advantage in a preliminary contact (Grove and Magi Levy, 1981).

Foot-in-the-door is nevertheless widely used, especially for marketing research surveys. Declining response rates and increasing resistance to surveys may make this technique even more popular in the future. An alternative technique is the use of cover letters for mail surveys, or advance letters for telephone surveys. Unlike with foot-in-the-door, there is empirical evidence that sending letters to prospective respondents does raise response rates (Dillman, 1978:243-245). *See also* CALLBACKS; INTERVIEWING.

FOREIGN ELEMENTS   *See* BLANKS.

FRONT-RUNNERS   Candidates who lead a field of rivals in the preelection polls. Front-runner status is usually determined by the trial heat question, matching competing candidates in head-to-head competition. The actual question varies among polling organizations, but some version of the following is typical:

> Q. If the election for President was held today, and the candidates were (x)_____, (y)_____, and (z)_____, for which one would you vote? (Crespi, 1989:16-18)

Sometimes there are two, three, or more combinations of candidates tested to determine how various matchups turn out.

The conventional wisdom is that front-runners for presidential nominations usually fall by the wayside. In any case, it is believed that being tagged a front-runner too early can ruin electoral ambitions. Most front-runners, in fact, try to lower expectations about their electoral prospects in order to avoid the front-runner label (Levy, 1984:88-89).

Most of the ominous traditional wisdom about front-runners is true, but only for the Democratic party; not the Republicans. In five of the last six elections, the early Democratic front-runners all lost their nomination fights. Yet among Republicans, we have to go back to 1964 to find a front-runner, Nelson Rockefeller, who did not eventually win. In each of the last six elections, Republican front-runners all won their races.

Why do Democratic front-runners almost always lose the nomination and Republicans almost always win? Richard Morin, director of polling for the *Washington Post*, lists five popular theories that attempt to explain this question:

1. *The Fresh Face Factor*--Democrats respond better to "late blooming candidates" (or tire more quickly of early favorites); Republicans stick with the familiar faces.

2. *The Information Gap*--Democrats know less about their candidates in the early contests and so are more likely to lack deep commitment to them. Republicans, on the other hand, "know more about their candidates and know it earlier." Consequently, they are more likely to stick with the first choice.

3. *Early Cash Syndrome*--Democrats' fund-raising gets started more slowly and lasts longer. So late-starting Democrats can still raise money to take a run at the front-runners. But Republican fund-raising starts faster, and front-runners are "more adept at milking party cash cows than are Democrats." So Republican front-runners leave little money available for their rivals.

4. *Party Demographics*--Democrats make up a much more heterogeneous cluster of voting groups than do Republicans. A front-runner coalition is often unstable because it has to be built among the support of "poorly-fitting and often competing voters blocs..." Republicans, however, are relatively homogeneous, so there is less stress and more stability in the coalitions of Republican front-runners.

5. *Different Primary Strategies*--Democrats play by party rules and traditions different than those used by Republicans. In particular, Democratic party reforms have opened the field to little- known or even unknown candidates. But Republicans rules and traditions favor established party figures and leading political figures. (Morin, Sept. 1987:37)

Why Republican front-runners survive, while Democratic front-runners fail, holds more than casual interest. Political power in the United States may be greatly influenced by the vagaries of front-runner status. In fact, most political analysts believe the Republican lock on the White House (five of the last six elections) owes partly to their consistently nominating front-runners, thereby ducking the vicious, expensive, and divisive convention fights now so associated with the Democratic party. *See also* TRIAL HEATS.

FRUGGING   *See* SUGGING.

G

GENDER GAP   Political differences between men and women--specifically, differences in voting patterns and in public opinions.   The gender gap is measured by polling.   In fact, we would have no evidence of the gender gap, but for polls--especially exit polls, which show how people actually voted and suggest what motivated them (M. L. Young, 1987:86).   Since 1980, these polls have consistently disclosed two key differences linked to gender.   First, women are more likely than men to vote for Democratic candidates; and second, women hold different opinions than men on a number of domestic and foreign issues. These differences--both the pro-Democratic voting and the issue differences--are on the order of 5 to 10 percentage points (Asher, 1988:187-191).

The gender gap shows up in virtually every social and political group, but it is most pronounced among westerners, younger women, whites, and unmarried voters.   The latter group is particularly important, registering a gender gap two to three times larger than among the overall population.

Six prominent gender gap issues separate men and women.   Three of these-- increased defense spending, nuclear power, and the death penalty--are more opposed by women than by men.   The other three--gun control, social security, and arms control--are more favored by women than by men (Heidepriem and Lake, 1987:6-7).   The so-called women's issues--the ERA, reproductive choice, and sexual discrimination--also show a gender gap, but one not as wide as on some other issues.

There is no settled explanation for the gender gap.   One popular idea is that the women's vote is motivated by economics.   Women, according to this view, have been more harshly treated economically than men, so they are simply pursuing their economic interests in the candidates they vote for and the issues they support (Frankovic, 1982:431-448).

Whatever causes the gender gap, its continuation could have profound political implications.   By the early 1990s, there were about ten million more women than men among the voting age population.   Moreover, women overall were registering and turning out to vote at heavier rates than men. In national elections, a combination of the gender gap and the larger number of women voters could give Democrats a sizeable voting edge over Republicans. This does not (as often forecast) mean the GOP and its candidates would no longer win national elections. What it does mean is that Republicans would no longer be able to win the really close national elections. Only in landslides--where the women's vote is not decisive--would Republicans remain competitive.

GENERIC WORDS   Words with broad meanings that may differ among respondents.   Generic words resemble what Stanley Payne has called blab words--words with vague, abstract, multiple, and often contradictory meanings (Payne, 1951:149). Researcher Patricia Labaw first encountered generic words in her political research:

> I asked the respondents to define what they meant by "honest" in a politician. I obtained at least four major definitions of honesty, and some of them were absolutely contradictory. ...In Hudson County...honesty means, he votes the way I do; in Princeton...honesty means, he votes his conscience;...in some communities...honesty means he is not on the take, not taking bribes; in other areas honesty means he tells the truth, tells it like it is. (Labaw, 1981:158)

Labaw acknowledges that generic words can be a problem in question writing. But she differs with writers like Payne who counsel avoiding them altogether. Instead, she advocates "asking the respondent to define generic words." So if a respondent says that "moderate" politicians represent his or her view; ask the respondent what the word moderate means.   Or if a banking client wants to improve the "quality" of services;   ask respondents what attributes make a quality bank.

Generic words address an old issue in polling, the so-called frame of reference problem.   When pollsters and respondents share an understanding about what a question means; they may be said to share a frame of reference (Schuman and Presser, 1981:51-53).   Pollsters always need to know "where respondents are coming from."   But there is more than one way to do this. Avoiding blab words is one method; using generic words after defining then is another. *See also* BLAB WORDS; GOOD WORDS.

GEO-DEMOGRAPHICS   A newer research tool that combines census data with public opinion surveys.   The principle behind geo-demographics is commonsensical: similar people cluster (live) near one another, and they share many opinions and behaviors. Geo-demographics categorizes people by demographic and lifestyle variables. The main ones used are education, occupation, income, hobbies, and spending patterns. Polling data is essential to geo-demographics. It identifies particular groups according to how they answer key questions. Then the neighborhoods and communities these people live in are located so that people can be contacted by phone or direct mail (Sabato, 1981:202-204). Pollsters doing political work have been especially enthusiastic about geo-demographics. One prominent pollster explains why:

> Never before have we had a situation where a pollster can tell a campaign, "Look, we have problems with people who live in new towns, who are white and upper-middle class," then tell the guy that 40 of those people live in this county, 60 here and 120 here. And here are their names, addresses and telephone numbers. (Nieburg, 1984:48)

Claritas is the trade name of the most widely known geo-demographic system. The claritas system divides the entire population into forty nonoverlapping clusters, each composed of people with similar backgrounds and lifestyles. Claritas uses colorful names to identify each of the forty clusters such as Blue Blood Estates, Hard Scrabbles, God's Country, and Bohemian Mix. Each cluster carries a profile of the people found in it. Cluster 27, for example, includes upper-class, mobile managers; Cluster 6 is made up of poor, grade-school-educated people living in rural neighborhoods. Polling data reveals which clusters are important, then geo-demographics locates the neighborhood and the communities where people in that cluster live (M. L. Young, 1987:121; Salmore and Salmore, 1989:182-183). *See also* DEMOGRAPHIC ITEMS; PUBLIC OPINION RESEARCH.

GOOD POLL Any poll designed and conducted in such a way that a prudent person would have confidence in the reported findings. Good polls observe accepted scientific procedures in drawing samples, asking questions, and analyzing data. Bad polls, conversely, flout the generally accepted conventions of scientific polling. In practice, some polls are very good, and a few are very bad. But most are a blend of both good and bad practice.

Still, there are fundamental differences between good and bad polls. David Gergen and William Schambra write that even laypeople can tell the difference-- when they know what to look for. Among the critical issues are method of sampling (should be probability), reputation of the pollster, and fairness of the questions (Gergen and Schambra, 1979:66-68, 70-72).

Another helpful approach to evaluating polls is determining if reasonable disclosure standards have been met in releasing the results. Polls should reveal actual questions asked, describe interviewing methods and dates, report completion rates, identify sponsor(s) and explain weighting procedures. Polls that do all this inspire more trust than polls that hold back information (Nieburg, 1984:259-264).

Veteran pollster Burns W. Roper recommends a practical rule of thumb for assessing accuracy: polls that ask factual questions are most accurate, next most accurate are opinion question polls, and least accurate of all are polls that ask speculative questions or questions about future intent. Roper also ridicules the idea that sampling error is a major quality issue in polling. An otherwise good poll, says the veteran pollster, is more likely to go bad due to faulty question writing (Roper, 1984:24-34). *See also* DISCLOSURE; SAMPLING ERROR.

GOOD WORDS   Words and phrases that convey concrete specific meanings when used in poll questions. Good words are opposite of blab words--the term invented by Stanley Payne to describe abstract, ambiguous, often polysyllabic words subject to multiple meanings. Blab words are words like reform, policy, fairness, government and leadership--all words so vague and general that a respondent's interpretation of them cannot be known for sure. Good words are words that tap basic language--words like baby, couch, drink, elephants, and so on. Used in polls, good words improve the chances that respondents understand the question--no small feat.

Unfortunately, good words are hard to find. Payne himself in *The Art of Asking Questions* disabused his readers of any hope that the search for good words would ever be easy:

> Most question worders, myself included, would welcome a list
> of "good" words--words that could without questions be used
> in any question. Essentially these words should be both single
> in meaning and generally understood....But the list of words
> which would fulfill al these requests would not be very long.
> Familiarity, wide usage, and single meanings do not go hand
> in hand. Quite the contrary, words that come into common
> use tend, in the process, to acquire a variety of meanings and
> nuances. (Payne, 1951:138)

If good words are rare, blab words are commonplace. And that disparity between the good and the blab point out the most critical methodological challenge facing contemporary polling: drafting questions that are intelligently understood by respondents, and consistently interpreted by pollsters. Question wording problems are no trivial matter: more than any other issue, they frustrate modern polling's efforts to become a precise science Robinson and Meadow, 1983). *See also* BLAB WORDS; GENERIC WORDS.

H

HAPHAZARD SAMPLE   *See* CONVENIENCE SAMPLE.

HARD DATA   Pollster jargon for respondent answers to factual or objective questions. Hard data comes from "hard" questions: how old are you? Are you employed? Do you own a car? Are you registered to vote? What is your annual income?

Hard data is factual and descriptive; its "hardness" derives from two characteristics: first, it provides specific, concrete, and tangible information. A researcher can specify exactly what is meant by being unemployed, having some college, being Hispanic, or not voting recently. Second, hard data can be verified by consulting records, family members, or other sources. If a respondent claims to be a college graduate, it can be checked. When someone reports they are registered to vote, it can be verified.

Hard data is not the only way to classify poll responses. There is also soft data, which is pollster jargon for answers given to opinion or subjective questions. Soft data comes from soft questions (Bohrnstedt, 1983:81), such as: are you in good, fair, or poor health? Do you think of yourself as a conservative, moderate, or liberal? What is the most important problem facing the nation today?

Soft data deals with opinions, attitudes, feelings, and impressions rather than facts or knowledge.

The hard-soft distinction has two practical implications. First, hard data is generally considered more trustworthy than soft data. Respondents are more likely to "get it right" and report it accurately. Second, hard data questions are usually easier to ask and answer than are soft ones--both respondents and interviewers are taxed less. Occasionally, the hard-soft distinction is treated as a synonym for classifying data according to whether it is quantitative or qualitative. Quantitative data is described as hard, and qualitative as soft.

As a general practice, however, treating hard-soft as equivalent to quantitative-qualitative is not sound. It is true enough that hard data is usually counted and, therefore, quantitative--but so is most soft data. In reality, hard-soft and qualitative-quantitative describe different aspects of survey data (Turner and Martin, 1984:8-10;407-410). *See also* DEMOGRAPHIC ITEMS; FACT QUESTIONS.

HARD ID   A popular way to describe the name recognition of a public figure. Hard ID refers to the proportion of respondents who have heard about a named person--and know enough to rate that person on a ten-point scale. The standard hard ID question is as follows:

> Next, I'll read some names of public figures. Please tell me on a 1 to 10 scale how negative or how positive you personally feel toward each person. A "1" indicates strong negative feelings, while a "10" indicates strong positive feelings. If you haven't heard of the public figure, just say so.

If 60 percent of respondents rate someone on the 1-10 scale, that person's hard ID is 60 percent. Soft ID consists of hard ID plus those respondents who say they have heard of the public figure, but can not give them a rating. These respondents "can't say" how they personally feel toward the public figure whose name they recognize. Soft ID runs about 5 percent higher than hard ID for most public figures. *See also* NAME RECOGNITION QUESTION.

HARRISBURG PENNSYLVANIAN   Generally acknowledged as the first newspaper in America to conduct and publish a presidential preference straw poll. *Harrisburg Pennsylvanian* surveyed groups of citizens in Wilmington, Delaware, during July 1824, asking about their presidential favorites (Gergen and Schambra, 1979:63). The results, "without discrimination of findings," revealed Andrew Jackson with a commanding lead (335 votes) over opponents John Quincy Adams (109 votes), Henry Clay (19 votes), and William Crawford (9 votes).

Jackson's front-runner status did not last. He eventually lost the election to John Quincy Adams after it was thrown into the House of Representatives-- the only U.S. election so decided. *Harrisburg Pennsylvanian* poll marked the beginning of an era of straw polling that lasted over one hundred years--until

1936, when the *Literary Digest* straw poll "elected" Alf Landon over Franklin Roosevelt. That fiasco soon produced demand for more scientific polls (Roll and Cantril, 1972:7). But until 1936, straw polls were virtually the only form of political polling done, and most of them-- just like the first--were conducted by newspapers. *See also LITERARY DIGEST*; STRAW POLL.

HEAD OF HOUSEHOLD *See* HOUSEHOLD.

HIRED GUN POLLS   Polls commissioned and carried out to promote a particular point of view. Hired gun polls are associated with reckless disregard for objectivity. Robinson and Meadow provide an example:

> Typical of the "hired gun" poll is a telephone survey done by George Fine Research for the Committee on the Present Danger, a group that favored a hard line on the SALT II TREATY. Respondents were asked to choose from four position statements the one that best represented their opinion....Three of the four options were negative...of the 71% willing to express an opinion (29% had no opinion on the treaty), an overwhelming 42% chose (the loaded) option. (Robinson and Meadows, 1983:14)

A synonym for the term hired gun poll is the term advocacy poll--although the hired gun metaphor connotes a much sleazier and less professional image. Selective reporting of poll results is one mark of hired gun polls. Another is questions worded to reflect the positions of sponsors. Both practices blatantly violate accepted ethical standards in the polling field.

Many writers view with alarm what they believe to be an increase in hired gun polling (Turner and Martin, 1984:84-86). But not everyone shares the concern. Harry O'Neill, for example, believes that advocacy research--which he defines as "providing a client with information to be used in advocating a particular point of view"--is legitimate and desirable. O'Neill argues that the topics of advocacy research are some of the most important political and social issues of the day. So it is fitting and appropriate that public opinion concerning them should be studied (Cantril, 1980:175-182).

O'Neill's perspective is probably not the majority view about polls designed to advance a cause. Still, his main point seems important. Hired gun polls should be judged by how well they are done rather than by how they are used (Crespi, 1989:40-42). *See also* ADVOCACY POLL.

HISTORICAL METHOD   A technique for inferring public opinion by looking to some historical circumstance. Historical method tracks from some specific documented event, back to the public opinion that would have accounted for it. Harwood Childs has described the causal chain assumed by the historical methods:

> The best index to public opinion is the accomplished fact. To find out what public opinion was, one need only start with an event, a legislative act, a meeting, a battle or any specific fact or event and then deduce what public opinion must have been. (Childs, 1965:66-67)

The historical method takes a retrospective approach to public opinion. By this view of things, historical events are simply logical consequences of whatever public opinion existed at the time.

The historical method is controversial. One of the issues it raises is the validity of using determinism to explain historical events. Nevertheless, the technique has some interesting applications. For example, the historical method might be used to infer the public opinion that resulted in Geraldine Ferraro's 1984 Democratic nomination for vice-president. Or the accomplished fact of federal tax reform legislation in 1986 might be used to deduce public opinion about the previously existing tax system. Still another example: the rising incidence of execution in the United States could be used to estimate public opinion about the criminal justice system.

The historical method need not be limited to the past. Future scenarios could be developed, then the public opinion needed to "explain" them could be described. For example, a balanced budget amendment might be added to the Constitution; what public opinion would be needed to bring this about? Another scenario: a black person is nominated for the presidency. What public opinion would have to exist to account for that result? *See also* WEIRD SCIENCE.

HOUSE EFFECTS   Any influence on survey findings due solely to the procedures used by the survey organization. House effects produce different answers to the same question asked at the same time (T. W. Smith, 1978:443). Many factors may explain the differences between polls. Slight differences in question wording, for example, can produce large differences in results; even the order in which questions are asked may influence the answers given. House effects, however, are strictly those differences traceable to a survey organization's unique procedures. The three main causes of house effects are believed to be: (1) different sampling methods, (2) different interviewing techniques, and (3) different approaches to analyzing data (Turner and Martin, 1984:161).

An example: say both the Gallup and the Harris organizations ask the following question at about the same time:

Do you think the use of marijuana should be made legal or not?

Gallup's answers are: should be legal, 65 percent; should not be legal, 35 percent. But Harris's answers are: should be legal, 55 percent; should not be legal, 45 percent--a 10 percent difference between the two polls. At least some and maybe all of the 10 percent can be attributed to house effects between the Gallup and Harris organizations.

How important are house effects, and how frequently do they occur? Systematic research has studied two types of polls where house effects would be most apparent: tandem studies, in which two or more survey organizations conducted interviews for the same study; and ad hoc occasions when two or more survey houses happened to ask the same question about the same time (Turner and Martin, 1984:149-154). This research has generally concluded that house effects do occur, but that they probably do not account for large differences between surveys. Moreover, most of the house effects that do occur can be traced to how survey organizations deal with "don't knows" (DKs) and "no response" (NRs) answers. Different ways of treating nonresponse probably accounts for most house effects (T. W. Smith, 1978:443-463). *See also* DK/NR; RESPONSE RATE; TANDEM SURVEYS.

HOUSEHOLD   People who live in separate dwellings, known as "housing units." Households refers to people, while housing unit refers to the physical structure lived in, such as a house or apartment (Backstrom and Hursh-Cesar, 1981:79-80).

Household is an important notion in polling. The household is one of survey research's most common units of analysis--the thing being studied. Other units of analysis, such as individuals, organizations, or events, are sometimes employed, but most often it is household that is used to define the population, draw the sample, and weight the results.

Using household (the people) as the unit of analysis requires defining housing unit (the physical structure), and there's the rub. Some survey organizations fail to define what a housing unit is, leaving the decision up to individual interviewers. Others use definitions difficult to understand, or too vague to apply; still other organizations change their definitions from study to study or even within the same study. Confusion frequently arises: do nontraditional sites like trailers, boats, tents, and even abandoned cars, constitute housing units? What about hotels and rooming houses? And how is "head of household"--a popular category of respondent--to be identified?

These problems in defining housing units and identifying households mean that standards of practice range considerably--particularly for deciding who belongs in sampling frames and how survey results should be weighted. One consequence is that two apparently similar studies may not be comparable at all because of differences in the population surveyed--differences attributed to how households and housing units have been defined (Martin, 1983:682-685). *See also* INTERVIEWERS.

HOUSING UNITS   *See* HOUSEHOLDS.

HUMAN SUBJECT AT RISK   *See* HUMAN SUBJECTS.

HUMAN SUBJECTS   People interviewed for a poll or survey. The use of human subjects raises several ethical issues in survey research. Underlying all of them is concern about people who may be "at risk"--that is, who may be exposed to potential harm because of the research (Welch and Comer, 1975:288-291). Three general principles provide ethical guidance to survey researchers in relations with their human subjects: (1) informed consent--respondents should be fully informed about the research; (2) respondent confidentiality should be protected; (3) respondent benefits should be explained and then provided. Each principle has produced fairly specific interviewer guidelines:

1. Informed Consent--Before being interviewed, respondents should give informed consent. They should understand any risks associated with the research and should know their participation is voluntary. Respondents should also be told what the research is generally about and who is conducting it.

2. Respondent Confidentiality--Researchers should follow reasonable procedures to minimize the chance the confidentiality will be violated. Access to data should be tightly controlled. Names and addresses should never be given to anyone outside the survey organization, nor should data be released that allows the identification of individuals or small groups.

3. Respondent Benefits--Respondents should be told of any benefits they will receive, without exaggeration or distortion. The promised benefits should be delivered. Sometimes cash incentives are paid to respondents. More often, benefits are intangibles: the satisfaction of expressing an opinion, or the gratification of contributing to social science. (Fowler, 1984:135-144)

During the late 1970s, the federal government adopted regulations that formalize these principles. Institutional Review Boards (IRBs) were established to certify that risks to respondents were minimal, and that respondents had given their informed consent to the research. Before long, however, IRBs became bogged down in a welter of bureaucratic rules and paper shuffling. Finally, revised regulations were issued exempting most surveys from formal human subjects review. Two major exceptions were created in the new federal regulations. The first is any circumstance where a breach of confidentiality would expose an individual to civil or criminal liability. The second exception is surveys that deal with sensitive subjects such as sexual behavior, drug use, alcohol abuse, and so on (Nieburg, 1984: Ch. 12). When either of these kinds of situations exists, a formal human subjects review is usually required. *See also* CONFIDENTIALITY; DISCLOSURE; INFORMED CONSENT.

HYPOTHETICALS   Poll questions that ask respondents to answer about some possible future condition. Hypotheticals are "what if" questions--what would you do if such and such were to happen, or if this or that product were available? (Hoinville, 1978:43-44). Consumers, for example, might be asked: "If you were buying a new car, what features would you want it to have?" Voters might be asked: "If the election were held today and the candidates were (X) the Republican and (Y) the Democrat, whom would you support?" Hypotheticals occur in almost every poll. Indeed, asking "what if" questions seems indigenous to survey work:

> Prediction of future behavior on the basis of survey questions plays, and must be expected to play, a central role in survey applications.   Market researchers would like--and try--to predict how people will react to a proposed change in the price of a product, to an alteration to its quality or packaging; how many people are likely to buy cars, radios or television sets in a given period, and so on. (Mosher and Kalton, 1972:326)

Pollsters usually weigh carefully answers to hypotheticals.   While respondents may give truthful replies, accuracy is a problem with all "what if" questions. Few respondents are really capable of forecasting their behavior or attitudes based on a hypothetical scenario. In fact, until a situation is real and immediate, many people have trouble answering questions about it at all. *See also* MR. SMITH QUESTION.

I

IMAGE QUESTIONS   Any questions asked by pollsters probing feelings about a political candidate's personality or character. Image questions use a variety of formats and approaches; most basic is the "like about," "dislike about" form. Respondents are asked what they like about candidate X, then what they dislike? (Agranoff, 1976:136-137). Some image questions ask respondents to evaluate candidates on their integrity, their performance in office, or their personal compassion.

Another standard image question is the job approval question, used to measure how well voters think an incumbent is performing. The major pollsters each phrase the job question a little differently. Gallup asks respondents:

> Do you approve or disapprove of the way (the incumbent) is handling his job?

Harris, however, poses the question this way:

> How would you rate the job (the incumbent) has been doing - excellent, pretty good, only fair or poor?

One popular device is ratings on a numerical scale. A respondent might be asked to rate a public figure on some attribute from +5 (best) to -5 (worst). A similar question asks respondents to picture a large thermometer scale, then say how warm or cold they feel towards a public figure. A politician who is rated low on approval or cold on the thermometer is said to have "high negatives." *See also* APPROVAL RATING.

INCENTIVES   Payments or gifts given to respondents. Incentives are not intended to be compensation so much as they are tokens of appreciation and regard. Researchers hope that a small gift or modest payment will make respondents feel positive about the study and willing to respond to it. The psychology of incentives is important to understand. Researchers describe them as "extrinsic" rewards--something that motivates respondents beyond the "intrinsic" benefits of being interviewed (Gorden, 1969:133-134; Nederhof, 1983:103-111).

Virtually any object can be used as an incentive. Popular items include money, stamps, pens, coupons, tickets, key rings, medals, magazines, and books. What do researchers look for in selecting incentives? Writers Alreck and Settle list six specific criteria: items should be inexpensive; they should not be connected to any questions asked; they should be useful; they should have some intrinsic value; they should be personalized; and they should be items that are perceived as luxuries instead of utilitarian objects (Alreck and Settle, 1985:215).

Incentives are not yet common in survey research, although the practice is growing. When used, they are frequently paired with mail polls, which is certainly a combination that makes sense. Mail surveys suffer from low response rates; incentives are supposed to increase those rates. The two together do appear to work. Various studies have found that incentives raise mail response rates by 25 percent or more (Johnson and Joslyn, 1986:97-98; Marsh, 1982:136).

Focus group research is another area where incentives are frequently used. Payments of ten dollars and up are offered to prospective respondents. In major cities, professionals are paid one hundred dollars or more to attend a focus group. Here incentives do function more as compensation, since focus group members frequently incur travel and other costs incidental to their participation. *See also* FOCUS GROUPS.

INCOME QUESTION   Asking respondents to report annual income during the polling interview. Income questions are considered among the most personal questions. Interviewers may ask about age, education, religion, political party, even personal life. But the income question incites more resistance and produces higher refusals than any of these. Herbert Weisberg and Bruce Bowen illustrate the kind of experience almost every pollster has had with the income question:

> In the early 1960's, the University of Michigan's Detroit area
> study surveyed attitudes relating to fertility. Their interview
> schedule asked Detroit women a number of intimate questions
> about how satisfied they were with aspects of their marriages.
> A number of refusals were expected, but few were obtained.
> The interviews sailed along smoothly until they reached the

> income question, which many women refused to answer
> because it was "too personal." Apparently, they considered
> income to be more personal than their sex life! (1977:53)

Information about income is vital to analyze polls. so despite its sensitivity, income questions are rarely omitted from questionnaires. Still, pollsters approach the income question carefully, and analyze answers to it with healthy skepticism. The conventional approach asks respondents to choose an income range corresponding to their family income. Interviewers read something like the following:

> Now, just for summary purposes, I need to know your
> approximate income. Is it (read rapidly) less than 10,000;
> 10,000 to 18,000, 18,000 to 25,000; 25,000 to 35,000;
> 35,000 to 50,000; more than 50,000?

The income question is traditionally placed toward the end of an interview, in order to reduce respondent resistance. By then some rapport between interviewer and respondent has been established. Even if the interview is broken off at that point, some data will have been collected. Refusal rates of 20 percent or more are not unusual for income questions. More disturbing, perhaps, respondents who do answer may exaggerate. One widely cited study of misreporting estimated that about one in four respondents inflate their income--on average by about 10 percent (Hoinville and Jowell, 1978:167-168). *See also* MISREPORTING.

INDEX   A composite measure of public opinion based on several related questions. Indexes have been constructed to measure such things as political interest, alienation, prejudice, media use, trust in government, and likelihood of voting. The methodological rationale for using an index is simple enough: single questions can not accurately measure complex opinions or attitudes, but an index that combines several questions can. Herbert Weisberg and Bruce Bowen explain this logic with an example:

> If you wanted to measure how cynical the person is about the
> government, you might find it necessary to ask a series of
> questions: "How much of the time do you feel you can trust
> the government to do what is right?" "Do you think that
> people in the government waste a lot of the money we pay in
> taxes, waste some of it, or do not waste very much of it?"
> "Do you think that quite a few of the people running the
> government are a little crooked, not very many are, or do you

think hardly any of them are crooked?" You might feel that no single question provides a perfect measure of cynicism, but these several questions could be combined into an index of how many cynical responses the person gives. (Weisberg and Bowen, 1977:44)

Indexes are "additive" measures. Several questions (or variables) are combined to yield the composite score. For example, a researcher may use an index to identify who are the likely voters among respondents to a poll. Five individual questions might be selected to predict likely voting: (1) being registered to vote; (2) knowing the location of the polling place; (3) expressing interest in the upcoming election; (4) planning to vote on election day; and (5) having voted in recent elections (Backstrom and Hursh-Cesar, 1981:220-224). A respondent who passed all five of these "screens" would be given an index score of five, someone who passed none would be zero, and so forth.

The term index is loosely used as a synonym for the term scale. An index and a scale do share common ground. Both are composites made up of two or more questions, and both rank respondents from low to high. But careful methodologists distinguish between indexes and scales (Babbie, 1973:255). Indexes average answers, but scales go further. They weight answers according to some criterion such as intensity. In effect, scales provide more information than indexes do. Not surprisingly, they also cost more to develop and use. Choosing between an index and scale often comes down to a practical question: is the additional information needed, or will an index serve the purpose just as well? *See also* SCALE; SCREENERS.

INDIGENOUS INTERVIEWERS   Interviewers who are matched with prospective respondents according to race, ethnicity, income, education, or other social factors. Indigenous interviewers come from backgrounds similar to those being interviewed. They may be ethnic Italians interviewing in south Philadelphia, Appalachian whites in Kentucky, or inner-city blacks in Washington, D.C. The argument for using indigenous interviewers is that certain populations, especially minorities, are unlikely to be candid with anyone perceived as an outsider. But if interviewers are people drawn from the population to be interviewed--if they are indigenous to it--they will be more successful at completing interviews and getting accurate answers to the questions they ask (Backstrom and Hursh-Cesar, 1981:242-245).

Experts at the University of Michigan, for example, have found that white interviewers of blacks get significantly different answers than black interviewers asking the same questions of other blacks. The same effect has been observed for whites. Even with questions not obviously race-sensitive, black interviewers get different answers from whites than white interviews do (Weiss and Hatry, 1971:35).

One of the perplexing things about findings like these is the issue they raise about poll accuracy: which response is the "true answer"? Is it the response given to indigenous interviewers (black to black, ethnic to ethnic, etc.), or is the "true answer" the response given when no racial or ethnic cues are present? Barry Sussman, while polling director of the *Washington Post*, told of his own efforts to grapple with this question--in this instance, two polls showing widely varying approval ratings among blacks for Ronald Reagan. One poll was mostly taken by black interviewers; the other was done by white interviewers. Sussman asked:

> Which response is the "real" one for blacks...the one given to
> a white interviewer, or to a black interviewer? I put these
> questions to a black colleague. He didn't have an answer.
> But then again, may be he would have, had I been black.
> (Sussman, 1986:37)

To some extent, using indigenous interviewers runs counter to accepted practice for surveys. The conventional wisdom is that the best interviewers are people whose personalities do not affect the way respondents answer questions. This maxim often results in the selection of interviewers who are middle-class, middle-aged, and female. But for studies involving special populations, indigenous interviewers may be a better choice--and this seems even more the case if "high threat" questions are asked (Bradburn, 1983:313). *See also* INTERVIEWERS.

INDIRECT QUESTION *See* PROJECTIVE TECHNIQUES.

INFORMANTS *See* RESPONDENT.

INFORMED CONSENT   The notion that respondents, before being interviewed, should understand any risks associated with a survey and know that their participation is voluntary. Informed consent is an ethical principle. It grew out of concern that human subjects of research (including surveys) were not always informed about the possible risks to themselves. Risks in surveys include such things as invasions of privacy, unauthorized disclosure of information, and the stress of being interviewed (Williamson, et al., 1982:95-96; Frey, 1983:178-180).

The informed consent principle is generally understood to require researchers to provide six types of information to prospective respondents:

1. Name of the polling organization
2. Name of the sponsor of the poll
3. Brief description of the research project
4. Indication whether answers will be confidential
5. Acknowledgement that participation is voluntary
6. And assurance that participants may refuse to answer any question. (Fowler, 1984:135-139)

In 1977, the federal government adopted legislation that required informed consent in research projects receiving federal money. Under the National Research Act, respondents had to give informed consent in writing--unless Institutional Review Boards (IRBs) had previously certified that risks to respondents were minimal.

Creating IRBs triggered an avalanche of bureaucratic regulation that threatened to disrupt serious social research. Under revised federal rules, most surveys are now exempt from formal review, and informed consent in writing is almost never required (Nieburg, 1984:238-245). Informed consent, as an operating principle, however, is still important. Most researchers observe it by informing prospective respondents at the beginning of the interview what the research is about and who is conducting it. Respondents are told their answers will be confidential (if they will be) and reminded that participation is voluntary. Respondents who then go on with the interview are presumed to have given their informed consent. *See also* CONFIDENTIALITY; HUMAN SUBJECTS.

IN-HOME POLL   *See* FACE-TO-FACE INTERVIEW.

IN-HOUSE POLL   A survey conducted by a business, nonprofit organization, government agency or other organization for itself. In-house polls use internal staff and resources to do the research instead of contracting with an outside company. Respondents may be employees, customers, clients, students, staff, legislators, or virtually any population whose opinions and attitudes are of interest. Many of America's largest corporations carry on extensive in-house surveys. These include AT&T, General Foods, CBS, NBC and the *New York Times* (Turner and Martin, 1984:348-349).

In-house polls run the gamut--from inexpensive questionnaires stuffed in pay envelopes to elaborate, sophisticated depth interviews. Quality also varies. At one extreme are carefully designed, faithfully executed, competently analyzed sample surveys employing much the same methods used by commercial pollsters. At the other extreme are sloppy, badly designed, poorly administered surveys that provide little or no useful information.

In-house surveys are often lumped in the same category as ad hoc surveys-- the latter are special purpose one-time studies, such as might be carried on by a municipality measuring the demand for recreation services. According to the *Handbook of Survey Research*, in-house and ad hocs together account for an entire sector of the social survey industry (Rossi, Wright, and Anderson, 1983:14). Thousands of ad hoc and in-house surveys are done each year. Virtually every major business polls its customers and employees from time to time. So do many governments, and nonprofits such as hospitals, schools, universities, and even churches. No one really knows how many such studies are done. One clue, however, is the number of them discussed on in the periodical literature. One scholar found that 30 percent of the surveys reported in sociology journals were not conducted by ongoing survey organizations. It is very likely that 30 percent is a conservative estimate of the actual proportion of surveys done ad hoc or in-house (Rossi, Wright, and Anderson, 1983:15). *See also* POLL COSTS; POLLING INDUSTRY.

INSTRUMENT   The questionnaire used by interviewers during a survey. Instruments are the "tools" with which information is collected and opinion is measured (Selltiz, Wrightsman, and Cook, 1976:542-563). Also referred to as the interview schedule, the instrument follows a more or less standardized sequence of question types. At least nine distinct kinds of questions are used:

1. *Introductions*--usually not formal questions, but opening statements designed to induce participation and gain the respondent's "informed consent."
2. *Screening questions*--often follow the introduction, and are designed to separate (screen) respondents by some qualification such as income or previous experience.
3. *Party affiliation questions*--asked in political polls about a respondent's partisan leanings--are they Democrats, Republicans, or what?
4. *Name identification questions*--these measure awareness of a product, a politician, a public figure, or an organization.
5. *Issue questions*--typically include a series of open and closed questions about current topics and public problems.
6. *Image questions*--measure feelings and attitudes about public figures, perceptions of institutions, and approval of politicians.

7. *Horse race questions*--used in political polls, ask which candidate will you vote for on election day, or which candidate would you vote for if <u>today</u> was election day.
8. *Media use questions*--what TV and radio stations do you listen to, when do you listen, and how often? Which newspapers and magazines do you use?
9. *Demographic questions*--respondent's age, sex, race, income, schooling, etc. (Karweit and Meyers, 1983:379-382)

Not all nine question types are used in every poll. For example, nonpolitical polls are unlikely to use horse race questions or political affiliation questions. The sequence of question types, however, is not random. Different questions are designed to achieve important goals as the interview progresses. Introductions are important for inducing participation and warming up both respondent and interviewer (Weisberg, Krosnick, and Bowen, 1989:78-83). Tougher questions, like issue and image questions, come toward the middle, when respondents are comfortable but not yet tired. And demographic questions come last, because they are most likely to elicit resistance or refusal. *See also* DEMOGRAPHIC ITEMS; INTRODUCTION; NAME RECOGNITION QUESTION; SCREENERS; TRIAL HEATS.

INTERCEPT SURVEYS   *See* EXIT POLLS.

INTERPRETATION   *See* ELABORATION PARADIGM.

INTERVIEW   *See* INTERVIEWING.

INTERVIEWERS   Survey workers who seek out and ask respondents questions during a poll. Interviewers are the critical resource in survey research. Success or failure in a study can often be traced back to the quality of the interviewing. There are three major sources of interviewers: (1) commercial interviewing houses, (2) in-house staff, and (3) volunteers. Each source has advantages and disadvantages (Backstrom and Hursh-Cesar, 1981:238-241).

First, commercial interviewing houses, provide experienced interviewers and reduce the administrative load of survey managers. But cost is high, and quality control can be a problem. In-house staff, a second source of interviewers, is less expensive and staffers may have background expertise. But in-house staff usually need extensive training and may be biased regarding the subject matter of the study. The third source of interviewers, volunteers, is low-cost, and volunteers are often highly motivated. But there are drawbacks here too. Volunteers must be recruited and trained. They are also notorious for their resistance to control and direction.

Many different types of people make successful interviewers.   Six characteristics in particular, however, seem associated with successful interviewing (Backstrom and Hursh-Cesar, 1981:242-245):

1. Age--Interviewers are generally between twenty-five and fifty-five years old. People younger than eighteen are rare; those over sixty-five may not be able to cope with the physical demands of interviewing.
2. Sex--Most interviewers are women and some researchers believe women are better than men. But there are no hard and fast rules here and more men are becoming interviewers.
3. Physical Characteristics--General good health and a neat, pleasing personal appearance is important.   Interviewers should also look as normal and average as possible.
4. Personality--The best interviewers are extroverted, interested in other people and good listeners. Neither very timid or extremely aggressive people make good interviewers.
5. Education--High school education is usually a minimum requirement. Interviewers with college backgrounds are more successful. But too much education can be a negative if the difference between respondent and interviewer is too great.
6. Race/Ethnicity--The general rule is that interviewers from the same race or ethnic background as respondents do better.   Whites are more successful with large general populations, while indigenous interviewers (blacks with blacks, for example) do better with minority populations.

In addition to these six specific factors, there are some rules of thumb about choosing interviewers. Obviously, people with previous interviewing experience will generally perform better than those without experience. Another guideline is that a special background in or direct knowledge of the survey topic is a plus. For example, a former prison inmate would be a better interviewer for a survey of ex-offenders than would be a graduate student in criminology. One of the best rules for selecting interviewers is also one of the simplest: people who are most like the people interviewed will produce the best interviews (Bradburn, 1983:313). *See also* BOILER ROOM OPERATION; INDIGENOUS INTERVIEWER; INTERVIEWER'S MANUAL; INTERVIEWING.

INTERVIEWER'S MANUAL   A field guide prepared for interviewers. Interviewer's manuals vary in format and content. Most review the basic principles of interviewing, describe common problems that will be encountered, and suggest field procedures that should be followed. Some manuals, in addition, give an overview of sampling procedures, weighting, and other technical matters (Worcester, 1972:136).

There are two basic types of manuals. One type is designed to be a reference book--the widely used University of Michigan's *Interviewer's Manual* is the leading example. These are compendiums of interviewing lore and practice applicable to most interviewing contexts. (Survey Research Center, 1976). The other type of manual is developed and written for a specific survey. Sometimes referred to as "interview specifications," these are more detailed, pay attention to operational matters, and tend to stress the unique conditions of the specific study for which they were written (Weinberg, 1983:349-350).

Interviewing manuals sometimes run to several hundred pages--making them bulky, heavy to carry in the field, and difficult to access for quick reference. Many users complain, in fact, that manuals are too long, with too much information not essential for interviewers to know. Addressing this point, Eve Weinberg has suggested a useful rule for deciding what goes into interviewer's manuals:

> Will it help the interviewers do a better job in carrying out the
> task of this survey? If the answer is "yes," include it; if "no,"
> leave it out. Following this adage will prevent manual writers
> from writing unnecessarily long manuals.   (Weinberg,
> 1983:349)

Following Weinberg's advice, manual writers not only won't have to write "unnecessarily long manuals," but manual readers won't have to read them, either. *See also* INTERVIEWERS; INTERVIEWING.

INTERVIEWING   The research technique that uses questions to collect information.   Interviewing relies on people self-reporting their behavior, attitudes, and opinions. It is this self-reporting, in fact, that distinguishes surveys from other kinds of social science data collection, such as observation, experiments, use of records, and so forth (Gorden, 1969; Kahn and Cannell, 1967).

Interviewing methods are traditionally classified into three modes: (1) face-to-face interviews, in which the interviewer seeks out and interviews respondents at home, in the office, while shopping, at school, or virtually any place physical contact can be established; (2) telephone interviews, in which the interviewer calls respondents and asks questions during a phone conversation; and (3) mail interviews, in which questionnaires are mailed to respondents, who are asked to read them, respond to the questions, and return their answer unassisted by interviewers (Weisberg, Bowen, and Krosnick, 1989: Ch. 5).

These three modes of interviewing each have particular advantages and disadvantages (Dillman, 1978:39-76). Face-to-face interviews, for example, are particularly good for long, complex questionnaires, and for interviews where rapport is especially important. But face-to-face interviews are also the most expensive, and the most subject to interviewer bias.

Telephone interviews are a good choice when a study must be completed fast, when relatively simple questions are asked, and when physical access to respondents is difficult. The drawback to telephone interviews is that they undersample people who can not be reached by phone, and they do not facilitate interviewer-respondent rapport.

Mail interviews are most appropriate when costs must be minimized, or when many complex, open-end questions are asked. The disadvantages of mail surveys include their very low response rates and lack of control over respondent selection.

At one time, face-to-face interviews were thought to be almost always the mode of choice--superior to telephone or mail in virtually every situation. But that is no longer the case. Today the practice is to consider each interviewing mode as more or less appropriate according to the conditions of a given study (Nieburg, 1984:111-116; Wilhoit and Weaver, 1980:14-18). *See also* FACE-TO-FACE INTERVIEW; INTERVIEWERS; INTERVIEWER'S MANUAL; SELF-ADMINISTERED INTERVIEW; UNSTRUCTURED INTERVIEW.

INTERVIEW SCHEDULE   *See* INSTRUMENT.

INTRODUCTION   A brief opening statement made at the beginning of a poll. Introductions are usually "scripted"--written in advance and read aloud by the interviewer. They are designed to gain the confidence and cooperation of respondents--many of whom will be wary or resistant to being interviewed. To accomplish this, introductions convey three kinds of information, delivered as succinctly as possible:

1. Notification that the interviewer works for a legitimate survey organization and is doing a bona fide survey;
2. Identification of the survey sponsor and/or the organization conducting the research;
3. Assurance that answers are confidential and participation is voluntary. (Sheatsley, 1983: 219-220; Backstrom and Hursh-Cesar, 1981:154-155)

Skillful introductions assure respondents the poll is legitimate, excite their interest, and enlist their cooperation. As a rule, long and involved explanations about the poll are not attempted. The prevailing view is that extended digressions tell respondents more than they want to know--and actually make it harder to complete interviews. Here is an example of a brief introduction that works smoothly into the first question:

> Hello. My name is (Interviewer's Name) and I'm from the Public Opinion Group, a national research firm. Currently we are doing a study of political attitudes people in your area have about the upcoming election. The questions will take only a few minutes, your answers are confidential, and you can refuse to answer any questions. OK? The first question is....

The introduction is prosaic, but crucial to the success of a survey. It is the first (and sometimes the last) opportunity to gain a prospective respondent's cooperation. To achieve this, the introduction must be short, but not too short. It must make the study sound important, but not demanding; it must also resolve any anxiety that the interview is merely a ruse for selling or for some other contrived purpose (Frey, 1984:174-176). *See also* INFORMED CONSENT; INSTRUMENT; SUGGING.

ISSUE POLLS   Surveys that emphasize questions about public opinion on the policy questions of the day. Issue polls might deal with such matters as public opinion on toxic waste, drunk driving, AIDS research, the Soviet Union, birth control, defense spending, or gun control (Salmore and Salmore, 1989:121-124). Polling on the issues is a demanding enterprise, as many scholars of public opinion have pointed out; making policy on the basis of polls is more difficult still.

John Robinson and Robert Meadow, working in the foreign policy area, have cited four problems associated with using polls to make policy (Robinson and Meadow, 1983:20-25). First are *time problems*--specifically those of conducting and reporting polls in time for them to have any relevance for policy debate. Second are *complexity problems*--most policy questions can not be boiled down to simple yes or no, agree or disagree, answers. Third are *conceptual problems*--most issues have multiple dimensions and require elaborate measurement. Fourth are *behavior problems*--people's real beliefs sometimes differ from the opinions they express.

Even when polls are good enough to use for policy formulation, they may not be used that way. Polls only infrequently have a direct influence on policymaking:

> Once reported, poll data enter a very dense stream of potential policy guidance, and policy makers must pay attention to these other sources as well....These sources include political actors...members of the executive and legislative branches, members of the permanent bureaucracy...foreign diplomats...and many other interest groups affected by specific policies. In this kind of policy setting, poll data must be very clear and decisive to be persuasive.   They rarely are. (Robinson and Meadow, 1983:24)

How then do policymakers actually use polls, if not to set policy?   No broad generalizations are possible, but polls are often used to implement political strategy rather than set policy. James Fallows, an assistant to former President Jimmy Carter, has been candid about his experiences:

> Polling data are useful (for those making policy decisions) to the extent that they tell you how to do things you have already decided to do for other reasons, and they are potentially demolishing and destructive to the extent that they take the place of other ways of deciding what you want to do. (Cantril, 1980:138)

So issue polls have limits as policy inputs.   There are methodological problems in producing them, and there are political problems in using them. In any case, policy makers, perhaps recognizing these constraints, tend to use issue polls to achieve tactical or strategic objectives. Rarely are polls alone used to make public policy (Roll and Cantril, 1972:55-63). *See also* POLL USERS; PUBLIC OPINION.

ITEM NONRESPONSE   A poll question skipped over or not answered by a respondent. Item nonresponse is any missing answer to a scheduled question (Mosher and Kalton, 1972:67-69). Pollsters calculate survey response rates at two different levels--one for the sample of respondents interviewed, and another for individual questions on the questionnaire. A poll may report a response rate of 80 percent, meaning 80 percent of eligible respondents were interviewed. But the same poll might report item nonresponse for Question 6 as 10 percent; for Question 23 as 7 percent; and for Question 31 as 15 percent.

Four interviewing problems can produce item nonresponse: (1) respondents may not understand the question; (2) they may not know the answer; (3) respondents may know the answer, but find the question embarrassing or offensive, and (4) interviewers may inadvertently omit the question or fail to record the response given. Any substantial amount of nonresponse signals problems. A rule of thumb is that item nonresponse of 20 percent or more points to a defective question (Wilhoit and Weaver, 1980:31). The question may be worded poorly, or interviewers may not be asking it skillfully.

Item nonresponse rates of 20 percent or more also mean that sampling error is significantly higher for that question than for other questions in the poll. Strictly speaking, any sampling error calculation for this question is dubious, since respondents may not be representative. Apparently, item nonresponse is one area where mail surveys outperform other interviewing methods. On sensitive questions, mail questionnaires consistently produce lower item nonresponse rates than either telephone or face-to-face interviews (Frey, 1983:47-48). *See also* COMPLETION RATE; NONRESPONSE; RESPONSE RATE.

J

JOE SIX-PACK   The mythical common person, ordinary guy, man in the street. Joe Six-pack is the rank and file citizen who views public affairs in a simple, uncomplicated way. Politicians use the term to ask: how do the Joe Six-packs of the world look at this, or, how do we explain this to Joe Six-pack? He is a composite figure, but the term Joe Six-pack often refers to working-class people, blue-collar workers, and the middle class--literally, the type of person who supposedly buys beer by the six-pack.

The contours of Joe Six-pack's mind have not been precisely mapped, but four characteristics are prominent:

1. Is not very interested in public affairs, nor very knowledgeable about them,
2. Possesses a direct, uncomplicated view of public life,
3. Holds opinions that tend to be conservative,
4. Is especially sensitive to tax increases and social spending.

Thinking about public opinion from the perspective of Joe Six-pack can be liberating. It provides fresh perspective on public issues, and inoculates against overreliance on conventional wisdom and so-called informed opinion. Keeping Joe Six-pack in mind also helps opinion analysts to translate concepts and ideas into "sixpackese."

The downside to linking public opinion to Joe Six-pack is that the stereotype falls far short of reality: the image is misleading and elitist. Ordinary Joes (and Janes) are not all selfish, insular people who ignore public affairs and eschew serious political debate. Moreover, virtually everyone becomes concerned with issues that matter to them, and are capable of working through even complex issues when convinced they are important. *See also* RESPONDENT; SALIENCE.

JUDGMENT SAMPLE   *See* PURPOSIVE SAMPLING.

JURY RESEARCH   A new and controversial use of polls and surveys. Jury research adapts the method of polling to the drama and combat of the courtroom. A widely cited example of jury research is the Eli Lilly civil case, in which the giant drug company was sued for marketing a drug subsequently linked to cervical cancer:

> Eli Lilly commissioned Season Wein Associates to conduct a survey to discover whether a jury was likely to acquit, with a view to deciding whether it should settle out of court or not. If the matter reached court the company had a profile of the kind of individuals who were most likely to acquit...and it also gave the defense a dry run of the kind of arguments that were most likely to sway the opinions of the jury. The research has to try to simulate the process of attitude formation accurately, so detailed questions are asked to test respondents reactions to alternative points of view. (Marsh, 1982:130)

Jury research has been used to help select prospective jurors, to argue for change of venue, to present evidence of prevailing public attitudes, and to simulate juror trial behavior. The basic jury research method is to identify the population from which jurors will be chosen, and then draw a sample of them, asking questions about defendants and trial issues (Berk, Hennessey, and Swan, 1977:143-148).

Jury research stirs deep controversy. Supporters of the practice argue that defense attorneys and defendants (the main users of jury research) have a basic right to the knowledge produced by surveys. The research helps attorneys understand the questions and concerns that jurors bring to the courtroom. Supporters also contend that jury research promotes public justice, by providing information that produces impartial jurors and fair trials.

Opponents of jury research see things quite differently. To them, studying juries gives defendants and defense attorneys an unfair advantage. Given enough money, attorneys can now buy information that allows them to stack the jury for their client. Opponents also ridicule the notion that using polls to study jurors improves public justice. In fact, they claim, jury research undercuts society's fundamental right to have trials heard by an impartial jury. *See also* FOCUS GROUPS.

K

KEY INFORMANT   *See* STRATEGIC INFORMANT SAMPLING.

KEY PRECINCT   *See* BELLWETHERS.

L

LAS VEGAS POLLS   Public opinion inferred from betting odds. Las Vegas polls are probability-based surrogates for survey research. The basic notion is that betting odds actually constitute a kind of poll-- a poll that measures the betting public's forecast about this or that coming event. The odds themselves are set by people risking money on their beliefs, so they are "a more dependable basis for prediction than the views of people who are not required to put their money where their mouth is" (Nieburg, 1984:148). For example, if an analyst wanted to know who was going to win an election, or by how much, she could simply consult the betting odds established on the outcome. Or if the question was public confidence in the maintenance of peace, one could examine the betting odds on war breaking out in the next year.

Using betting odds as surrogate polling has some limits--the most obvious being limits on the kind of opinion that can be measured. Las Vegas polls can measure only the things people are willing to bet on. Still, that constitutes a long list that includes elections and some policy issues. Another limitation of Las Vegas polling is scope. These polls measure expectations, rather than opinions--not which candidate will you vote for, but which candidate do you think will win. Las Vegas polls predict what will happen, but traditional polls report choices about what should happen. With a Las Vegas poll, one knows peoples' opinion about what other people will do. With a traditional poll, one knows peoples' opinion about what they will do (M. L. Young, 1990:551). *See also* WEIRD SCIENCE.

LATE DECIDERS   *See* EARLY DECIDERS.

LEADING QUESTION   A survey question phrased in such a way that
respondent answers are influenced by the question wording. Leading questions
"lead" respondents to the answer (Alreck and Settle, 1985:110-111). Gordon
describes three general forms of leading questions:

1.   Context leading biases responses by giving information as part of the
     question. Respondents, for example, might be told that 80 percent of
     the federal budget is defense related, then asked if the defense budget
     should be cut.
2.   Loaded questions use emotionally charged words or phrases likely to
     skew answers for or against some alternative. For example: "Do you
     advocate increasing the drinking age to stop the loss of human life from
     drunk driving?"
3.   Restrictive questions exclude certain answers so respondents are limited
     to the alternatives provided. (Gordon, 1969:357)

Sometimes leading questions find their way onto questionnaires through
inadvertence. Pollsters fail to adequately pretest their instruments, and include
questions flawed in one way or another.   Other times, however, leading
questions are planned: they are included at the request of sponsors who favor
certain policies and hope to produce data that supports their position.
     Neither poor pretesting nor pandering to sponsors justifies leading
questions. However, there may be one situation when leading is sound practice,
and that is   research of a personal and intimate nature.   These studies can
require leading questions to overcome respondents' defenses about reporting
intimate information.   The classic illustration is Kinsey's sexual behavior
research, where the "burden of denial" was placed on the respondent regarding
experience with common sexual practices.   Kinsey, for example, asked
respondents at what age they first masturbated rather than whether they
masturbate.   Leading questions used this way may actually reduce bias by
"leading" respondents to believe the truthful answer is also an acceptable answer
(Payne, 1951:182). See also DOUBLE-BARRELED QUESTION; PRETESTS;
SOCIAL DESIRABILITY BIAS.

LEAKED POLLS   Polls informally released by sponsors or others hoping
thereby to influence opinion, attract attention, or build support for some
candidate or cause. Leaked polls are almost always contrived and orchestrated
by political operatives.   In fact, leaking is a widely used political strategy
(Ehrenholt, 1986:779; Roll and Cantril, 1972:22-33).
     Leaking a poll has four main purposes:

1.   Fund raising--It is axiomatic in electoral politics that candidates with

good polls see a surge in contributions, while candidates who lag or fall back in the polls have trouble attracting backers. Leaking a poll that shows a candidate doing well can stimulate fund raising.

2. Media attention--Another reason for leaking is the favorable media attention it can bring. The press adjusts political coverage roughly according to how viable a candidate appears to be. Also-rans are usually accorded perfunctory coverage--or even no coverage at all. Positive polls can turn this situation around.

3. Momentum--A third reason polls are leaked is to create "momentum," or achieve a bandwagon effect with voters. There is no evidence that polls directly influence voters, but many campaigners continue to believe they do--and continue to leak polls for that purpose.

4. Dissimulation--Finally, polls are released to confuse and mislead opponents--to create "disinformation" and sow confusion among political adversaries. Using polls to deceive opponents is condemned under the ethical codes of all major professional polling groups.

Leaking polls also raises concerns about disclosure of the methodological details of the poll--sampling, question wording, response rate, and so on. Since leaks are usually done circumspectly--perhaps giving the poll to a friendly reporter--disclosure standards are often flouted. (Sabato, 1981:317-318).

Journalists have become more and more sophisticated about leaked polls, sensing (often correctly) that they are being manipulated by the leaker. The leaking issue is now taken seriously enough by journalists that the American Newspaper Publishers Association has published a book, Newsroom Guide to Polls and Surveys, instructing reporters on the esoterics of polling, and how to evaluate polls leaked to them (Wilhoit and Weaver, 1980:5-45). *See also* BANDWAGON EFFECT; DISCLOSURE.

LEANERS   The term used to describe voters who "lean" toward one candidate or another--but cannot say for certain which way they will vote.   Leaners initially tell pollsters they are undecided for who to vote, but after a follow-up probe question, they are able to name a favored candidate (M. L. Young, 1987:91).

The following question sequence is standard example of how to locate leaners:

(Trial heat question) "If the election was held today and the candidates were George Bush, the Republican, and Bill Bradley, the Democrat, which would you support?"
(Follow-up question for undecideds) "Well, which candidate

are you leaning to as of now, Bush the Republican, or Bradley the Democrat?"

Those voters who cannot specify a candidate preference until a follow-up question are classified leaners. Those who cannot choose even after a follow up are labeled undecideds. The general rule is that identifying leaners reduces the undecideds by about half. *See also* TRIAL HEATS; UNDECIDEDS.

LETTER OF TRANSMITTAL *See* COVER LETTER.

LIES, DAMN LIES, AND STATISTICS   A famous phrase attributed to Mark Twain. The full remark was that "there are three kinds of lies: lies, damned lies, and statistics." The phrase has become code for criticism of polling and pollsters. Poll antagonist Michael Wheeler, in fact, entitled his widely read attack on polling *Lies, Damn Lies, and Statistics* (1976). In it, he lambasted the polls and the pollsters for a variety of sins--all allegedly perpetrated to bamboozle the public into thinking that polls are accurate and trustworthy. Some of Wheeler's complaints have been dismissed as unfair or exaggerated, but other critics of polling--including academics, journalists, politicians, and even pollsters themselves--have also been heard from (Young, 1990:234-237; Marsh, 1982; Robinson and Meadow, 1983; Gallup, 1972:155-171).

These critics level four main charges at polling. First, polls are said to influence voters in undesirable ways. Among the charges is that polls cause undecided voters to switch to leading candidates, discourage supporters of trailing candidates, and reduce financial support for candidates who do not show well.

Second, polls are said to be irrelevant. The thrust of this complaint is that polls deal with frivolous matters, do not address the really important issues, and tend to focus on the hoopla and horse- race aspects of politics. A related criticism is that polls only confirm commonsense--or that their findings are trivial and even silly. Academic polls in particular are often scorned for their impracticality.

Third, polling is said to be unethical. This criticism is that polls violate the privacy of those sampled by exposing their political opinions. Another issue turning on the morality of polling is the charge that polls can be rigged to show the results the pollster or sponsor wants. Pollsters can manipulate their results by asking loaded questions, using biased samples, weighting data to skew poll results, and misrepresenting "likely voter" or "undecided" categories of respondents.

Fourth, critics say that polling is not really scientific.   This is the methodological criticism of polls.   Its theme is that polls are so inaccurate and riddled with error that they provide little valid information about peoples' real preferences.   Typical of methodological criticisms are claims that gross errors in sampling and weighting infect most polls.   Other methodological criticisms are that questions are poorly worded, interviewers are badly trained, and respondents answer questions when they have little knowledge about the topic.

Poll apologists counter all this criticism by characterizing much of it as self-serving, as the mark of people embarrassed or inconvenienced by poll findings (Field, 1983:221-228).   Some of the specific technical complaints, such as those about sample size and weighting, are dismissed as being uninformed or unsophisticated about polls.   Poll advocates argue that most of the remaining issues can be resolved by full disclosure of the procedures used in each poll. And, in fact, all major polling organizations now have ethical codes that require this disclosure (Roll and Cantril, 1972).   *See also*   DISCLOSURE; POLL REGULATION.

LIKELY VOTERS   The pollster's label for those eligible voters who will probably vote on election day.   Likely voters are those who "pass" voting screens--typically a battery of questions designed to measure proclivity to vote (Welch and Comer, 1975:369-370).   Some version of the following six voting screen questions is standard: (1) Are you registered to vote? (2) Do you know where your polling place is located? (3) How interested are you in the election? (4) How probable is it you will vote? (5) Did you vote in the last election for U.S. senator? (6) Did you vote in the last presidential election? (Backstrom and Hursh-Cesar, 1981:169-171).

Pollsters employ different criteria to distinguish likely voters from unlikely voters.   Generally, however, someone is designated a likely voter who is registered to vote, has voted in recent elections, and who reports high interest in this election.   Unlikely voters, on the other hand, are not registered, do not know where to vote, have not voted in recent elections and are not particularly interested in this one (M. L. Young, 1987:91).

Likely voter screens bear decisively upon the accuracy of political polls. With today's nonvoting rates of 50 percent or higher, it is difficult to screen out everyone who will not vote.   Just how difficult is seen by some figures from the Gallup organization.   Even the touted Gallup voting screen reports only an 87 percent success rate--that is, one in eight (13%) of people labeled likely voters do not actually vote.   *See also* SCREENERS.

LIKERT SCALE   A standard question style used by pollsters. Likert scales are very popular. Named after behavioral scientist Rensis Likert, they measure intensity of opinions and attitudes (Nieburg, 1984:145-148). Standard usage is to put the question in statement form, asking respondents whether they agree or disagree with the statement:

> Now I'm going to read a series of statements. After each, would you tell me if you strongly agree, agree, are undecided, disagree or strongly disagree.
>
> Inflation is the country's number one problem.
>
> SA   A   U   D   SD
>
> Taxes should be raised to meet the deficit.
>
> SA   A   U   D   SD
>
> Drug abuse is caused by decline of moral standards.
>
> SA   A   U   D   SD

Statements can be switched between positive and negative, and agree-disagree may be replaced by scales such as support-oppose, accept-reject, or like-dislike (Anderson, Basilevsky, and Hum, 1983:252-255).

There are other methods of measuring the intensity of attitudes or opinions. A common one is the ten-point scale. "On a scale of one to ten, with one being none at all and ten being a great deal, how interested are you personally in the upcoming presidential election?" One major advantage of Likert scales, however, is the facility with which respondents pick up on them. After the first one or two questions has been answered, a series of statements can be run through quickly. The enduring popularity of Likert questions also owes to their ability to measure intensity of feeling about this issue or that problem. Survey research has surprising few tools that measure the strength of opinions and attitudes. The Likert scale does this, and does it efficiently (Selltiz, Wrightsman, and Cook, 1976:418-421). *See also* AGREE-DISAGREE; SCALE.

LISTING   *See* SAMPLING FRAME.

LITERARY DIGEST   A now defunct magazine best remembered for its straw polls of presidential elections in the 1920s and 1930s. The *Literary Digest* has become a symbol for flawed polling, because it predicted that Democrat Roosevelt would be overwhelmed by Republican Landon in 1936. Instead, Roosevelt won forty-six states and 63 percent of the vote, handing Landon one of the worst defeats in presidential election history. The *Literary Digest* itself was lampooned mercilessly, and soon after ceased publication (Roll and Cantril, 1972:10).

The failure of the *Literary Digest* poll is usually attributed to its use of a bad sampling frame--1936 automobile registrations and telephone book listings. Millions of Roosevelt supporters in 1936 were too poor to have phones or own automobiles, so sampling only people that did would not produce a cross section of likely voters. Making things even worse, the *Digest* poll was based on some specious logic still common in straw polling: the bigger the sample, the more accurate the results. Ten million questionnaires were mailed out, and over two million people responded--producing a huge sample, but one badly slanted toward affluent Republican voters (Hennessey, 1985:62-64).

Even today, mention of the *Literary Digest* evokes skepticism about polls. One scholar, however, has made the intriguing argument that the magazine is remembered for the wrong reason. Perhaps it was not bad polling, but bad polling analysis that derailed the *Digest's* 1936 survey. Richard Link, writing in *Public Opinion Magazine*, acknowledges that the *Digest's* sampling design was less than ideal. But the more serious problem, he thinks, was that the magazine never weighted the data. Using the actual 1932 voting results to weight the 1936 poll findings, Link explains, would have made the difference. A total of 19 states would have been moved from Landon's column to Roosevelt's. Roosevelt would have been forecast to win; and the *Literary Digest* would not have become a notorious example of bad polling (Link, 1980:55). *See also* STRAW POLL; WEIGHTING.

LOADED QUESTION   *See* LEADING QUESTION.

LONGITUDINAL SURVEYS   Surveys that collect data at regular intervals over a long period of time. Longitudinal surveys include three optional study designs: trend studies, cohort studies, and panel studies (Babbie, 1973:63-65).

First, trend studies are separate samples of the same population taken several times over a period of months or years. Any poll that asks different respondents the same question poll after poll is a trend study (Babbie, 1982:61-62).

Second, cohort studies are surveys of people who have had some common life experience, such as being born or graduating from high school in the same year. These cohorts are studied as they age, with each successive survey based on a new sample from the original population (Plano, Riggs, and Robin, 1982:22).

Third, panel studies survey the same group of respondents, called panels, for two, three, four, or more "waves" of interviewing. Unlike either trend studies or cohort studies, panels do not draw separate samples for each new survey. The same respondents are interviewed each time (Johnson and Joslyn, 1986:111-112).

Survey researchers contrast longitudinal surveys with cross-sectional surveys. Longitudinal surveys have been described as the "long view," while cross-sectionals have been labeled the "wide view." Longitudinal refers to data collected at several points in time, while cross-sectional refers to data collected just once. A single poll is a cross section--but repeated annually for five years, it becomes longitudinal. *See also* COHORT STUDIES; PANELS; REFERENCE PERIOD; TREND STUDIES.

M

MAIL SURVEYS   *See* SELF-ADMINISTERED SURVEYS.

MANDATE   A charge from the electorate to enact or dismantle some public policy. Mandates are traditionally associated with dramatic election outcomes--either overwhelming victories or wrenching defeats.   President Reagan's impressive reelection victory in 1984, for example, was interpreted as a mandate to continue the Reagan agenda.   But there are some serious problems with inferring mandates from popular elections. The ambiguity of party platforms and imprecision of candidate positions often make it uncertain just what a party stands for or a politician is advocating.   Even worse, voters themselves often lack a deep understanding of election issues (M. L. Young, 1987:22).

Polls, however, are not elections, and unlike elections, they can be definitive about public opinion.   Surveys can reveal specific preferences, how strong they are, and even why people hold them (Crespi, 1989:18-20).   But even polls have some limits as popular mandates.   One problem is the limited scope of polls.   Polling can portray the broad policy direction people prefer, but few polls explore the issues in enough depth to spell out the detail and specificity policy makers need to implement policy.   A second constraint on poll mandates is their advisory status: if polls are indeed referendums, they are nonbinding ones.   Unlike electoral victories, polls confer no power and award no office.   And no elected official is responsible for acting on them.   Both elections and polls have limitations in revealing public mandates--elections because we don't always know what they mean, and polls because they don't always mean what they say.   The nature of mandates and how to measure them remains elusive in American political life.   *See also*   CONTINUING ELECTIONS; PLURALISTIC IGNORANCE; PUBLIC OPINION.

MARGINALS   The overall numbers produced by polls. Marginals are summary figures--52 percent support candidate A and 48 percent support candidate B; 60 percent favor policy X while 40 percent oppose it. A leading text gives this precise definition:

> The figures showing the responses of the total sample are called "marginals." They are the end figures for any table that add down the columns or across the rows to 100 percent of the sample. (Backstrom and Hursh-Cesar, 1981:339)

Marginals are usually thought of in terms of percentages, but they can also be presented in terms of raw numbers.   Earl Babbie (1973:240), in fact, simply refers to marginals as "frequency distributions."

Either raw number frequencies or percentage frequencies make up the marginals. The following example, taken from a statewide sample of 1,000, includes both "raw" marginals and percentage marginals.

Q. Do you favor or oppose Governor Casey's plan to reduce property tax, eliminate miscellaneous taxes and raise local income taxes?

Response	# of People	Percent of Sample
Favor Plan	540	54%
Oppose Plan	350	35%
No Opinion	110	11%
	1,000	100%

The "raw" marginals show that the sample of 1,000 breaks down as follows: 540 favor the governor's plan, 350 oppose it, and 110 do not have an opinion. The percentage marginals show that the governor's supporters (54%) outnumber opponents (35%) almost five to three, while one in nine people (11%) have no opinion. The raw number marginals will always add up to the total size of the sample; the percentage marginals will always sum to 100 percent. *See also* CROSSTABS.

MARKET RESEARCH   *See* POLLING INDUSTRY.

MEANINGFUL RELATIONSHIP   *See* STATISTICAL SIGNIFICANCE.

MEDIA POLLS   Opinion surveys sponsored by broadcast or print media. Media polls can be distinguished from those polls reported on by media, but commissioned by someone else.   Over five hundred media outlets today regularly sponsor polls.   Among these are the three high-profile network polls: the ABC-*Washington Post* poll, the CBS-*New York Times* poll, and the NBC-*Wall Street Journal* poll.   Other well-known media polls include the *Los Angeles Times* poll, the *New York Daily News* poll, the *Detroit Free Press* poll, the *Chicago Tribune* poll, and the *Boston Globe* poll.   Syndicated polls such as the Harris poll and the Gallup poll are also media-sponsored (Sudman, 1983b:490- 496).   Newspapers and broadcast media who wish to sponsor polls have two basic options available to them: they can hire outside pollsters, and then have the poll done under a contractual arrangement, or they can train reporters and then conduct the poll "in house."   These two options are also mixed in various ways.   For example, a media outlet might hire an outside pollster as consultant, then do the poll in house (Ismach, 1984:106-118).

A number of issues have been raised about the appropriateness and accuracy of media polling. For example, it is felt that journalists' norms of objectivity are fatally compromised when the press both pays for and publishes the same poll. Critics also charge that media research is conceptually and methodologically flawed: its questions are simplistic, its analysis is superficial, and it uses little or no theoretical perspective (Wheeler, 1976:15-37, 270-287).

Two main reasons probably explain the widespread popularity of media polls.   First, a newspaper or broadcaster sponsoring a poll earns considerable positive publicity.   The outlet has its name mentioned every time the poll is reported.   And there is an aura of prestige around any news organization important enough to have its own poll.   Second, polls are more and more an important category of news. Findings from media polls now inform editorial commentary and influence political endorsements.   And they provide an important resource for journalists in their adversarial relationship with government leaders.   Finally, media polls bring power to the press--power to define and reflect public opinion and to advocate policy based on it. The media has always sought to interpret public opinion. Media polling lends scientific legitimacy to that journalistic tradition (Atkin and Gaudino, 1984:143-154). *See also* NETWORK POLLS; PRECISION JOURNALISM.

METALLIC METALS ACT   The topic of a now-classic poll question designed to find out if people bluff when asked their opinion on things they know nothing about.   In 1947, Sam Gill asked a group of people about the

"Metallic Metals Act," a made-up piece of legislation, and 70 percent of the sample volunteered an answer (most of these said it would be a good thing, but should be left to the states). Only 30 percent of Gill's sample when asked about the nonexistent act had no opinion about it (Payne, 1951:18).

The story of the Metallic Metals Act question has been used to argue that most people will make up answers if faced with an issue they have not thought about. These respondents fabricate opinions and invent attitudes that allow them to answer the question and avoid embarrassment. But the answers given are essentially random in the sense that the next time the same question is asked, a different answer may be given. This is what Philip Converse referred to as the nonattitudes problem: people answering questions even though they know little or nothing about the issue at hand. Converse argued that the nonattitude problem was common in polls and resistant to pollsters prophylactic effects to avoid it (Converse, 1964).

But more recent research by Schuman and Presser presents a more complicated picture. These authors looked at Gill's study and concluded it was defective on several grounds:

> Examination of this original report reveals... that it is hardly more than an anecdote: the population sample is identified only as a "group of people" and the size of the sample is never given. (Schuman & Presser, 1981:147)

Schuman and Presser replicated Gill's study with a new question. Instead of the Metallic Metals Act, respondents were asked if they were in favor of or opposed to repealing the (fictional) Public Affairs Act of 1947. In this experiment, only a third of the respondents expressed opinions about the nonexistent legislation (compared to Gill's reported 70%). Moreover, the proportion offering opinions fell below 10 percent when filter questions preceded the Public Affairs Act question.

The data from Schuman and Presser, along with additional evidence, suggests that about one-third of poll respondents will express an opinion even when lacking basic knowledge about the issue. This is far better news than the 70 percent reported by Gill. Nevertheless, one-third or so still pretend, and even when filter questions are used, about 10 percent of respondents manufacture opinions. Questions like those on the Metallic Metals Act and the Public Affairs Act are formal examples of what pollsters call "sleepers"--dummy questions designed to detect respondent guess work. Sleeper questions mention a phony name or pose a fictional issue, then ask people to answer a question about it. A rule of thumb in political polls is that about one in ten respondents will claim to recognize the name of an imaginary public figure (M. L. Young, 1987:104). *See also* HARD ID; NONOPINIONS.

MISREPORTING   Providing inaccurate or misleading information to pollsters.   Misreporting is a euphemism for lying.   It is any purposeful deception or exaggeration (M. L. Young, 1987:93).   Misreporters misstate their age, inflate their incomes, claim education they do not have, and express opinions they do not hold.   Even socially neutral questions produce some misreporting.   One study reported, for example, that 10 percent of the respondents lied about having driver's licenses, 9 percent claimed library cards never issued to them, 5 percent lied about owning a car, and 3 percent said they owned homes when they did not (Hennessey, 1985:78-79).

Misreporting becomes more frequent as questions become more ego-threatening.   Up to one- third of respondents exaggerate education, up to one-fourth overstate income, up to one-fifth will claim to be registered to vote when they are not, and up to one-sixth will misrepresent their age.

There is disagreement about the causes of misreporting.   Some writers ascribe most of it to honest mistakes, fatigue, and boredom.   But other writers argue that misreporting cannot all be involuntary.   Misreporting occurs, they say, because many people simply lie when they find the truth to be embarrassing (Fowler, 1984:91-95; Marsh, 1982:17-18).   There is also disagreement about the effect of misreporting on polling data.   Some researchers believe misreporting distorts polling data and undermines polling accuracy.   But others take a more benign view, arguing that most misreporting has trivial influence, because it eventually "washes out" as nonsampling error (Lewis and Schneider, 1982:42-47).   *See also*   METALLIC METALS ACT; NONSAMPLING ERROR; RESPONDENT.

MR. SMITH QUESTION   A special trial heat question that describes a hypothetical (Mr. Smith) candidate.   Mr. Smith questions are a kind of market test of the "political product" before introduction:

> (Mr. Smith)...puts Candidate A against Candidate B (and sometimes C or D)...in a poll to check a candidate's generic appeal on issue positions and personal characteristics....The standard methodology is to present a potential voter with an often lengthy paragraph describing "candidate A's" personal characteristics and positions on issues.   The respondent is asked what he likes and doesn't like about the candidate and then often is asked an open-ended question of why these qualities are or are not appealing.   (Bogart, 1984:30)

Here's an example of a Mr. Smith question taken from a gubernatorial poll done in Pennsylvania:

Next I'll read a description of a possible candidate for governor of Pennsylvania.

Candidate A is a fifty-year-old Republican from central Pennsylvania who has built a successful small business. From 1980 to 1988, he served four terms in the Pennsylvania House of Representatives, but did not seek reelection for a fifth term because he believes public officials should be limited to the number of years they can hold office. **Candidate A** believes that the cost of running our state government is far too high and that legislators' salaries, pensions, and expense accounts are "out of control." He has been called a "maverick" because of his challenge to legislative pay raises which the General Assembly gave themselves. In fact, when the last pay raise was passed against his protest, he refused to accept his, and argued against the pay increase in Commonwealth Court. **Candidate A** also fought against pension increases for state lawmakers and judges, and refused his state pension when he retired from the General Assembly. **Candidate A** is divorced and has five children. (Source: Young, 1989)

Mr. Smith questions are also known as no-name questions, Q-vignettes and hypothetical candidate questions.

Another version of the genre is the attribute list. Interviewers read a list of candidate characteristics--race, sex, age, ethnicity, political experience, ideology, education, marital status, and so on. After each quality, respondents are asked to say whether they are more or less likely to support a candidate having that trait (Morin, Aug. 1987:37). Pollsters armed with such data can compare the strengths and weaknesses of real candidates and try to predict voter reaction to different choices.

Campaign strategists cite two conditions when Mr. Smith questions are most useful: when a relatively unknown challenger is running against a well-known incumbent, and during candidate recruiting, when a party needs to identify the qualities a successful candidate should have. Another time Mr. Smith questions can be helpful is during multicandidate primaries. When there are several candidates in a race, it is difficult to imprint a strong impression on prospective voters. A Mr. Smith portrait of the ideal candidate can help a real candidate stand out among a crowded field. *See also* HYPOTHETICALS; IMAGE QUESTIONS.

MODERATORS   *See* FOCUS GROUPS.

MOST IMPORTANT PROBLEM QUESTION   A standard question asked by Gallup and other survey organizations, going back to 1935. The most important problem question is the second most frequently asked question in American polling--only questions about presidential popularity are more common. Gallup's standard formulation is: "What do you think is the most important problem before the American people today?"

Tom W. Smith has organized answers given to Gallup's most important problem question into seven broad categories. These include:

1. Foreign affairs--military matters and space
2. Economics--inflation, unemployment, and trade
3. Social control--crime, riots, drugs, and moral decay
4. Civil rights--race and civil liberties
5. Government corruption--inefficiency and red tape;)
6. Energy--OPEC, oil supplies, and hoarding
7. Miscellaneous--poverty, health, environment, and pollution (T. W. Smith, 1985:264-265).

Smith's analysis indicates that public perceptions of the most important problem shifts as objective conditions change in the country. Usually concern about the economy is the priority problem--unless foreign crises or war intervenes, such as World War II, the 1950s cold war, or the Iranian hostage ordeal.

Gallup also asks two other most important problem questions--one about regional concerns: "What do you think is the most important problem facing this section of the country today?"--and the other about family problems: "What is the most important problem that you and your family face today?" Since the late 1940s, the most important regional problems have been the economy, civil rights, and housing--fluctuating over time much as top national problems have. But top family problems have been remarkably consistent:

> In stark contrast to the fluctuation in the top concern on the national, sectional, and local question, economics has always been the most important personal problem. Despite the civil rights movement, the social disorder of the sixties and the energy crisis of the seventies, people have always placed their pocketbook first when they consider their personal problems. (T. W. Smith, 1985:404)

An interesting methodological issue is connected to the most important problem question. Usually the question is asked in open end format. But in an experiment, Schuman and Presser constructed a closed version with eight alternative answers. Asking the question in closed format changed some of the results. In the open version, unemployment (19%) received the largest number of votes as the most important problem; in the closed, it was crime and violence (35%). Trust in government received 3 percent in the open format, but 10 percent in the closed. Morals and religion were 6 percent in open format, but 9 percent in closed. On the other hand, answers such as inflation, busing, and racial problems received comparable responses in both open and closed formats (Schuman and Presser, 1981:82-85). Schuman and Presser speculate that some respondents answering the open format question may have simply excluded local problems from consideration, while the closed format listed local problems as possible answers. In any case, there is now evidence that answers given to the most important problem question are influenced by the question format. *See also* ISSUE POLLS.

MULTISTAGE SAMPLING   Drawing a probability sample in two or more successive stages. Multistage sampling is not really a distinct type of sampling-- it incorporates such common sampling techniques as simple random sampling, stratified sampling, and cluster sampling. Rather, multistage sampling is a general procedure for "sampling down" to ever smaller populations until individual respondents can be interviewed.

Multistage is mainly used in situations where a large area is to be surveyed- -such as an entire country or a large state. In these circumstances, typically no reliable listing of the population exists. In fact, the most common form of multistage sampling is known as "area sampling." It is used to sample geographic units--countries, states, cities, census tracts, neighborhoods, and so on (Fowler, 1984:28-31).

A hypothetical area sample illustrates the multistage sampling process. Stage one draws a sample of all the counties in a state; stage two then selects several municipalities within each sampled county. Stage three then draws a sample of census tracts within the chosen municipalities. Stage four picks a sample of blocks or block groups within the sampled census tracts. And so it goes, until finally individual respondents are selected (Wilhoit and Weaver, 1980:23-24).

One very important point about area sampling: at each stage, the geographic units at that stage (counties, municipalities, etc.) must have a chance of being selected that is exactly equal to their share of the overall population. This requirement is known as PPS, or "population proportionate to size." If a county includes 5 percent of the state's population, its chance of ending up in the sample must be exactly .05, or 1 in 20. Otherwise the multistage sampling process uses a biased sample of respondents (Sudman, 1978:131-134).

A major attraction of multistage sampling is its efficiency. It avoids laborious listings of large populations. Even more important, however, multistage designs allow populations to be sampled that otherwise could not be reached. The main drawback to multistage sampling is its complexity and the increased sampling error associated with it. Since each stage is an independent sample, the sampling error is cumulative (Warwick and Lininger, 1975:108-109). *See also* CLUSTER SAMPLING; SIMPLE RANDOM SAMPLING (SRS); STRATIFIED SAMPLING.

MUSHINESS INDEX   A battery of four questions used to measure the firmness of public opinion. The mushiness index predicts how likely people are to change their mind about their opinions (Sabato, 1981:109).   First, respondents are polled on some issue or asked whether they favor or oppose some policy. Then the four questions of the mushiness index are asked, using a 1 to 6 point rating scale:

1.   On a scale of 1 to 6, where 1 means that the issue affects you personally very little and 6 means that you really feel deeply involved in this issue, where would you place yourself?
2.   On some issues people feel that they really have all the information that they need in order to form a strong opinion on that issue, while on other issues they would like to get additional information before solidifying their opinion. On a scale of 1 to 6, where 1 means that you feel you definitely need more information on the issue and 6 means that you do not feel you need to have any more information on the issue, where do you place yourself?
3.   On a scale of 1 to 6, where 1 means that you and your friends and family rarely, if ever, discuss the issue and 6 means that you and your friends and family discuss it relatively often, where would you place yourself?
4.   People have told us that on some issues they come to a conclusion and they stick with that position, no matter what. On other issues, however, they may take a position but they know that they could change their minds pretty easily. On a scale of 1 to 6, where 1 means that you could change your mind very easily on this issue and 6 means that you are likely to stick with your position no matter what, where would you place yourself? (Nieburg, 1984:162-163)

The mushiness index was developed by the polling firm of Yankelovich, Skelly and White. It is scored from 4 to 24, with 4 being very mushy and 24 being very firm. The more personal involvement, conviction, and information a respondent reports, the higher will be their overall score; conversely, respondents who feel little stake in the issues and believe their information is lacking will be labeled mushy. Mushy opinion is synonymous with soft opinion. Pollsters have long been aware that opinion can be volatile, particularly where information is lacking. But the mushiness index is the most elaborate approach so far developed for measuring the probability that opinions will actually shift. Mushiness apparently differs according to the type of policy issues being studied.   Opinion seems to be most mushy on foreign policy questions, somewhat mushy on issues that involve both foreign and domestic questions, and least mushy on domestic and social policy questions (Robinson and Meadow, 1983:133-134). See also HARD DATA; LIKERT SCALE; SOFT SUPPORTERS.

MYTHS OF POLLING   Those widely accepted but seriously mistaken beliefs about polls--what they do, why they are done, and how they are used. Polling is now big business. The industry annually grosses an estimated $5 billion in the United States alone. Polls have become a familiar fixture of American business and political life. For all of this success, however, there have grown up some incredible half- truths, and plain falsehoods, about the nature of polling. Here are five of the worst myths about polling:

(1) SAMPLING ERROR MYTH

MYTH--Sampling error, the statistical precision of a poll, is the source of most poll mistakes.

FACT--Sampling error is important, but nonsampling error--quality of questions, competency of interviewing, and so on--is a much greater threat to poll accuracy.

(2) EXPERT MYTH

MYTH--Polls are so technically involved, what with question wording, sampling design, statistical analysis, and so on, that only a polling expert can tell the good from the bad.

FACT--There is much nontechnical information that a layman can look to for a sense of the quality of the poll, such as poll sponsorship and wording of questions.

(3) HORSE RACE MYTH

MYTH--The most important question in polls is the "horse race question." Finding this out is the main purpose of polling.

FACT--Pollsters consider the horse race question one of the least important.   It is the press, seeking drama and excitement, that emphasizes the horse race question in their poll coverage, often leading with it in stories and news accounts.

(4) BIG SAMPLE MYTH

MYTH--The larger the population surveyed, the larger must be the sample interviewed.

FACT--For most polls, population size and sample size are not closely related. Pennsylvania, with 12 million people, requires a sample size of 1,200 (+/- 1-3% sampling error). The entire United States can be surveyed with about 300 more respondents.

(5) BANDWAGON MYTH

MYTH--Polls make people jump on the bandwagon to support candidates and opinions shown popular in the polls.

FACT--There is no solid evidence of a bandwagon effect on the electorate. Examples of politicians who pulled ahead after being behind in the polls are abundant. So are examples of candidates losing after being far ahead in polls.

The myths about polling have considerable staying power. Pollsters, academics, and others have been debunking them for some time--with limited success. The bandwagon myth, for example, still persists despite being exorcised in virtually every book on polling published in the last twenty years. *See also* BANDWAGON EFFECT; NONSAMPLING ERROR; SAMPLE SIZE; SAMPLING ERROR; TRIAL HEATS.

N

NAME RECOGNITION QUESTION   A question that measures awareness of a public figure.   The name recognition question produces the touted "numbers" or "recognition score."   This is the proportion of the electorate who say they know who a public figure is.   These scores can range from virtually zero for unfamiliar figures to ninety-five or higher for widely known politicians (Sabato, 1981:177).   Sometimes name recognition questions try to gauge more than simple recognition.   One example is the personal dimension scale (PDS), which combines name awareness with a measure of the negative and positive feelings evoked by candidates:

> Next, I'll read some names of public figures.   Would you please tell me on a 1-10 scale how negative or how positive you personally feel toward each person.   A value of "1" indicates strong negative feelings, while a value of "10" indicates a strong positive feeling.   If you don't feel one way or the other, give the figure a "5" or a "6."   If you haven't heard of the public figure, just say so.   The first public figure is....(Boyd, 1989)

In practice, PDS scores stretch from around 3 (very low) to around 8 (unusually high).   Pollsters consider the 5 range a neutral zone for candidate feelings.

Politicians often look to name recognition scores to gauge a candidate's prospects.   But this is not consistently good practice.   In the early trial heats, these scores can be misleading.   Even overwhelming leads can vanish as races heat up, opponents become better known, or voters simply begin to pay more attention (Crespi, 1989:58-59).   Nevertheless, name recognition is an important asset in electoral politics.   In many local races, the widely recognized candidate is at a particular advantage because their opponents will never become well known during the campaign. Many voters will end up voting for the widely recognized candidate because it is the only name they know. *See also* APPROVAL RATING; TRIAL HEATS.

NATURAL STRAW POLLS   Trackings of the mail received by a public figure.   Natural straw polls count letters, cards, and other unsolicited correspondence--perhaps classifying it as pro or con, favorable or unfavorable, on some issue or topic.   Unsolicited mail is notoriously unrepresentative.   Still, many public officials tend to read it, and some certainly are influenced by it. H. L. Nieburg reports that the White House logs about 10,000 pieces of mail a day, a process that occupies the time of thirty clerks.   Established procedures have been developed to process this load: an incoming letter is opened, the subject noted, and pros and cons are counted.   A weekly tally is subsequently filed with White House staff (Nieburg, 1984:61).

Other public officials who get mail usually pay some attention to it--perhaps on the theory that someone who cares enough to write is someone who matters. Not all unsolicited mail, however, is treated seriously.   A conspicuous example of mail that is not is that sponsored by PACs and other interest groups.   Known as generated mail, these letters, cards, and telegrams are typically orchestrated to coincide with a critical vote on pending legislation.   Legislators and others discount generated mail considerably; as a rule it is not considered a reliable indication of public opinion (M. L. Young, 1987:120-121). *See also* STRAW POLL; WEIRD SCIENCE.

NAYSAYER   *See* YEA SAYER.

NCPP   The National Council on Public Polls.   NCPP was founded in 1968 to promote the interests of organizations that conduct public polls.   NCPP membership is made up of organizations rather than individuals.   Charter members included the California Poll, the Gallup Poll, the Harris Surveys, the Iowa Poll, Market Opinion Research, the Roper Poll, and the Texas Poll (Roll and Cantril, 1972:160).

NCPP underwent a schism in 1979, when the membership adopted a tougher ethics code.   The original NCPP standards were very similar to those of AAPOR.   Adhering to the notion of disclosure, members were pledged to include six key pieces of information when releasing polling data: (1) identity of the polling organization; (2) specification of the population surveyed; (3) size of the final sample; (4) method of interviewing used; (5) exact question wording; and (6) timing of the field work (Turner and Martin, 1984:66-67).

The tougher standards also required that a NCPP member make full disclosure if a private client leaked just part of a poll or misrepresented poll findings. The other new provision established a Committee on Disclosure with responsibility for adjudicating alleged violations (National Council on Public Polls, 1979).

The new ethics provisions sparked opposition. Two important members, NBC News and Cambridge Survey Research, eventually resigned because of them. Cambridge complained that the new items required NCPP members to police clients, while NBC viewed the Committee on Disclosure as an infringement on network editorial judgment.

There are some informal links between NCPP and AAPOR. In fact, the initial organizational meeting for NCPP (hosted by George Gallup, Sr.) coincided with an annual AAPOR meeting. The disclosure codes of both organizations are similar, although NCPP is somewhat stricter. And there is membership overlap in the two organizations: many pollsters active in NCPP also belong to AAPOR (Nieburg, 1984:258-259). *See also* AAPOR; CASRO.

NEDZI TRUTH IN POLLING   *See* TRUTH IN POLLING BILL.

NETWORK POLLS   Refers to those broadcast media polls originally sponsored by the major TV networks: ABC, CBS, and NBC. Each of the three eventually took on a print partner. ABC's partner is the *Washington Post*, CBS combined with the *New York Times*, and NBC now works with the *Wall Street Journal* (Ismach, 1984). Survey research methodologist Seymour Sudman has evaluated the network polls on seven "aspects of survey quality," which range from "selection of topics" to "reporting of limitations." His findings provide a fascinating comparison of the three major network polls (Sudman, 1983:490-496):

1. Selection of Topic--All three network polls continuously measure presidential approval and consumer economic trends. A number of topics have been covered by all three polls (such as abortion, gun control and social security, however, a surprising range of topics have been researched by only one or two network polls.

2. Sampling Execution--Many of the polls are done in one or two days, few last longer than five or six days. This relatively short interval probably means that "contact" rates are relatively low--many perspective respondents are never reached by interviewers.

3. Sample Design--All three polls employ random digit dialing. NBC uses unweighted quotas to achieve equal members of men and women--

a procedure which probably reduces the quality of that network's sampling design.

4. Interviewing--ABC uses Chilton's for interviewing; NBC and CBS recruit and train interviewers in-house. All three networks limit efforts to "convert" refusals.

5. Questionnaires: Questions are pretested and none show blatant bias. However, results of split sample tests of different question wording is not reported regularly. Nor are knowledge screening questions used enough.

6. Analysis--All three polls employ basic descriptive analysis, but not much more. Even simple scales and indices are avoided. This "simple-minded analysis" is apparently motivated by a judgment of what the audience will understand.

7. Reporting of Limitations--The *New York Times* disclosure is the best because it includes the idea of nonsampling error as well as sampling error. ABC and NBC include statements which only refer to sampling error.

Sudman's conclusions regarding quality are mixed. All three network polls are competent, yet each has technical weaknesses that mar their performance. The are good, but not perfect. How about the lesser-known media polls? How would they rate on the same criteria? Sudman did not review them, so we cannot tell for sure. But it is doubtful that other media polls would look any better than the network polls do (Levy, 1984). *See also* MEDIA POLLS; PRECISION JOURNALISM.

NEWS HOOKS   *See* NEWS PEGS.

NEWS PEGS   The major backdrop news stories around which lesser stories are written and reported. News pegs are the big events of the day--political developments, government decisions, critical economic news, and important international events. Some news pegs hang on for weeks or even months; others last only a day or so. Among the prominent news pegs during the 1980s were Chernobyl, the Challenger Disaster, the Iran-Contra hearings, the AIDS health crisis, presidential elections, Soviet glasnost, and eastern European upheaval. Reporters build stories on news pegs. These stories themselves are called news hooks because they are linked (hooked) to the day's news pegs (Graber, 1980:60-66).

Here is a simple example involving polling: say the week's top news events concern the legal problems of a top aide to the president--that would be the news peg. A polling organization might release a poll showing that 65 percent of the electorate is alarmed about ethics among government officials--that would be a news hook. The relationship among news pegs, news hooks, and polls is more than casual. David Paletz and his associates have produced some revealing research that shows polls are much more likely to be reported when they function as news hooks (Paletz et al., 1980:495-513).

Paletz and his associates examined newspapers and television practices separately. With respect to newspapers (*The New York Times*), they found that about one-third of the polls reported were news hooks tied to the day's news pegs. But it was television where polls more often were presented as news hooks. About 70 percent of the polls reported on TV (the "CBS Evening News") were tied to the day's news pegs. Paletz and associates write:

> Television journalists even deliberately forced connections. In reporting results from the CBS/*New York Times* Poll, the anchorman would introduce the reporter who would link an item from the poll to the previous story, then continue with unrelated data from the poll. (Paletz et al., 1980:502)

These findings explain why some polls are widely reported on, but others ignored.   Apparently, the substance or intrinsic importance of the poll is not so important. Polls that fit the news peg background are more often reported by the press, while polls that fail as news hooks are more often ignored. *See also* MEDIA POLLS; NETWORK POLLS.

NEW YORK DAILY NEWS   *See* STRAW POLL.

NEXT BIRTHDAY METHOD   A respondent selection technique that randomly chooses the household member to be interviewed. Next birthday method selects for interviewing the adult living in a household who has the next birthday. Selection is straightforward. The interviewer simply asks to speak to the member of the household over eighteen who has the next birthday.

The next birthday method is one of several procedures commonly used to select the actual respondent.   The most widely used respondent selection technique is probably the Troldahl-Carter method, also known as the Kish Grid (Troldahl and Carter, 1964:71-76).

A study by Charles Salmon and John Nichols, appearing in *Public Opinion Quarterly*, compared next birthday with the Troldahl-Carter method and two other less widely used techniques. They reported that the next birthday method yields a higher completion rate than the others--and a more representative sample

(Salmon and Nichols, 1983:270-276). Next birthday has one other advantage, too: it does not require potentially embarrassing questions early in the interview as does, for example, the Troldahl-Carter, which asks how many women are living in the household. *See also* TROLDAHL-CARTER METHOD.

NONCONTACT   A prospective respondent who was not interviewed because he or she could not be contacted. The noncontact rate (NCR) is calculated as the (numerator) number of prospective respondents not contacted over the (denominator) total number of eligibles. Thus a sample of 1,000 eligibles reporting 300 noncontacts would have a 30 percent noncontact rate. Noncontacts are directly related to the refusal rate. Any interview not obtained from an eligible respondent is either attributed to direct refusal or counted as a noncontact (Frey, 1983:40-43).

Typical causes of noncontact are people who are away from home, people who have moved, and people who are too sick or infirm to participate in an interview. Research indicates that the noncontact rate varies with the mode of interviewing. It is lowest with mail surveys--especially those where cover letters are addressed personally to prospective respondents. It is highest for telephone surveys, where many obstacles--no answers, busy signals, answering machines, and so forth--can prevent interviewers from contacting respondents. Face-to-face interviews produce a lower noncontact rate than telephone interviews. This may be changing, however, as people become less available for interviewing in their homes (Weisberg, Krosnick, and Bowen, 1989:95-101). *See also* COMPLETION RATE; NOT AT HOMES; REFUSALS; RESPONSE RATE.

NONOPINIONS   Respondent answers that are based on little knowledge or thoughtful understanding. Nonopinions are essentially random responses (Weisberg, Krosnick, and Bowen, 1989:71-72, 124-126).

The term nonopinion (nonattitude is a loose synonym) comes from a classic article by Philip Converse. Converse analyzed answers given by a survey panel during three successive "waves" of interviewing. He discovered that on some questions there were very low correlations from interview to interview. Respondents' answers tended to change from one time to the next, but in no predictable way. Converse reasoned that this pattern of answering could be explained only by assuming that many respondents had no real opinion at all. They answered randomly each time the question was asked (Converse, 1969).

Converse--and this is an important point often overlooked--did not argue that all public opinion was random or meaningless. What he said was that some questions bring forth nonopinions; to these questions respondents give meaningless answers, usually because they do not want to appear uninformed.

Nonopinions threaten any poll that asks public policy questions. Some people will give their opinions even though they are not informed on a topic--they will approve a policy rather than admit they do not know about it, or they will identify public figures they have never heard of. A common example of nonopinion is encountered by pollsters measuring candidates' name awareness among voters. Earl Babbie recounts his experience:

> In a political poll in Honolulu years ago, I asked a sample of voters whether they were familiar with each of 15 political figures. One of the names was Tom Sakumoto. Nine percent of the sample said they were familiar with him. Of those, about half said they had read about Tom in the newspapers, and half said they had seen him on TV. Some characterized him as a liberal, others as a conservative. Some like him, others weren't impressed. The one thing no one mentioned about Tom was that he was made up! There was no political figure of that name in the state. Nonetheless, a substantial portion of the sample provided information about him. (Babbie, 1973:143)

There are some methodological solutions to nonopinion. Gallup's much discussed, but seldom used quintamensional would certainly identify most respondents giving random answers. Less cumbersome and more accessible techniques such as filter questions and screeners are probably better alternatives. But improved methodology alone will never eliminate nonopinion answers. The problem will remain as long as pollsters continue to ask people's opinion about matters that pollsters think are important--but that many respondents do not (Schuman and Presser, 1981: Ch. 9). *See also* METALLIC METALS ACT; PHANTOM PUBLICS; PLURALISTIC IGNORANCE; RESPONDENTS; SPIRAL OF SILENCE.

NONPROBABILITY SAMPLE   Any sample that flouts the established laws of probability theory--the most important of which demands that every person in the population be given an equal chance of ending up in the sample. Nonprobability sampling has a long--if not always glorious--history and tradition. Indeed, there is an almost bewildering variety of sampling techniques labeled nonprobability. Some sorting out, however, is possible. Three main types of nonprobability sampling can be distinguished: convenience samples, purposive samples, and quota samples. The three form a rough hierarchy from least to most sophisticated (Warwick and Lininger, 1975:73-74; Chein, 1976:517-521).

Convenience samples are also known as haphazard samples and accidental samples. These include respondents who are chosen because they are readily accessible. Street corner straw poll interviews of passersby are convenience samples. So are studies that rely on volunteers (Williamson et al., 1982:105-106).

Purposive samples are also known as judgment samples. These rely on researchers' judgment about who should be a respondent. "Expert choice" samples, in which someone with specialized knowledge chooses the respondents, is a purposive sample. So are "snowball samples," in which respondents themselves refer other respondents for interviews (H. W. Smith, 1975:117-118).

Quota samples are drawn to replicate the population according to key demographic categories: income, education, race, and gender are most common. Quota samples violate probability rules because interviewers determine who becomes a respondent (Hennessey, 1985:56).

Since none of the nonprobability methods use random procedures, it is impossible to know how well their samples represent the target population (Fowler, 1984:55-59). Nevertheless, nonprobability sampling is widely used. Practical reasons--chiefly lower cost and expediency--explain much of this popularity. But there are some circumstances in which nonprobability samples are justified on research grounds alone (Mosher and Kalton, 1972:90-93). For example, they are especially appropriate for exploratory studies where great precision is unnecessary and some flexibility is useful. Nonprobability samples are also indicated in situations where only very small samples are possible. In fact, nonprobability samples may actually be more representative than probability samples when thirty or fewer respondents are to be interviewed. *See also* CONVENIENCE SAMPLE; PROBABILITY SAMPLE.

NONRESPONSE   A condition in which one or more questions have not been answered by the designated respondent. Nonresponse is a serious problem because it threatens the representativeness of the sample: respondents who don't answer may have different opinions than respondents who do not answer may have different opinions than respondents who do, but their opinions are not represented in the poll (Wilhoit and Weaver, 1980:29-31).

Five kinds of nonresponse can be distinguished according to their main source:

1.   *The unsuitables*--nonresponse from people unsuitable for interviewing, such as the sick or infirm.
2.   *The mobiles*--nonresponse from people who have moved since the sampling frame was created.
3.   *The refusals*--nonresponse from people who refuse to be interviewed.
4.   *The aways*--nonresponse from people away from home for extended periods.

5. *The absents*--nonresponse from people temporarily away from home. (Mosher and Kalton, 1972:169-170)

One established method of dealing with nonresponse is to list nonrespondents as an independent subsample, then contact and interview some of them so they can be compared to people who originally responded (Raj, 1972:158). The logic is that if those nonrespondents finally interviewed are like the original respondents, then the survey is probably representative even with most nonrespondents still missing. In practice, however, it is difficult to sample and locate nonrespondents. Their inaccessibility continues to make them hard to contact and interview. One imaginative approach to nonresponse is to conduct a "sensitivity analysis"--that is, calculate "how different the nonrespondents would have to be from the respondents" to make a difference on the decisions to be made with the polling data (Tull and Hawkins, 1980:141-142). *See also* COMPLETION RATE; DK/NR; REFUSALS; RESPONSE RATE.

NONSAMPLING ERROR   Poll error caused by the practical problems encountered in conducting polls. Nonsampling error comprises a very long list of hazards that can bias polls. These include faulty questions, defective sampling frames, faked interviews, misreporting, specious analysis, improper coding, and tabulation errors (M. L. Young, 1987:94; Backstrom and Hursh-Cesar, 1981:56).

Researchers divide nonsampling error into two general classes: random error and systematic error. Random nonsampling error occurs by chance--for example, clerical errors committed in recording information from a questionnaire. Because random errors tend to cancel each other out, they are considered relatively benign. But systematic error--poorly worded questions are one example--is more serious. It accumulates, instead of "washing" itself out, as does random error.

Nonsampling error is often linked to sampling error. But the two have little in common beyond their mutual threat to polling accuracy. Sampling error is a statistical measure determined by the size of the sample and the sampling method employed. It can be estimated with some precision and it can be controlled. Nonsampling error, on the other hand, cannot be precisely measured, and often escapes detection. It is not influenced by the size of the sample and is not easily controlled.

Most pollsters consider nonsampling error to be a much more serious threat to polling accuracy than sampling error. Strenuous efforts are made to minimize it. Nevertheless, polls are reported as if all nonsampling error was random (and therefore cancelled itself out), or otherwise had been eliminated. Unfortunately, this is not always the case (Mosher and Kalton, 1972:385-392, 482-483). *See also* SAMPLING ERROR.

NONVERBAL TECHNIQUES   Interviewing tactics that use nonverbal communication instead of spoken or written language. Nonverbal techniques conventionally include four distinct modes (Gordon, 1969: Ch. 15):

1. *Kinesics*--a nonverbal technique that uses body movement to communicate--standing, walking, sitting, eye movement, and so on. For example, respondents who use extensive hand movements may be exhibiting aggressive behavior, while a respondent who avoids eye contact may be expressing anxiety or embarrassment.
2. *Proxemics*--a nonverbal technique that uses personal space to communicate--sitting close by or far away, moving toward or from, and so on. An interviewer who positions herself too close to or too far from a respondent is violating proxemics. And a respondent who backs away may be reacting to threatening questions.
3. *Chronemics*--a nonverbal technique that uses time to communicate. Two chronemic techniques are most common: pacing and silent probes. Pacing involves the rate of speech adopted by the interviewer. Talking too fast can trigger anxiety, even anger, while talking too slowly may cause ennui. Silent probes are chronemic tactics in which interviewers use pauses and other kinds of silence to signal expectations.
4. *Paralinguistics*--a nonverbal technique that uses voice volume and pitch to communicate. Voices can be loud or soft, high or low, and so on. Both interviewer and respondent convey paralinguistic meanings. Respondent feelings especially may be revealed by paralinguistic interpretation.

Nonverbal techniques differ from verbal in one obvious way: verbal techniques use words to communicate, nonverbal ones do not. But there is another, less obvious, difference between the two. Nonverbal messages are both sent and received subliminally. Neither party to the communication may be consciously aware of them.   Nevertheless there is some evidence that interviewers can be trained to recognize and use nonverbal interviewing techniques. Indeed, nonverbal techniques may come to have as much influence on polls as the more conventional verbal techniques (Kahn and Cannell, 1967). *See also* INTERVIEWING; PROBING; PROJECTIVE TECHNIQUES.

NOT AT HOMES   Prospective respondents who are not available when an interviewer calls. Not at homes pose two polling problems: they threaten to reduce the survey's response rate, and they compromise the representativeness of the sample (Backstrom and Hursh-Cesar, 1981:103-104):

1.   Response rate problem--Not at homes reduce survey response rates unless they are eventually contacted and interviewed. A respondent who is not reached on the first try requires one or more callbacks to complete the interview. After two or three unsuccessful calls, a not at home is usually counted as a nonresponse (Wilhoit and Weaver, 1980:29-31).

2.   Representativeness problem--The other problem caused by not a homes is their threat to sample representativeness. People who are not at home when interviewers call tend to be different than people who are at home. Specifically, not at homes tend to be younger, more affluent, and male. Since these groups spend less time at home, they are often underrepresented in general population surveys.

Weighting the not at home group is the general solution to the representative problem. One widely used technique is the Politz-Simmons method, which asks respondents interviewed how often they are at home "normally at this time of day." If a respondent reports being at home regularly, then poll responses are "weighted down." Those who say they are rarely at home have their responses "weighted up." The Politz-Simmons method assumes that the people rarely at home are a lot like the not at homes. Since the not at homes cannot be interviewed, the rarely at homes stand in for them (Tull and Hawkins, 1980:143). *See also* NEXT BIRTHDAY METHOD; RESPONSE RATE; TROLDAHL-CARTER METHOD.

O

OBJECTIVE DATA   *See* SUBJECTIVE DATA.

OMISSION   *See* TELESCOPING.

OMNIBUS POLL   Several short polls integrated into one questionnaire. An omnibus poll is a sort of anthology--a collection of small surveys tied together by a common theme or purpose. Omnibus polls are fielded by research concerns or academic institutions, which sell question space to individual "subscribing" clients (Worcester, 1972:202-205). A distinguishing characteristic of omnibus polls is their periodicity: they run regularly on a monthly, quarterly, semiannual, or annual basis. Widely known omnibus polls in the U.S. include the Minnesota State Survey and the University of Alabama Capstone Poll. Typical of these, the Penn State at Harrisburg "policy omnibus" is quarterly, has about fifty questions and about ten subscribers--mostly agencies of state government, state think tanks and public interest groups.

The appeal of omnibus surveys is their relatively low cost. Subscribers realize substantial savings over what their series of questions would cost in an independent poll. Efficiency is also an advantage. The typical omnibus can be produced quickly because time-consuming sampling, fieldwork, and data analysis are organized in advance (Marsh, 1982:222). Still other advantages are quality and consistency: since the omnibus is run periodically, most design glitches have been worked out.

Omnibus polls do have some tradeoffs. One is the limit on the number of questions a subscriber may sponsor (often measured in interviewing time). Also limited are the complexity and scope of the questions. Respondents encounter so many different topics that some simplification is necessary. Complex questions and abstruse issues do not fit well (Worcester, 1972:211-213). Finally, omnibus polls require considerable standardization. Unusual sample designs, specific interviewing dates, or screening for rare populations is normally not feasible. *See also* CARAVANING; PIGGYBACK POLL.

OPERATIONALIZE Researcher jargon for translating abstract concepts into specific questions. To operationalize in polling means to word questions so that the researcher is precisely measuring variables such as trust in government, feeling of well being, socioeconomic status, and likelihood of voting. The process of arriving at a measure for a variable is operationalizing that variable. Even straightforward concepts are challenging to operationalize, as Lawrence Clark illustrates with the concept of vegetarianism:

> A vegetarian is "one who believes that plants afford the one proper food for man." In order to develop a good survey, we have to operationalize that definition. Are vegetarians people who have not eaten meat for the past week? Past month? Past year? Do we include people who normally do not eat meat but who eat meat when invited over to someone's home for dinner?...Do we include people who fluctuate between eating meat depending on which diet they are following?...In each of these cases, decisions must be made as to whether or not the behaviors are of interest and should be included in the survey. (Clark, 1976:10)

In practice, most poll concepts require two or more questions. Operationalizing the concept "voter exposure to media," for example, might require the following four questions:

1. Did you read about the campaign in any newspaper?
2. Did you listen to any speeches or discussions about the campaign on the radio?
3. Did you watch any programs about the campaign on television?
4. Did you read about the campaign in any magazine?

Respondent answers to these four questions would measure the concept "exposure to media." Four yes answers might be taken to indicate high exposure; two or three yes answers, medium exposure; and none or one yes answers, low exposure (Selltiz, Wrightsman, and Cook, 1976:40).

Appreciating the nature of operationalization gives insight into an inherent limitation of polling. Researchers are really interested in abstractions--opinions about this issue, attitudes toward that problem, and so forth. But what researchers actually measure are not these abstracts, but specific questions that operationalize these abstractions. It is these specific questions, the way they are worded and how they are asked, that determines what any concept really means. This is why the questions used must always be examined before the meaning of poll findings can be understood (Wilhoit and Weaver, 1980:5-13). *See also* INSTRUMENT.

OVERNIGHTS Polls completed in a single day, then reported the following day. Overnights (flash polls and spot surveys are both synonyms) are full field surveys of reasonably large samples--up to 1,200 for national overnights. They are usually done in response to some fast breaking news event of unusual importance and wide interest--presidential debates, for example, or an important speech. The Iran-contra hearings in 1987, according to *Washington Post* correspondent Richard Morin, inspired at least ten overnights. Overnights differ from more leisurely polls in a couple of ways. One of these is timing. Overnights are conducted while events are still fresh and feelings still strong. Consequently, they are more likely to reflect respondents' gut reactions. Another difference with overnights is their disregard of callbacks. Each telephone number is tried only once. This practice almost invariably skews the sample, possibly resulting in an oversample of women, Democrats, older persons, or college-educated people (Morin, Aug. 3, 1987:37).

Overnights should not be confused with either tracking polls or media rating overnights. Tracking polls resemble overnights in that both are done daily. But tracking polls are done continuously over many days or weeks, so each day's tracking poll has only an incremental influence on the overall results. With overnights, the poll is completed the day it is started, and reported the next day (Levy, 1984:89-91). Media rating overnights rate program audiences for the commercial networks. These overnights come from Nielsen and Arbitron meters installed in homes in the nation's largest media markets. These ratings cover programming from 6:00 a.m. to 1:00 a.m. the previous day, and are usually distributed to subscribers early the following morning (Belville, 1981). *See also* TRACKING POLLS.

OVERREPORTING Answers from respondents that exaggerate or overstate some personal experience. Overreporting occurs, for example, if someone reports voting more frequently than they actually do, or claims to read more books than they have. A special type of overreporting is telescoping. This is a reporting error made by respondents who mistakenly remember an event occurring more recently than it actually did occur. For example, a trip to the dentist that happened six months ago is reported as happening only three months ago (Tull and Hawkins, 1980:259).

The opposite of overreporting is underreporting. This is when a respondent omits part or all of a personal experience. Forgetting a shopping trip, the use of some product, or having listened to a particular program are examples of underreporting. It seems clear that much over- and underreporting is due to memory error, rather than conscious deception--people simply forget what happened or when. But respondents are probably more likely to overreport and underreport certain kinds of information. Specifically, overreporting is more likely for experiences that are flattering or socially desirable--like voting, church attendance, and support for charities. Underreporting is more common for events that embarrass or threaten one's self image--like drinking, use of drugs, and financial troubles (Turner and Martin, 1984:116-117, 268).

A distinction is maintained between the terms overreporting or underreporting and the term misreporting. Misreporting has the same effect as over- or underreporting--a loss of information. But the state of mind is different. Misreporting is purposeful deception, while over- and underreporting are due to memory errors (Hennessey, 1985:92-95). *See also* MIS-REPORTING; TELESCOPING.

OVERSAMPLING   A procedure in which an overly large number of people from some key population group is sampled systematically. Oversampling is also known as booster sampling and disproportionate sampling. Its purpose is to collect enough interviews from the oversampled group to allow statistical analysis of data for that group (Worcester, 1972:86). Oversampling is most often done with rare populations or ethnic minorities. Warwick and Lininger provide this example:

> In a survey of Chicago, for example, it may be theoretically or practically important to study the Italian subgroup in that city. In a small sample relying on equal probabilities of selection, the number of selected cases from the Italian subgroup may be too small to permit reliable analysis. Under these conditions, the areas of the city where persons of Italian decent tend to live might be treated as a separate stratum and over sampled. (Warwick and Lininger, 1975:98)

Two basic situations justify oversampling. First, a demographic group might be relatively rare in the overall population, say 1 or 2 percent. If a group this small were not oversampled, there would not be enough interviews to perform statistical analysis. The second situation that justifies oversampling is when a demographic group is especially important to the survey--a critical ethnic group, for example, in a political poll. Only a small margin of sampling error can be tolerated. So the important group must be oversampled to ensure that the small level of sampling error is not exceeded (M. L. Young, 1987:95).

In special circumstances, undersampling instead of over sampling is appropriate. Undersampling entails sampling a disproportionately small number of people from some large and homogeneous subgroup. A survey of religious groups in Utah, for example, might undersample Mormons. The rational for undersampling is that the subgroup involved is unusually homogeneous. It requires fewer interviews because its members are so similar (Nieburg, 1984:184). Both oversampling and undersampling require weighting the overall sample. Oversamples must be "weighted down"; the most common technique is randomly to delete the excess respondents, or to assign each respondent some value less than one. Undersamples are "weighted up"; each respondent is assigned some value more than one. Both oversampling and undersampling are legitimate procedures. Any poll, however, that employs either of them should disclose its weighting procedure. *See also* WEIGHTING.

P

PANELS A specialized poll in which respondents are interviewed again and again as part of an ongoing study. Panels use the same respondents for two, three, four, or more interviews (Johnson and Joslyn, 1986:111-112). The panel method was developed by the renowned sociologist Paul Lazarsfeld. His classic study of voting behavior, *The Peoples Choice*, (1944) is still a leading example of the technique. Lazarsfeld and his colleagues interviewed over six hundred people in Erie County, Ohio, once a month for six months. Respondents were asked about their voting intentions and the things that influenced their thinking about the upcoming election (Williamson et al., 1982:130).

Today panels are widely used in consumer research, audience research, and political polling. They have one paramount advantage over other polls: panels monitor change in individuals from poll to poll. This allows researchers to find out who is changing, who is not, and why. By contrast, nonpanel polls allow only net change to be measured from one poll to the next. Knowing only net change may obscure enormous shifting back and forth of opinion between surveys (Clark, 1976:20).

Of course, panels also have drawbacks. The most serious is the mortality problem--which is people dropping out of the panel. Mortality is a serious threat to the representativeness of panels, since people who drop out of panels are usually different than those who remain. The other problem with panels is their potential for reactivity; that is, respondents may become biased from repeated interviewing. This problem, known technically as the interaction effects of testing, can occur if respondents change simply because they have been interviewed. They may pay more attention to news, be more aware of issues, or think more about the matters on which they are questioned (Babbie, 1973:64,65,43; Weisburg, Krosnick, and Bowen, 1989:133-134). *See also* CONDITIONING; DROPOUTS; LONGITUDINAL SURVEYS; TREND STUDIES.

PARTIAL INTERVIEWS   Interviews started with respondents but never completed.   Partial interviews occur for several reasons.   Respondents may simply change their mind about continuing--and abruptly terminate after only one or two questions.   Some respondents may cooperate for a while, but become tired or bored before the interview is over.   Still other respondents may have to run an errand or make a phone call.

About 5 percent of all interviews become partials.   Most of these occur in telephone surveys rather than during face-to-face interviews (Frey, 1983:220). The method of accounting for partial interviews is unsettled among pollsters. The general practice, however, is to salvage an interview if it produces significant amounts of information.   When this is done, any unanswered questions from the partial interview are treated as missing data in subsequent analysis (Babbie, 1973:264-266).   *See also* COMPLETION RATE; RESPONSE RATE.

PARTY AFFILIATION QUESTIONS   Standard questions asked in political polls about a respondent's partisan leanings.   Party affiliation questions may be simple and straightforward, as in this example:

> Generally speaking, in politics do you consider yourself to be a Democrat, a Republican, an Independent, or what?   (Backstrom and Hursh-Cesar, 1981:168,206)

More complex questionnaires go further, asking respondents about choices made in past elections, attitudes toward political parties, and ideological disposition.   One poll, for example, uses four separate questions to assess party affiliation:

1.   Which of these statements best describes how you usually vote--mostly Republican; sometimes Republican; mostly Democratic; sometimes Democratic; or for the man, the candidate?
2.   In what political party are you registered--Republican, Democrat or Independent?
3.   In this state, thinking of the Democratic and Republican parties, would you say there is a great deal of difference in what they stand for; a fair amount of difference; or hardly any difference at all?
4.   Do you consider yourself to be very liberal; fairly liberal; moderate; fairly conservation; or very conservative?   (Selltiz, Wrightsman, and Cook, 1976:311,312)

Despite general decline in voter enthusiasm for political parties, partisan affiliation is still the best predictor of voter behavior on election day.   Voters who say they are Republican (or conservative) are more likely than other voters to vote for the Republican candidate(s). Similarly, voters who say they are Democrats (or liberals) are more likely to vote for the Democratic candidate(s). When a voter says she is a "strong" Republican or a "strong" Democrat, that voter is virtually certain to support the party's candidate once inside the voting booth (M. L. Young, 1987:198-199; Crespi, 1989:60-61). *See also* SOFT SUPPORTERS.

PEOPLE METER   A newer audience measurement device that rates television viewing. People meters are small, hand-held keyboard devices. They require a TV viewer to press a button before viewing. Separate buttons are provided for each person in a household (Belville, 1981:285). People meters replaced A. C. Nielsen's audimeters in late 1987. Audimeters, which were attached to TV sets in 1,700 sample households, automatically measured whether a set was turned on and to what channel it was tuned. Audimeters dominated audience measurement for many years, but they had limitations. By themselves, they did not record how many people were watching or who they were: people meters do (M. L. Young, 1987:64).

Not surprisingly, the shift in measuring systems has brought changes in program ratings. People meters rate some programs higher than audimeters, others lower. Specifically, programs targeted to younger urban viewers do better than before, but programs targeted to older rural viewers do worse. Some of the ratings gap between the newer and older systems may owe to the technology involved. Younger viewers may be more comfortable with using the hand-held keyboard--hence, younger-oriented programs score better (Winfrey, 1987). One other issue, so far unresolved, is whether people meters will produce the consistent cooperation needed to measure viewing accurately. The older Arbitron system was automatic, but people meters require individual effort from every member of the household. *See also* COINCIDENTALS.

PERCENTAGE POINTS VS. PERCENTAGE   An interesting if arcane argument about how to describe the accuracy of polls. Pollsters typically evaluate their own polls in terms of the percentage points between forecast and actual results (Crespi, 1989:53-54). Thus, if Gallup predicts a Bush over Dukakis win of 54 to 46, but Bush actually wins 56 to 44, Gallup would claim an error margin of two percentage points. Critics of this practice, however, argue that using percentage points understates true error. Instead, they say, percent error should be the standard. So in the example above, Gallup's error would actually be about 5 percent - the 2 points Bush scored higher divided by 54, the original Bush forecast.

Both sides have some support here, but the pollsters, rather than their critics, probably have the strongest case. This, in fact, is what Harold Mendelsohn and Irving Crespi conclude after reviewing both sides of the argument:

> Standard statistical practice and theory indicate that the use of percentage points is proper and accurate. For example, consider the case in which a poll reports 80 percent for candidate A and 20 percent for candidate B, but the election returns are 90 percent to 10 percent. using the percent criterion, the error for candidate A would be 11 percent, but for candidate B it would be 100 percent. The percentage-point criterion, in contrast, shows an error of ten percentage points no matter which candidate is considered. Clearly, the latter method is less subject to misinterpretation and confusion. (Mendelsohn and Crespi, 1970:68)

Mendelsohn and Crespi add that "every statistics textbook deals with sampling error in terms of percentage points." So pollsters do seem on solid ground describing their accuracy in percentage points rather than percents. *See also* SAMPLING ERROR.

PERIODICITY   *See* SYSTEMATIC SAMPLING.

PERSONAL DIMENSION SCALE   *See*   NAME RECOGNITION QUESTION.

PHANTOM PUBLIC   Walter Lippman's satirical allusion to the notion that average people formulate public opinion. The phantom public to Lippman was a convenient specter conjured up in the minds of theorists, editorial writers, public relations workers, and others who had need for it. Lippman popularized the term as the title of his 1925 book about public opinion. In *The Phantom Public*, Lippman ridiculed the notion that average people produced public opinion. He argued instead that most people have neither the training nor the inclination to deal with complex policy issues. Most of their time is given over to the demands of daily survival, and even people who follow public affairs are handicapped by the quality of information available in the press (Lippman,

1925).   The average person, harrassed for time, paid little attention to government or politics.

He exhausted his energies earning a livelihood, and once home from work, he was likely to take off his shoes and indulge his feet as he looked at the comics rather than to attempt to inform himself on the "weighty" matters currently confounding Washington. Even if he were willing to devote his spare time to the study of public issues, the information available to him was both inadequate and unenlightening.   Nor was the amorphous public, even if informed, capable of taking the initiative in any public action (Welch & Comer, 1975:15).

Lippman especially criticized the media for not clarifying important public issues, and then creating phantom publics by labeling their own private views as views of the general public.

The notion of phantom publics is still relevant today. Now, however, it is more likely pollsters than editors who are chided for conjuring up bogus public opinion.   Pollsters who tap nonopinions by asking questions people are not qualified to answer, are producing phantom publics. So are pollsters who frame questions so carelessly that public opinion seems unstable from poll to poll (Robinson and Meadow, 1983). Indeed, much of the inaccuracy, inconsistency, unreliability, and so forth that polls are criticized for is traceable to the influence of these modern day phantom publics. But these modern phantoms may be even more sinister than the phantoms of Lippman's era, because they make their appearance garbed in the guise of science. *See also* JOE SIX-PACK; NON-OPINIONS.

PIGGYBACKING   *See* PIGGYBACK POLL.

PIGGYBACK POLL   A poll sponsored by two or more clients, each with space reserved for their specific questions. Piggyback poll is a rough synonym for omnibus poll.   One distinction sometimes drawn between the two is regularity.   Piggyback surveys are irregular or ad hoc arrangements of convenience, while omnibus studies run on some periodic schedule such as quarterly or semiannually. Expected quality is connotative difference. Omnibus polls are usually fielded by major research concerns-- increasing expectations of careful design and professional field work. Piggybacks, on the other hand, may be coupled to any poll, grafted on as it were, wherever convenient (Backstrom and Hursh-Cesar, 1981:45-46,171-238). *See also* CARAVANING; OMNIBUS POLL.

PILOT STUDY   *See* PRETESTS.

PLURALISTIC IGNORANCE   An important theory about public opinion and the social forces that shape it. Pluralistic ignorance describes the condition in which a majority of people are mistaken about prevailing public opinion, that is, they are ignorant about what most other people believe. "Individuals believe X, but are convinced that the large majority of people believe Y" (Sheatsley, 1983:204).   A frequently cited example of pluralistic ignorance is racial attitudes.   Survey data shows that a majority of whites express considerable tolerance on racial issues, but also believe incorrectly that most other whites are intolerant (O'Gorman, 1979:48-59).

The pluralistic ignorance notion is often fitted to another theory about public opinion--the "spiral of silence."   According to the spiral of silence theory, actual support for any opinion thought to be minority opinion is likely to be understated, while actual support for opinion thought to be majority opinion is likely to be overstated.   Pluralistic ignorance describes a public confused about what is actual public opinion.   The spiral of silence predicts that the same public will be reluctant to express opinions believed to have majority backing (Noelle-Neumann, 1984).

The troubling implication of all this is that opinions believed to be those of the majority are likely to seem much more popular than they actually are, while opinions believed to be those of the minority are likely to seem much less popular than they actually are.   Here's a hypothetical illustration: most people's opinion is that religious organizations should <u>not</u> be tax exempt (prevailing opinion), but they believe wrongly that a majority of people disagree with their view (pluralistic ignorance).   So, the opinion thought to be minority opinion (i.e. religious organizations should not be tax exempt) is actually the majority opinion, but people will be reluctant to express it (spiral of silence) because it is thought to go against prevailing opinion.

There is some evidence--from survey data and small group experiments--that pluralistic ignorance is common; people regularly confuse majority opinion for minority opinion, and minority opinion for majority opinion.   Interestingly, one group seems immune to this tendency: public officials and leading political figures are typically able to accurately sense prevailing public opinion--a talent undoubtedly helpful in maintaining their leadership positions.

Some writers suggest that polls can act as a corrective to the effects of pluralistic ignorance-- faithfully informing the public of true majority opinion.   This may happen, but so far there is no evidence that it does.   What we do know, in fact, is that the general public does not pay too much attention to polls. Neither public opinion nor political behavior is much influenced by polls-- or what people learn from them (Fields and Schuman, 1977:444-445). *See also* ATTENTIVE PUBLIC; PUBLIC OPINION; SPIRAL OF SILENCE.

POCKETBOOK INDEX   *See* WEIRD SCIENCE.

POLITICAL POLLSTERS   Those pollsters and firms who work mainly or exclusively for political clients.   Political pollsters poll for political parties, PACs, and candidates for elective office.   Of the approximately 250 survey research firms operating around the country, only a handful concentrate on political work.   Of these, just six firms dominate the political market.   Three of them normally work for Democrats (William Hamilton Associates, Cambridge Survey Research, and Peter Hart Research Associates); the other three usually work for Republicans (Market Opinion Research, V. Lance Tarrance & Associates, and Decision Making Information) (Sabato, 1981:72).

At one time, the role of political pollsters was subordinate to that of media consultants and other political operatives.   But not today.   Pollsters have emerged as the grand strategists of American politics.   Part of this transformation has been due to the growing sophistication of polling, but most of the enhanced role of pollsters is due to pollsters themselves understanding politics better (Levy, 1984:86-96).

The attention accorded to the political pollsters seems grossly disproportionate given their minuscule share of the national polling industry. Political polling makes up only a tiny sliver of the up to $5 billion spent annually on surveys.   Less than 1 percent of polls done in the U.S. are political work.   The other 99 percent deal with consumer behavior, not politics or public affairs (Field, 1983:203).   Nevertheless, political pollsters have gained stature and visibility over the last decade or so, not only relative to other pollsters, but also within organized politics.

Many political pollsters are well known and widely publicized--figures like Bill Hamilton, Robert Tetter, Arthur Finkelstein, Lance Tarrance, and Peter Hart.   A few have even become celebrities: Pat Caddell and Richard Wirthlin are examples.   *See also* POLLING INDUSTRY.

POLITZ-SIMMONS METHOD   *See* NOT AT HOMES.

POLL COSTS   The money required to plan, design, carry out, and analyze a public opinion survey.   Poll costs range from several hundred dollars to several hundred thousand dollars.   Three variables heavily influence final costs: the size of the sample, the length of the questionnaire, and the method of interviewing (Sabato, 1981:75-81):

1. <u>Sample Size</u> varies from as little as a few dozen for small tracking polls to 1,500 or more for national surveys. Polls done locally range from 450 up, while 600 to 850 respondents is the normal range for statewide polls. In general, the larger the sample, the higher the costs of a poll. Some economies of scale, however, are realized as sample size increases. Consequently, larger polls often have lower costs per respondent.

2. <u>Questionnaire Length</u> runs from a single page of ten or fewer questions to multiple-page schedules of hundreds of questions. Benchmark polls often have one hundred or more questions. Intermediate-sized questionnaires might have thirty or so questions. Tracking polls, which typically feature less than ten questions, are the shortest of all. In general, the longer the questionnaire, the higher the poll costs. As with sampling, however, there are scale economies. With longer instruments, the marginal cost of additional questions decreases-- sometimes quite substantially.

3. <u>Interviewing Methods</u> affect costs directly. Three modes of interviewing are available: face-to-face, over the telephone, and via mail. Conventionally, mail is considered the cheapest, with in-person the most expensive and telephone interviewing the middle choice. One careful study done at the University of Michigan Survey Research Center estimates the cost per telephone interview at 45 percent of the in-person interview (Groves & Kahn, 1979: Ch. 7). This means a twenty-minute telephone poll costing $20,000 could cost as much as $45,000 if conducted face-to-face.

A less systematic way to calculate poll costs is to draw on the numerous rules of thumb available regarding the cost of polls. The following nine are especially helpful (M. L. Young, 1990:47-49):

1. <u>Billing Practice</u>--Pollsters bill their services in thirds: one-third due on signing the contract, another third due when interviewing begins, and the final one-third due when findings are presented.

2. <u>Poll Value</u>--A poll loses half its value after fifteen days and 95 percent of its value after sixty days.

3. <u>Campaign Budget</u>--Total polling costs run 5 to 10 percent of political campaign budgets.

4. <u>Cost Range</u>--Poll costs range from $15 to $35 per interview for telephone interviewing, and from $35 to $150 for a face-to-face interview.

5. Dollar Per Minute--The cost of a telephone survey is about $1.50 per minute per respondent; face-to-face is about $3.40 per respondent.

6. Cost Differential--Face-to-face interviews cost more than twice what telephone interviews cost. $45 per respondent face-to-face would cost only $20 by telephone.

7. Hours Per Interview--Each completed telephone interview requires three-and-a-half hours' work, including administrative support. Each completed in-person interview requires about nine hours work.

8. Cost Allocation--About 50 percent of the cost of a poll is allocated to interviewing. The other 50 percent covers planning, data processing, analysis, and other fees.

9. Size of Population--Size of the survey population is essentially irrelevant in determining cost. For any given accuracy level, a town of 25,000 will require almost as many interviews as a metropolitan area ten times larger.

See also COST ITEMS; POLLING INDUSTRY.

POLLING INDUSTRY   The hundreds of private firms, nonprofit organizations, media outlets, and university institutes that produce public opinion research in America.   The polling industry employs forty to sixty thousand people and boasts five distinct sectors (Rossi, Wright, and Anderson, 1983:9-15; Turner and Martin, 1984:341-350):

1. The Academic and Nonprofit Sector includes the national survey organizations affiliated with universities, such as NORC (University of Chicago), ISR (University of Michigan), and Rand Corporation. Also included are the regional and local survey operations found at dozen of state and private universities.

2. The Private Sector includes larger firms like Gallup, Louis Harris and Associates, Chilton Opinion Research Corporation, as well as hundreds of smaller firms across the country like Peter D. Hart, DMI, and MOR.

3. The Mass Media Sector includes about two hundred newspapers, magazines, networks, television and radio stations that conduct polls. Most prominent are the large, well-known media polls like the CBS-*New York Times* poll, the ABC-*Washington Post Poll*, the *Boston Globe* poll, the *Chicago Tribune* poll, and the *Los Angeles Times* poll. There are also dozens of regional, state, and local polls that are sponsored by print and broadcast media.

4. The Government Sector includes those surveys conducted by federal, state, and local agencies. A considerable share of government-sponsored surveys are contracted out to academics or the private sector. Some federal agencies, notably the U.S. Census Bureau, and a handful of state and local agencies carry on regular survey work. Government surveys tend to deal with Objective Facts such as employment status and housing conditions.

5. The In-House Sector includes two kinds of surveys: ad hoc and in-house. Ad hoc studies are irregular or one-time polls--for example, a city studying the satisfaction of its citizens with community services, or an academic doing a survey of local conditions. In-house surveys are regular polls, but they are not done by polling organizations. Most of these are large corporations who do their own work rather than contract out.

The exact size of the polling industry is not established, but there are at least 250 firms across the country. One source estimates that survey organizations annually contact 32 million households and conduct 100 million interviews. Industry revenues are also conjectural. One dollar range given is $2.5 to $5 billion (Rossi, Wright, and Anderson; 1983:9-10).

Somewhat surprisingly, it is market research instead of the higher profile political polling that accounts for most survey research activity. Political polling, in fact, generates only a small fraction of industry revenues. In 1980, for example, an estimated $20 million was spent for all political polls. For the same year, an estimated $1 billion dollars was spent for market research--about fifty times the amount spent on politics (Field, 1983:203). The dollar share among types of political polls is also worth noting. In 1984 about $65 million was spent on all political polls. Almost half of this (46%) was spent on congressional and state offices; about one-third (35%) was spent on media polls; and less than one-fifth (19%) was spent on presidential primary and general election polls. See also COST ITEMS; POLITICAL POLLSTERS; POLL COSTS.

POLL/MEDIA CYCLE   The rise and fall of political popularity caused by the interaction effects of polls with mass media. The poll/media cycle is a sequence of phases in which poll results increase (or decrease) the media attention a candidate receives. This resultant media coverage in turn raises or lowers the next round of poll results for that candidate; these new polls then influence the next round of media coverage, and so forth (Roper, 1980:46-49).

Presidential primaries illustrate clearly the poll/media cycle. Those candidates starting high in the polls usually receive the most media attention;

their high polls then attract even more press coverage, which in turn raises their poll standings even higher. Conversely, those candidates starting low in the polls usually receive the least media attention, which holds down their subsequent poll results. William C. Adams explained the pattern of circularity in *Public Opinion* magazine:

> The overall pattern is interactive: prior visibility begets high poll ratings which beget media coverage/legitimacy which begets improved poll standings which beget media coverage/legitimacy. For those with little initial standing, the pattern is fairly stable. Low visibility begets under five percent in the polls which begets little media attention/credibility which begets continued low standings in the polls. In every phase the poll media cycle depresses or stimulates the other two key elements in campaign dynamics: money and volunteers. (Adams, 1984:10)

The poll/media cycle raises an old issue in polling--the effect polls have on the outcome of elections. Studies of the bandwagon effect, the alleged influence of polls on voters, have found no evidence of any direct polling effects. Voters are not usually influenced to vote one way or another because of polls (Field, 1983:211). Indirect effects from polls, however, are more likely. Apparently polls do influence the amount of money contributed to a campaign, the media coverage a campaign receives, and the morale of campaign supporters.

These indirect effects are what *Los Angeles Times* writer David Shaw dubbed the "Three M's of polling: money, media, and morale" (Gallup, 1972:222-227). The "Three M's" fuel the poll/media cycle. Candidates having "good" polls raise money, attract media coverage, and keep campaign supporters, and these resources, in turn, help them continue to score high in the next round of polling. Meanwhile candidates with "bad" polls continue to lose ground because they cannot raise money, attract media coverage, or maintain the morale of supporters. *See also* BANDWAGON EFFECT; THE THREE M's.

POLL REGULATION Bringing polling under government control through reporting requirements, licensing, or other means. Poll regulation in the United States is minimal, but not for any lack of interest. Proposals to regulate polls have been made after every national election since at least 1948. That year, after the polls "elected" Dewey, Congress held hearings on a bill that would have regulated syndicated pollsters. But nothing came of it.

Since 1948, the most serious national effort has been the Truth in Polling Bill, proposed in the late 1960s and early 1970s. Known as "Nedzi," after its chief sponsor, Congressman Lucien N. Nedzi, it would have required pollsters to file their polls with the Library of Congress within seventy-two hours of completion (Hollander, 1971:335-341). Nedzi sparked considerable debate. Most pollsters opposed it, arguing that self-regulation and voluntary disclosure were far more practical than government regulation.

There have been sporadic attempts in a few states to go beyond the industry's standard disclosure requirements. California once considered a bill that would have registered and licensed pollsters. New York introduced legislation that would have required reporting of respondents' names. Neither of these passed. But Texas did approve legislation that would have had the effect of preventing the publication of preelection polls. Governor Connally vetoed it before it could become law. Washington state had a law regulating exit polling until it was struck down by an appellate court. And New York still has a statute requiring candidates who are releasing poll results also to explain the basic methodology used (Nieburg, 1984:252-259).

State laws like those in Washington and New York, however, are unusual. Most proposals to regulate polls simply call for some form of disclosure regarding the poll--when was it done, how large was the sample, what were the questions, and so forth. Advocates of disclosure argue that neither the media nor the public can intelligently evaluate polls unless pertinent technical information is released (Turner and Martin, 1984:61-67).

Polls have acquired real power and influence in the past fifty years. It is hardly remarkable that proposals to regulate polls continue to be made. Thus far, however, self-regulation through voluntary disclosure--not government regulation--has held sway. There is still some sentiment for outside regulation, but prospects for it are not strong. In fact, it seems likely that constitutional guarantees regarding free speech bar any further restrictions on polling (Young, 1990:494-495). *See also* DISCLOSURE; TRUTH IN POLLING BILL.

POLL RIGGING   Determining the outcome of a poll by manipulating the sample. Poll rigging is a recurring nightmare among pollsters. It would require penetrating survey security processes--such as communicating with respondents in advance, or substituting a phoney sample for the real one (Wheeler, 1976:115-121). Attempts to rig polls occur only infrequently, but polling organizations still take steps to keep samples secure.

So far there has been no disclosed instance in which a major poll has been successfully rigged. But there was an attempt in 1966 to rig the Nielsen broadcast ratings. Rex Sparger, the perpetrator, had acquired extensive knowledge of the Nielsen system while staffing a congressional subcommittee. Hugh Belville picks up the story:

> Sparger somehow acquired the names of some Nielsen service
> men and either trailed them as they made service calls on

sample homes or stole files of names left in service men's unlocked cars. In any event, (he) acquired the identity of 58 (Nielsen) households in Ohio and Pennsylvania. He approached (the) executive producer of a forthcoming special...(who) agreed to send questionnaires to each of the 58 homes designed to influence them to watch the show. Each questionnaire...was accompanied by $3.00 (with another) $5.00 promised for completion and return. (Belville, 1981:321)

Nielsen's security system quickly uncovered the rigging attempt. The entire affair was eventually settled in civil court, but the experience stands as a reminder: polls and surveys can be rigged, by someone both skilled and motivated enough to do it.

POLL USERS   Pollsters, government officials, business people, journalists, and others who use the results of survey research. Poll users are a diverse lot. They can, however, be grouped into four broad categories: mass media users, academic users, public officials, and political managers (M. L. Young, 1990:112-114):

1. Mass Media Users include both print and electronic outlets. Members of the media use polls to forecast elections--the time-honored function of press polling. More recently, however, other journalistic objectives have been pursued with polls. These include providing editorial guidance, developing story material, and, of course, increasing circulation.

2. Academic Users include university research institutes, as well as individual professors. Academicians emphasize the scientific function of polling. They use polls to build theory and empirically test propositions about voting, public opinion, and social behavior.

3. Public Officials typically use polls to sell programs rather than develop policy; or as former presidential assistant James Fallows put it, polls "tell you how to get from A to B," but not that "B is where you want to go" (Cantril, 1980:134).

4. Political Managers include political party strategists, PAC officials, political consultants, and campaign managers. Political managers use polls as a source of strategic information--to help identify key issues, pretest advertising themes, and monitor public opinion. They also use polls for decision making, consulting them about allocating campaign monies, scheduling, and media time buying.

One suggested new use of polls would parallel the relationship that business now has with market research. Pollster Irving Crespi argues that government officials could govern more effectively if they drew upon survey research. Private business found out decades ago that success depended upon consumer approval; now bureaucrats need to learn the same lesson (Crespi, 1979:15-19). *See also* POLLING INDUSTRY.

POLL VS. SURVEY   *See* SURVEY VS. POLL.

POPCORN POLL   *See* SILLY POLLS.

POPULATION   *See* ELEMENTS.

POSTAL CHECKS   A procedure used to verify that respondents were actually interviewed. Postal checks consist of so-called sample verification-- sending a postcard to a respondent who is asked to report whether or not an interview was accomplished. Sometimes postal checks also include question verification--inquiring if the interviewer asked the scheduled questions and recorded accurately the response given (Mosher and Kalton, 1972:293-294).

Occasionally, 100 percent postal checks are conducted, usually for small samples. More commonly, some kind of sampling selects the respondents to be recontacted. Two approaches are popular:

1. The 20/100 method--a sample of about 20 percent of all interviewers are selected, and 100 percent of their work is checked.
2. The 100/20 method--100 percent of all interviewers are selected, but only about 20 percent of their work is checked. (Worcester, 1972:140-141)

The main drawback of postal checks is that at least some of them are never returned by respondents. The nonresponse rate ranges from 20 percent to 50 percent, sometimes more. Follow-up mailings can reduce this considerably. But in practice, there is always some fraction of reported interviews that cannot be verified. *See also* CHEATER QUESTION.

POSTCONVENTION POLLS   Polls taken in the first week to ten days following a political party convention. Postconvention polls almost always show marked gains in support for the presidential candidate just nominated, which gradually slips back to preconvention levels or even lower. The postconvention phenomenon owes to the intense media attention that parties and their candidates receive during conventions. After the convention, media coverage lessens and poll standings return to normal (Aldrich, 1980).

Just after conventions and during primary campaigns are two of the least auspicious times to take polls. In the case of primaries, the problem comes from underexposure: neither candidates nor issues have received enough media converge to come to the attention of most voters. The result--poll-measured opinion is volatile, and support for specific candidates tends to be "soft." Postconvention polls present just the opposite problem--overexposure. Presidential candidates receive saturation media during their conventions-- coverage that is flattering and even glamorous. The consequence is a kind of postconvention euphoria that gives nominees a "bump" up in the polls. Eventually, however, the excitement wears off, the glow fades, and the polls slide back down.

Most major party conventions produce these postconvention effects, but not all do. Occasionally something more akin to depression then euphoria occurs when feuding party factions collide in full view of national television audiences. This happened to Barry Goldwater and the Republicans in 1964 in San Francisco. It also happened to Hubert Humphrey and the Democrats in 1968 in Chicago. Neither Goldwater nor Humphrey ever recovered from the bitter conflicts that erupted during their party's convention. *See also* DELEGATE POLLS; PRIMARY POLLS.

PRECISION JOURNALISM   The use of polling and other social science methods to research and write news stories. Precision journalism was once virtually synonymous with the use of polls in news reporting. But more and more the term refers to a wide array of qualitative and quantitative tools (Meyer, 1973). Arnold Ismach makes this point in an article discussing polling as a news gathering tool:

> Public polls are not the beginning and end of precision journalism effects. Instead, as they gain resources and build confidence, the media are increasingly moving toward more refined research approaches--content analysis, behavioral studies, index construction, and even experiments--to develop for themselves and their audiences information that is not ordinarily available from any other source.   (Ismach, 1984:112)

The mass media is rapidly adopting the tools of precision journalism. The major broadcast networks and the elite print press have all established polls. There are also more than five hundred regional broadcast and print media outlets that produce polls on a regular basis. All of this "precision" has influenced press coverage. In fact, according to Charles K. Atkin and James Gaudino, the explosive growth of public opinion polling has transformed the mass media. Political news coverage, particularly, has been significantly altered by polls (Atkin and Gaudino, 1984:119-128). Findings from surveys also now play a role in editorial comments and endorsements--and they provide an important resource for journalists in their adversarial relationships with government leaders.

The influence of precision journalism on the media has a counterpart in the influence of the media on polling itself. Polling has been affected by the ways journalists now use it. According to pollster Burns Roper, a few of journalism's effects have been positive. Media "embracing" of polls, for example, has promoted broader acceptance of polling. But most of the consequences of precision journalism have been bad for polling--and some have been very bad. Among the harmful effects, Roper claims, is that the media initially retarded the growth of polling. Even today, the press often abuses the tool, or uses it in trivial and unimportant ways (Roper, 1980:46-49). *See also* MEDIA POLLS.

PRECODING   Inscribing questionnaires with instructions about how respondents' answers are to be recorded. Precoding involves two related steps: assigning number codes to each possible answer a respondent might give, and designating the location on the computer record where that answer will be stored for later analysis (Dillman, 1978:222-277).

Here is an example of precoding for a single questions:

> Q. Which of these actions would you support to reduce
>   the deficit?
>   (39)
> 1. Reduce defense spending
> 2. Raise taxes
> 3. Reduce social program spending
> 4. A combination of these three actions
> 5. Don't know/no response
> 6. Refused

The number 39 in parentheses and the numbers 1 through 6 beside the answers illustrate precoding instructions. The number 39 indicates which column on the data entry card is used to record and store answers to this question. The numbers 1 through 6 indicate which numbers may be entered in that column. For example, if a respondent answers the deficit question with "raise taxes," the number 2 corresponding to that answer would be punched in column 39 (Babbie, 1973:152-155).

Precoding can be done only for closed questions, that is, questions that list all possible responses on the questionnaire. Open questions must be coded after interviewing is over. Then major answer categories are designated and assigned numerical codes similar to those used in precoding. *See also* CODING.

PRESTIGE EFFECTS   *See* RESPONSE SET.

PRETESTS   Trial runs for a planned poll. Pretests are troubleshooting pilot surveys designed to uncover defects in the questionnaire or other aspects of a study before it goes into the field (Mosher and Kalton, 1972:48-51). One prevailing rule of thumb is that pretests should include twenty to fifty interviews with prospective respondents. An even better guide is to ensure that each major group in the study population is exposed to the pretest. Pretests also allow practice for the interviewers who will be doing the main survey (Sudman, 1978:87,88).

Two problems exist with pretests as they are commonly carried out. The first is scope. In principal, pretests can provide evaluations of each phase of the planned study: the questions, the sampling, the interviewing, the field operation, and so forth, can all be pretested. In practice, however, this broad preview rarely happens.   More commonly, pretests simply review the questionnaire. The second problem with pretests is the quality of the work done.   Pretests are often carried out carelessly or even skipped.   It is not completely clear why this is the case, since leading writers stress the importance of pretesting--characterizing it as a dress rehearsal for the main study. Even among pollsters themselves, it is axiomatic that poor pretesting is a major cause of bad polls (Babbie, 1973:205-222; Warwick and Lininger, 1975:161-162). *See also* INSTRUMENT; INTERVIEWING; RESPONDENT.

PRIMARY POLLS   Election surveys conducted during a primary election campaign. Primary polls are much like any other poll--samples are randomly drawn, interviewing methods are comparable, and the questions themselves differ only slightly from other polls. Nevertheless, primary polls are wildly unreliable and misleading. It is common for them to show sudden shifts in opinion or wide swings in support for a candidate--even in surveys taken only days apart. And primary polls are often inaccurate. In fact, they have a notorious reputation for missing the election-day winner (Sabato, 1981:85; Gallup, 1972:179-180; Wheeler, 1976:275-279).

Three explanations are usually given for the inconsistency of primary polls. First, it is pointed out, primary voters lack the party cue available in general elections. In primaries, the candidates are all Republicans or all Democrats, so voters, bereft of a party anchor, put off their decision--or else base it on surface impressions, subject to change.

A second reason primary polls are often wrong is that primary elections bring out a tiny and unrepresentative electorate. Only a fraction of eligible voters cast ballots in these party contests--as few as 20 percent or less. Pollsters, therefore, must screen out nonvoters who do not turn out and vote on primary election day. Doing this well is one of the most difficult tasks in polling.

A third factor cited to explain the poor record of primary polls is the mass media. Many voters first learn of the campaign through media coverage and paid political advertising. But the press coverage voters depend upon is concentrated in the last few weeks of most primary campaigns. Voters consequently make up their mind late--and their commitments tend to be unstable (Roll and Cantril, 1972:18-22; 30).

The generally poor record of primary polls does not mean that all primary polls are unreliable. Not all are, nor is all the data from them subject to sharp change. Many "baseline" conditions measurable in primary polls are relatively stable. Ratings of well-known incumbents, political party preference, and prevailing opinion on longterm issues are examples. Primary polls are as reliable for this kind of information as polls taken at other times (Salmore and Salmore, 1989:115-122). *See also* LIKELY VOTERS; POSTCONVENTION POLLS.

PRIMARY SAMPLING UNITS   *See* CHUNKS.

PRIVATE POLLS   Surveys done for individual clients that are not released to the news media or formally publicized. Private polls distinguish themselves from public polls in two main ways: sponsorship and utilization.

Public polls are typically sponsored by a media outlet, public organization, or business group that releases results. Private polls, on the other hand, are usually commissioned by such clients as political parties, PACs, and political candidates.

Public polls--many of them conducted by well-known, national firms like Gallup or Harris--are used to inform readers, influence policy, and disseminate information.   Private polls, on the other hand, are used to promote political objectives--typically those of a candidate for political office (Harris, 1963:3-8).

Public polls have the glamour, but private polls seem to have the greater utility.   In fact, the many uses of private polls have become much better understood recently.   Scholars have now identified at least ten specific uses to which private polls are put (Altschuler, 1982:168-187; Field, 1983:205-206). These are:

1.   Understanding Candidate Image--exploring   the   strengths   and weaknesses of political candidates.
2.   Key Demographic Breakdowns--describing the electorate in terms of important groups and coalitions.
3.   Assessing the Candidacy--deciding whether to run or not--the feasibility of candidacy.
4.   Issue Definition--determining which issues are important, and how to present them.
5.   Endorsement--testing whose endorsement is helpful, and with what groups.
6.   Opposition Research--researching an opponents vulnerabilities, as well as one's own.
7.   Resource Allocation--determining on which radio and television outlets to buy time, and when.
8.   Themes and Slogans--testing prospective campaign themes.
9.   Measuring Progress--using tracking to monitor reaction to advertising, debates, opponents changes, and so on.
10. Party Preference--determining the overall allocation of party strength, where it is concentrated, and how strong it is.

The many and versatile uses of private polls underscore a curious fact about modern political polling.   Most of it is private--a good guess is that seven of every ten political polls is private.   Yet it is the public polls--Gallup, Harris, the media polls, and so on--that get virtually all of the attention   (King and Schnitzer, 1968:431-436).   *See also* POLITICAL POLLSTERS; POLLING INDUSTRY.

PROBABILITY PROPORTIONATE TO SIZE (PPS)   *See* MULTISTAGE SAMPLING.

PROBABILITY SAMPLE   Any sample that chooses respondents according to probability theory. Probability samples are drawn so that every element (person) in the population has a known and equal chance of ending up in the sample. There are four main versions of probability sampling: simple random sampling, systematic sampling, stratified sampling, and cluster sampling. A fifth type, multistage sampling, is a hybrid of the main four (Babbie, 1973:91,102).

Simple random sampling is the sampling method that underlies all other forms of random sampling. It is simple and straightforward: each member of the population is "listed" with a unique number, then a random procedure selects actual respondents for interviews. Unfortunately, simple random sampling is often impractical because of the difficulty associated with producing a complete list of any population (Weisburg, Krosnick, and Bowen, 1989:35).

Systematic sampling builds on and improves the basic idea of simple random sampling. Again, everyone in the population is listed. Then a sampling interval is calculated according to how large a sample is planned (for example, the interval might be every 100 persons on the population list). Next the initial respondent is chosen using a "random start." Finally, the rest of the sample is selected, using the sampling interval and counting from the initial respondent (Backstrom and Hursh-Cesar, 1981:59-60).

Stratified sampling divides the target population into layers, called strata, before sampling begins: male/female, black/white, urban/suburban/rural, and so on. Virtually any population characteristic can be used to form strata; race, income, education, and gender are the most common. The objective is strata that reflect real differences between people. The main advantage of stratified sampling is efficiency: it reduces sampling error compared to other sampling methods (Roll and Cantril, 1972:82-89).

Cluster sampling locates respondents in groups (clusters) rather than one at a time. Population clusters such as schools, offices, neighborhoods, and so forth are identified, then groups of five to ten respondents are interviewed in each cluster. The major attraction of cluster sampling is economic: it produces faster, cheaper interviews, because respondents are concentrated. The trade-off, however, is increased sampling error, because people who are grouped together are more homogeneous. Consequently it takes more respondents to equal the representativeness of other sampling methods (Warwick and Lininger, 1975:98-101).

Multistage sampling is a process in which sampling is done in stages-- usually involving some combination of systematic sampling, stratified sampling and cluster sampling. Multistage sampling is mainly used where large geographic areas (such as a county) are being surveyed, and no good population listing exists. The major advantage of multistage sampling is that it makes it possible to poll large dispersed populations. The drawback is increased sampling error and greater complexity compared to simpler methods (Fowler, 1984:28-31).

Probability sampling costs more than nonprobability methods and is more involved to carry out. Nevertheless, probability methods have become the preferred sampling technique. There are two main reasons for this: first, probability methods are more likely to be representative of their populations than are nonprobability methods; and second, probability methods allow sampling error to be calculated. Pollsters using probability methods can estimate the difference between sample findings and actual population values. *See also* CLUSTER SAMPLING; MULTISTAGE SAMPLING; SIMPLE RANDOM SAMPLING (SRS); STRATIFIED SAMPLING; SYSTEMATIC SAMPLING.

PROBING An interviewing procedure designed to dig past the initial answer given by respondents, in order to produce final answers that are full and complete. Probing is used almost exclusively with open-end questions. There are a variety of probing techniques discussed in the survey research literature: Gordon (1969) lists five separate types of probes, the *Interviewers Manual* (Survey Research Center, 1976) reviews six types, and Warwick and Lininger (1975) go into seven types.

Three examples illustrate the range of probes commonly used: encouragement probes, silent probes, and echo probes. First, encouragement probes emphasize positive feedback. Interviewers signal approval of what was said and interest in hearing more--with expressions like "go on," "I see," "yes, yes," and "uh huh,"--or (in face-to-face interviews) nonverbal cues such as leaning forward, smiling, or simply nodding.

Second, silent probes utilize natural lulls in the conversation. After a respondent has answered a question, interviewers pause and wait for amplification or clarification. Silent probes work because people are inclined to fill conversational gaps by continuing to talk.

Third, echo probes repeat the respondent's exact answer turning it into another question--such as, "You think taxes are too high?" A related technique is the repeat probe, which requires interviewers simply to repeat the original question itself. (Gordon, 1969; Survey Research Center, 1976; Warwick and Lininger, 1975).

Probing puts some burden on interviewers, who are required to produce a verbatim record of answers given. But even extensive probes can be captured efficiently in a few lines of writing--as is evident in this example from a leading survey research text. The words in parentheses are "probe symbols," which allow the pollsters later to reconstruct the sequence between interviewer and respondent:

(Question:) In your opinion, what are two or three of the most important problems facing the American people today?

(Answer:) Taxes are important. (Taxes?) They're too high, especially the sales tax. (High?) Its up to six percent. (Else?) Nothing, that's all. (Other?) Well, welfare's pretty important. (Why?) The poor people ain't getting the help they should. (Help?) You know, like food stamps and stuff like that. (Stuff?) Oh, I don't know. They should get free food stamps, that's all. (Else?) That's all I can think of. (Other?) No, just those two. (Backstrom and Hursh-Cesar, 1981:271)

Some writers emphasize the distinction between probing and prompting. Probes should never lead or imply an answer, while prompting actually suggests possible answers. Another difference: prompts are often printed on questionnaires, and interviewers are instructed to use them if a respondent hesitates. Probes, however, usually require the interviewer to supply the response needed to elicit full and complete answers. *See also* INTERVIEWING; NONVERBAL TECHNIQUES.

PROJECTIVE TECHNIQUES   A class of research methods in which respondents are asked to react to some vague stimulus--such as a word, phrase, or picture. Projective techniques follow a notion well established in clinical psychology: people interpret ambiguous situations by projecting their own feelings onto them; the more nebulous the situation, the more people reveal themselves in describing or discussing it. Writers generally recognize four types of projective techniques. These differ according to the stimulus given respondents (Tull and Hawkins, 1980:364).

First, word association techniques ask a respondent to report the first thing that comes to mind after hearing a word or phrase. The stimulus words might include specific products, objects, or even names of well-known people.

Second, completion techniques provide an incomplete sentence and ask respondents to complete it. Respondents are asked to finish sentences such as: "Men who wear hats are ....."; "Fast food restaurants attract ....."; "Politicians in this state always...."; "People who drive Fords ....."; and so on. Sometimes stories are used instead of sentences. The interviewer might describe an imaginary scenario, such as a shopping trip, a buying decision, or a voting dilemma, then ask respondents to furnish an ending.

Third, construction techniques provide a picture of some sort, then ask respondents to construct something based on it. Cartoons are an example. One of the characters may be shown talking or engaged in some activity. Another character will have a "bubble" over its head, which the respondent fills in.

Fourth, expressive techniques involve respondents acting out roles of some sort. When the role depicts themselves, the technique is referred to as "psychodrama"; when somebody else is depicted, it is called "sociodrama." Both versions of expressive technique encourage respondents to project their own feelings and values into the roles they assume.

Projective techniques are probably applicable to most types of public opinion study. Their use, however, has been largely restricted to marketing research (Worcester, 1972:35-37; Hoinville, 1978:14-15). The most common projective technique used in opinion polling is the indirect question, also known as the third-party question. In these, the interviewer asks the respondent to speculate on the views of some third person, such as "your neighbors," "most voters," "other people," "average guys," and so on. For example, a poll studying rates of income tax compliance might ask, "How do you think most people feel about cheating on tax returns?" Third-party questions assume that respondents will reveal their own deeper feelings and opinions in the process of speculating about other people's feelings and opinions (Mosher and Kalton, 1972:326-327). *See also* NONVERBAL TECHNIQUES; PROBING.

PROMPTING   *See* AIDED RECALL.

PSEUDO OPINION   *See* NONOPINIONS.

PSEUDOSURVEY   Any survey that violates the principals of scientific polling. Pseudosurveys resemble authentic polls, but are flawed in some way. Three types of pseudosurvey can be distinguished: sham polls, silly polls, and straw polls.

First, sham polls are pseudosurveys that fraudulently present themselves as bona fide. The practice of sugging (selling under the guise of a survey) is a sham poll. So are phoney questionnaires accompanying fundraising appeals. Many congressional mail polls are also sham polls--electioneering, not public opinion is their real interest (Turner and Martin, 1984:73,268).

Second, silly polls are pseudosurveys clearly designed to be humorous or make a point. Unlike sham polls, these make no pretense of scientific practice. Silly polls include perennial election- time amusements such as popcorn polls, bumper sticker polls, and toilet paper polls (M. L. Young, 1989:551-552).

Third, straw polls are surveys that do not conform to the strict principle of probability sampling. Strictly speaking, any nonprobability poll is a straw poll, but the term usually refers to those straw pc'is conducted by newspaper and broadcast outlets before an election. The *New York Daily News* straw poll is probably the best known of these. Some straw polls are serious attempts to measure public opinion--and may even turn out to be accurate. But straw polls are properly classified as pseudosurveys, since they are not based on a random sample (Hennessey, 1985:42-43). *See also* CALL-IN POLL; SILLY POLLS; STRAW POLL; SUGGING.

PUBLIC AFFAIRS ACT   *See* METALLIC METALS ACT.

PUBLIC OPINION   The moving force behind it all--the raison d'etre of surveys and polls. Public opinion is to polls and surveys as sex was to Kinsey, religion is to the theologian, zoos to the zoologist, and politics to the political scientist. V. O. Keys once declared that public opinion was "those opinions... which governments find it prudent to heed." This is the practical formulation of things--public opinion is the opinion that counts (Key, 1967:14). But Key's definition does not please everyone. There is, in fact, very little consensus on what constitutes public opinion. One leading textbook remarks: "there are almost as many definitions of public opinion as there are writers on public opinion" (Hennessey, 1985:4). Even a brief sampling bears this out:

> ...Writer David Truman declares: 'public opinion consists of the opinions of the aggregate of individuals making up the public under discussion...(not)... all the opinions held by such a set of individuals, but only those relevant to the issue that defines them as a public.' Arthur Kornhauser states that 'public opinion may best be though of as the views and feelings current in a specified population at a particular time in regard to any issue of interest to the population.' Bernard Hennessey himself simply declares that public opinion is "the complex of preferences expressed by a significant number of persons on an issue of general importance. (Hennessey, 1975:8)

Problems in defining public opinion have led some writers to eschew definitions and discuss the "qualities" of public opinion. Three qualities are commonly described: first, distribution of opinion--opinions may be widely distributed, meaning shared by most people; or they may be narrowly held, meaning few people express them. Second, stability of opinion--some opinions are volatile, subject to sudden change, they are "soft." But other opinions change slowly, if at all; they are "hard." Third, intensity of opinion--some opinions are held weakly; they are "shallow." But other opinions are strongly held; they are "deep" (Erikson, Luttbeg, and Tedin, 1988:39-69).

What, then, is public opinion, given the abundance of definitions and scarcity of agreement on any of them? From one perspective, public opinion is simply the latest poll findings. In fact, the term public opinion in common usage has become a de facto synonym for polls. Equating polls however with public opinion does have its limits. Only the very naive believe that polls can perfectly portray public opinion. Still, in the every day practice of public opinion, the concept demands an adequate working definition. And for many purposes, that definition today is that public opinion is what the polls say it is (Crespi, 1989:89-90). *See also* PLURALISTIC IGNORANCE; PUBLIC OPINION RESEARCH; SPIRAL OF SILENCE.

PUBLIC OPINION QUARTERLY (POQ) The leading scholarly journal on polls and public opinion research. *Public Opinion Quarterly (POQ)* is now published by the American Association for Public Opinion Research (AAPOR), whose offices are in Princeton, New Jersey. *POQ* tends toward the academic and theoretical, but it also publishes articles dealing with applied and practical aspects of public opinion research. The roster of contributors is filled with well-known and widely respected academics and practitioners (Childs, 1965:49-64). *POQ* editorial objectives were summed up by new editor Howard Schuman in 1987:

> POQ has been deeply interested from the start in both theory and method, both ideas and current issues, both basic and applied research. And although the sample interview survey and its close relatives are often the method employed in empirical reports, articles that illustrate the nature of public opinion by other means--experimental, qualitative, historical, or whatever-- are equally welcome....a further distinguishing characteristic...is making articles as clear and accessible as possible to a wide range of readers. (1987:1)

Some recent articles give the flavor of *POQ*. The summer 1987 issue includes pieces on political tolerance, the impact of investigative reporting on public opinion, the Knowledge Gap Hypothesis; an evaluation of response order effects, experiments with the middle alternative in questionnaires, and a Meta analysis of return postage in mail surveys. The same issue included two special reports on "The Polls" and several book reviews of two to four pages' length.

Several other periodicals and magazines publish material on polling and public opinion research. Prominent among these is *Public Opinion* magazine, published every other month by the American Enterprise Institute (AEI), in Washington, D.C. *Public Opinion* features timely pieces on polling, public opinion, and public policy written by academics, pollsters, journalists, and AEI resident scholars. The articles tend to be shorter and somewhat breezier than articles appearing in *POQ*. The magazine's material rarely deals with abstract theoretical issues, instead concentrating on analytical and reflective pieces linked to some contemporary issue or event.

Other magazines or periodicals that regularly include polling-related material, are the *National Journal, Congressional Quarterly Weekly, Gallup Reports*, the *Journal of Politics*, and the *Washington Monthly*. Among national print media, the *New York Times*, the *Washington Post*, the *Wall Street Journal*, and the *Los Angeles Times* also frequently publish stories about polling. *See also* AAPOR.

PUBLIC OPINION RESEARCH   In general, any technique or procedure used to discover or explain public opinion. The term public opinion research, in common usage, is a synonym for poll or survey (Babbie, 1973:41-52; Backstrom and Hursh-Cesar, 1981:1-9, 15-23). Thus anyone conducting a poll or survey is doing public opinion research, and that research is generally understood to be based on probability sampling and formal questions of some sort.   Face-to-face, telephone, or self-administered interviewing all qualify (Fowler, 1984).

The techniques counted as public opinion research probably should include more than traditional surveys. Already, gray areas such as focus groups and "Q sorts" are emerging, labeled vaguely as qualitative or "soft" methods. But within and outside the profession, there is still unease about using nonquantitative methods to study opinion. There probably should not be. A large group of alternative methods do exist. These techniques, and others like them, offer a rich variety of options for performing public opinion research (Childs, 1964:66-69). *See also* SURVEY RESEARCH; SURVEY VS. POLL; WEIRD SCIENCE.

PURPOSIVE SAMPLING   A type of nonprobability sampling that uses judgment--the researcher's or someone else's--to determine who is to be interviewed. Purposive sampling offers several variations. These include such sampling strategies as "expert choice" and "snowball sampling." Bellwether samples, in which typical political precincts are selected to represent a cross section of the electorate, are also examples of purposive sampling (H. W. Smith, 1975:117-118).

Some writers treat the term nonprobability as a synonym for the term purposive.   But there is an important distinction.   Purposive samples are carefully chosen to represent some target population, while nonprobability samples include all types of nonrandom samples, those chosen intentionally as well as those chosen haphazardly or accidently (Warwick and Lininger, 1975:73-74).

Purposive samples are best for doing exploratory research--that is, surveys that concentrate on defining the broad scope of a problem or issue. Purposive samples are not so good for counting or describing how specific attitudes and opinions are distributed within a population. Purposive samples also have the same statistical limitations as any other form of nonprobability samples: there is no method to evaluate how well they represent the target population. They may turn out to be a perfect replica of that population, or they may resemble it very little; there is no way to know (Chein, 1976:52). *See also* CONVENIENCE SAMPLE; NONPROBABILITY SAMPLE; QUOTA SAMPLE.

Q

QUBE POLL   An opinion survey conducted by using cable television to pose questions to viewers.   QUBE allows subscribers in Columbus, Ohio, to view debates, speeches, or other public forums, then "vote" their opinions with an electronic keyboard attached to their TV.   QUBE has been promoted as a prototype system that would permit virtually instant two-way communication between TV viewers and operators. The concept's potential for opinion research has been widely discussed--attracting both supporters and opponents (Sabato, 1981:71).

Supporters enthuse about electronic polling and a promise of wider democracy. Public opinion, they believe, can be known instantly--and it will have greater influence on the formulation of public policies. Opponents counter that QUBE-type polling, if widely used, could provoke despotic rule by majority whim. Public policy would be less stable, and subject to sudden shifts in mass opinion.

Pollsters themselves have serious methodological reservations about electronic polls. This type of survey is essentially a straw poll; only QUBE subscribers may participate, and only some of them do. As with all straw polls, the results are suspect, because the sample is nonrandom. Albert H. Cantril, president of the National Council on Public Polls (NCPP), emphasized this point after being asked to comment on a recent QUBE poll:

> Such a survey cannot even be construed as a measure of sentiment in Columbus. At $10 a month, poor people were not likely to subscribe to cable, skewing the results. Since those who watch and those who decide to respond are self-selected, this presents a fatal systematic error, even if demographic questions are added to see whom they represent. (Nieburg, 1984:63)

One does not need to be a QUBE critic to agree that cable interactive polling still offers more promise than performance. The methodological problems are serious, and some of the novelty has worn off. Nevertheless, interest in QUBE and polls like it will doubtless continue. Tieing the computer, television, and opinion research together is an exciting prospect--if not yet reality (Nieburg, 1984:123). *See also* SAMPLING ERROR.

QUESTIONNAIRE   *See* INSTRUMENT.

QUESTION ORDER EFFECTS   Any influence on respondent answers traceable to the order in which questions were asked. Question order effects are a subtle but critical source of bias in polls. Simply put, the sequencing of questions and the organization of the questionnaire can determine the answers respondents give. It also can affect respondent candor and even raise the rate of refusals (Bradburn and Mason, 1964:4).

Pollsters recognize the importance of question order, and have developed several rules of thumb to guide questionnaire construction. The following five are widely observed (Weisberg and Bowen, 1977:53-55; Sheatsley, 1983:220-223):

1. The instrument should begin with easy, general questions that relax the respondent and promote rapport.
2. Open-ended questions should be asked before closed-ended questions on similar topics. This rule prevents information given in the closed-ended question from influencing the open-ended response.
3. Questions on the same topic should be asked together. Questionnaires should be organized so that each series of questions flows well and is easy for both the interviewer and respondent to follow. Transition sentences between topics are particularly helpful.
4. Topics and question types should shift often enough to maintain respondents' interest and enthusiasm. Repeated questions on the same topic or use of the same question format dulls respondent interest and can even lead to premature termination of the interview.
5. Personal questions, controversial questions, or embarrassing questions should be asked at the end of the interview. By this time growing rapport makes it more likely that respondents will answer. And if respondents do terminate the interview, most of the poll will have been completed.

A special kind of question order problem is context effects--the influence that is exerted on poll answers by where a question is positioned in the questionnaire, and what questions precede it (Schuman and Presser, 1981:12,311-319). Context effects have been studied extensively. It is known, for example, that placing a question toward the end of a poll rather than at the beginning can produce dramatically different responses. A similar effect comes from placing questions in one cluster of items rather than another.

Today virtually all pollsters are aware of the dramatic differences produced by variations in question phrasing, sequence and design.   Some methodologists, in fact, suggest that only question wording itself has greater influence on poll results than does question order effects. *See also* INSTRUMENT.

QUINTAMENSIONAL   A five-part question sequence designed to capture the complexity of public opinion on some issue.   The quintamensional is attributed to George Gallup, who advanced it as a way to explore the diverse facets of opinion on many issues (Gallup, 1947:pp. 385-393).   In Gallup's formulation, the first question in a quintamensional should measure awareness--has the respondent heard of such and such?   Then comes a question about general opinion on the matter--what do you think should be done about this issue? Third is a question about some specific proposal--do you favor or oppose the idea?   Fourth comes a question about the reason for approval or disapproval; fifth and final is a question that taps intensity--how strongly do you feel about your opinion on this issue (Payne, 1951:112)?

The following is an illustration of the quintamensional format as used in a series of questions about Pennsylvania's state-controlled liquor and wine monopoly:

(Awareness)

Q1.   Will you tell me what you may have heard or read about Pennsylvania's Liquor Control Board (LCB) and the state store system?

(General opinion)

Q2.   What, if anything, should the Governor and General Assembly do about the LCB and the state stores?

(Specific opinion)

Q3.   One proposal being discussed is abolishing state stores in Pennsylvania and turning the sale of spirits and wine over to private retail outlets like grocery stores and wine shops.   Would you favor or oppose doing this?

<u>(Reasoning)</u>
Q4.   Would you tell me the reasons you feel the sale of spirits and
        wines should (should not) be turned over to private retail outlets?

<u>(Intensity)</u>
Q5.   How strongly do you feel about your opinion here--very strongly,
        somewhat strongly, or not strongly at all? (Backstrom and Hursh-
        Cesar, 1981:217)

Together all five questions of the quintamensional measure the major
dimensions of public opinion. In theory, the five-question series is an elegant
approach to capturing the richness and diversity of public opinion. In practice,
however, the quintamensional has not been widely used. Certainly the process
is time-consuming and expensive. But the most important inhibiting factor may
simply be lack of demand for a method that measures opinion so exhaustively
(Robinson and Meadow, 1983:126). *See also* PROBING; PUBLIC OPINION.

QUOTA SAMPLE   A major type of nonprobability sample, one that selects
respondents according to demographic categories--sex, age, income, race,
political party, and so on. Quota samples aspire to be miniature portraits of the
population being polled (Selltiz, Wrightsman, and Cook, 1976:517-521).

Three basic steps are involved in quota sampling. First, census data or
other sources of information are consulted to determine the proportion of the
overall population in key demographic categories--the percentage of men, blacks,
city dwellers, Jews, and so forth. Second, interviewers are then assigned quotas
so that the completed survey will include the correct proportion of respondents
in all key population groupings--so many men, so many blacks, so many city
dwellers, and so on. Finally, interviewers are sent into the field, where they
choose the actual respondents based on the quotas assigned. The quotas, of
course, overlap, so that respondents often fill two or more quota categories--
such as white college women, Southern black Democrats, and so on (Mosher
and Kalton, 1972:91-92).

Bernard Hennessey describes a national quota sample:

> In a national sample of 2,000, the pollster may decide to
> interview 1,000 men and 1,000 women; 250 farm dwellers,
> 900 town and small city dwellers, 850 big city and suburban
> dwellers, 450 from the lowest income class, 1,200 from the
> middle income class, 350 from the highest income class, 900
> Democrats, 700 Republicans, and 400 Independents or Third
> Party supporters. Interviewers then select in their areas a
> certain number of persons who fall within these categories--for

example, 10 farm women and 17 farmers, 12 persons from low income areas, 20 Democrats....During the field work phase, interviewing plans are constantly being adjusted by interviewers and the central office to ensure proper stratification of the whole sample. (Hennessey, 1985:56)

Quota sampling was disgraced in the United States after the 1948 presidential election, when it was used to "elect" Tom Dewey over Harry Truman. Nevertheless, versions of it are still used today and, in fact, quota sampling has some attractive qualities.

One of these qualities is simplicity. Quota sampling is considerably easier to design and carry out than is probability sampling. It is also less expensive. Interviewer time and travel is reduced, because callbacks are eliminated and appointments with respondents are not usually necessary (Alreck and Settle, 1985:83-85). Then, too, quota sampling has a certain appeal because it produces a replica of the population in precisely the correct demographic proportions. Even probability samples do not usually achieve this without weighting.

The charms of quota sampling are countered by many serious methodological problems. The gravest of these is the bias that occurs when interviewers choose who to interview. Invariably, interviewers select respondents who are accessible and are like themselves. Quota samples consequently become skewed toward better-educated, white, and middle-class respondents (Worcester, 1972:82-84).

Another problem is knowing the demographic categories to use for quotas. Pollsters do not always know what factors influence opinion or which groups are most important to interview. Even when researchers understand which quota categories are important, there still are practical limits to how many categories an interviewer can be assigned. In practice, quotas are usually based on only a few classification groups, while other demographics that also may be important are ignored. *See also* NONPROBABILITY SAMPLE.

R

RANDOM DIGIT DIALING (RDD)   A popular technique used to draw a sample for a telephone poll. Random digit dialing was developed because telephone directories are often out of date or too incomplete to use as the sampling frame (Glasser and Metzger, 1972:59-64).   Almost 95 percent of American homes have phones, but about 30 percent of these have unlisted numbers. Moreover, about one in five directory listings are out of date because people have moved.   Yet another problem with telephone directories is that some homes have multiple phones (M. L. Young, 1987:100-101).

The basic version of RDD uses a computerized "random number generator" to list the telephone numbers that will be called. The virtue of this approach is that it is simple, and every working number has an equal probability of selection (EPSEM).   The great drawback, however, is that up to 90 percent of the numbers called will be commercial or nonworking.   A more efficient approach combines RDD with directory sampling. The add-a-digit dialing method (ADD) achieves this: an actual telephone number is drawn from the directory, then the last digit is replaced with a randomly selected number.   Versions of ADD produce about 50 percent working telephone numbers (Frey, 1983:67-68).

One other variation of RDD is the Waksberg technique.   It exploits the common practice of assigning telephone numbers in blocks of one hundred. For example, if the number 523-6931 was dialed and found to be working, probably the series from 6901 to 7000 has been assigned to other telephone subscribers. Interviewers then simply call random numbers only within those blocks of one hundred that have at least one working number. Initial working numbers could be screened by random calling or by consulting telephone directory listings (Waksberg, 1978:40-46).

Random digit dialing is not fool proof. Two problems in particular are cited: first, RDD misses people who live in houses without telephones--only about 5 percent of the national population, but a much higher proportion of poor and minority groups. Second, RDD produces too many calls to nonworking or commercial numbers. Even embellishments like add-a-digit dialing still require two numbers be called for every one that is usable.

RDD has one other limiting circumstance. It was designed to overcome directory deficiencies. But in some cases, particularly rural areas, directory coverage is close to 100 percent--virtually everyone has a phone, and few numbers are unlisted. In this situation, the additional cost of RDD is not justified, since the telephone directory itself can be the sampling frame. *See also* ADD-A-DIGIT DIALING; EPSEM; SAMPLING FRAME.

RANDOMIZED RESPONSE TECHNIQUE (RRT)   An interviewing technique designed to encourage candid answers to personal or sensitive questions. RRT records answers without the interviewer knowing for sure which answer the respondent gave. Respondents are thus assured they are anonymous and their responses are confidential (Zdep and Rhodes, 1976:531-537). The RRT method has two steps. First a respondent is given two questions; one is personal (a yes or no question), and the other is a factual question with known probabilities (such as, "Were you born in April?"). Second, the respondent is told to choose which of the two questions to answer according to some random device such as a coin toss. For example, "Answer the first question if a head comes up, but answer the second if it's tails." It is important that the probabilities of the coin flip or other random device be known (Tull and Hawkins, 1980:264-265).

The randomized response technique yields two pieces of information: (1) the probability that a respondent will answer either the first question or the second question (it's 50 percent for both if a coin is flipped); and (2) the probability of someone answering yes to the matter-of-fact question (it's approximately one in twelve, or .083% for those born in April). With these two probabilities, it requires only simple algebra to compute the proportion of people answering yes or no to the sensitive question. RRT has been used to study a wide range of sensitive subjects, including tax evasion, shoplifting, child abuse, and drug use. Some reservations have been raised about the technique--the chief one being that respondents may suspect a trick and therefore cheat on their answers (Mosher and Kalton, 1972:328-330). Overall, however, randomized response technique seems to be successful in overcoming nonresponse to personal questions (Johnson and Joslyn, 1986:176-178). *See also* CONFIDENTIALITY; INTERVIEWING.

RANDOM PROBE   *See* PROBING.

RANDOM SAMPLING   *See* PROBABILITY SAMPLE.

RANDOM START   *See* SYSTEMATIC SAMPLING.

READING THE INTERNALS   Pollster jargon for understanding and interpreting a poll. Reading the internals means going beyond the surface information of a poll--the externals--to the deeper implications in the data. Doing this requires logical inference and some ability to think strategically. It also requires an ability to exercise the imagination and envision how problems today can be turned to opportunities tomorrow. For example, Edward King of Massachusetts, running for governor, did a baseline poll in 1979 only to find himself trailing incumbent Michael Dukakis, 64 percent to 11 percent. Discouraging, of course. But reading the internals of that poll convinced King he could win:

> The survey internals showed that large percentages of Democratic primary voters said that "under no circumstances would they support a candidate who opposed minimum jail sentences for violent crimes, opposed the death penalty, or favored abortion"--all positions taken by Dukakis. King's manager said of these findings, "That's when we discovered we could get significant defectors from Dukakis if we could let people know where he stood and where we stood on the issues." (Salmore and Salmore, 1985:123)

Reading the internals is more art than science. No two pollsters do it exactly alike. Some use statistical procedures to uncover patterns in the data. Others look to favored indicators and scales, such as approval ratings, name identification scores, or reelect questions. Still other pollsters simply immerse themselves in the data until they feel comfortable with it. More than anything else, reading the internals means having political judgment--understanding not just what the data says, but what it means, and being able to translate statistical abstractions into concrete, specific strategies (Crespi, 1989:89-92). *See also* CROSSTABS; MARGINALS.

RECALL   *See* AIDED RECALL.

REELECT QUESTION   A standard used in political polls.   The reelect question gauges support for incumbents up for reelection.   Pollsters consider it a reliable indicator of political strength or weakness Salmore and Salmore, 1989:117-118).   Here's a popular version of the question: "Looking ahead to next year's race for governor, do you think you would vote to reelect Bob Casey, or is it time to give a new person a chance to do the job better?"

The reelect question is reported in terms of respondents who say yes they plan to vote to reelect the incumbent: a 60 percent reelect score means 60 percent of respondents say they will vote for the incumbent.

One rule of thumb among pollsters is that reelect scores over 60 percent make incumbents hard to beat, while scores under 40 percent signal trouble ahead.   Another rule of thumb uses ratios.   Strong incumbents have a reelect ratio of 2:1 or better; a 1:1 ratio is cautionary, and 1:2 predicts electoral disaster.   One of the lowest reelect scores ever recorded went to three-term incumbent mayor Ed Koch of New York City.   Koch scored 17 percent reelect just four months before New York's 1989 mayoral election, which he lost.   *See also* APPROVAL RATING; NAME RECOGNITION QUESTION.

REFERENCE PERIOD   The interval referred to by poll questions. Reference periods may be the day of the poll; it may be last week, last month, or even last year.   If respondents are asked, for example, which candidate they support "as of now," the reference period is the day that question was asked. But questions about behavior during the previous month would make the previous month before the poll the reference period.

Longer reference periods tax respondents' memories.   On the other hand, shorter reference periods can produce a telescoping effect--respondents include things in the reference period that actually occurred sometime earlier (Raj, 1972:169).   A distinction is made between fixed and moving reference periods. Fixed periods are intervals with definite end points, such as "between last Sunday and Tuesday."   Moving reference periods are intervals with no definite end points, such as "the previous month."

The term time reference is also used in polling.   But its meaning is quite distinct from reference period.   Time reference is the period in which polling field work was done.   If a poll begins February 10 and ends February 15, the time reference is that five-day period.   Time references in practice range from a single day to ten days and longer (Turner and Martin, 1984:296-297).   *See also* LONGITUDINAL SURVEYS; TELESCOPING.

REFUSALS   Eligible respondents who are contacted but refuse to be interviewed.   Refusal rates are calculated as the (numerator) number of eligibles who decline to be interviewed, over the (denominator) total number of eligibles in the sample (Frey, 1984:40-43). A sample of 1,000 eligibles reporting 150 refusals would have a 15 percent refusal rate. The refusal rate has a direct relationship to the noncontact rate (NCR). Any interview not obtained from an eligible respondent is counted as either a noncontact or a refusal.

Refusal rates are rising. Once rates of 5 percent to 10 percent were anticipated. Today rates of 15 percent to 20 percent are common, and refusal rates of 40 percent are not rare. No one knows for sure why refusals are increasing. The length of interviews and the personal tone of many questions may explain some of it. Certainly many people are simply uncomfortable with being interviewed--and more today feel they cannot spend the time. Then, too, there are more polls than ever (Gordon, 1969:310-312; Martin, 1983:701-703). Several writers tie rising refusal rates to "sugging"--phoney calls people get from sales solicitors pretending to be carrying out a poll. People victimized by this practice may resist a legitimate interviewer conducting a real poll (Baxter, 1964:124-134).

Interviewers are often taught refusal conversion techniques, which aim to turn an initial refusal into an interview. Skillfully used, these may reduce refusals by about 3 percent. Prevailing practice among pollsters is to report refusal rates, but not to be too concerned until the rate gets above 20 percent. The comforting assumption is often made that people who refuse are not greatly different from people who cooperate. But empirical evidence for this view is mixed. *See also* COMPLETION RATE; NONCONTACT; RESPONSE RATE; SUGGING.

REPLICATION   *See* ELABORATION PARADIGM.

RESPONDENT   Someone interviewed for a poll or survey. Respondents answer questions put to them by interviewers, thereby becoming the subjects of the research. Informant is a loose synonym, but in strict usage the informant is that person with whom the interviewer first speaks at the door or on the phone. The respondent is the person eventually chosen to be interviewed. The number of respondents in a poll varies. Around 250 is the smallest for general population surveys, while 3,000 or so is the largest. Local polls average about 450, statewide polls about 850, and national polls about 1,500 (M. L. Young, 1987:101-102).

Pollsters classify respondents according to an almost bewildering variety of categories. Depending on the answers they give, respondents might become ticket splitters, don't knows, leaners, soft supporters, likely voters, strong Republicans, or undecideds. Recent work by the Gallup organization using factor analysis has added major respondent classifications, such as enterprisers, moralists, bystanders, and seculars (Times Mirror, 1987). In addition, respondents are still classified along traditional demographic lines according to gender, age, income, educational level, ethnic group, and religion (Backstrom and Hursh-Cesar, 1981:160-176).

Respondent selection procedures also vary considerably. Some methods simply call for the interviewer to talk to the first person who answers the phone or comes to the door. But other approaches require the interviewer to select the respondent based on some random process. One widely used selection procedure is the Troldahl-Carter method, which designates respondents according to the number of men living in the household. Still another technique is the next birthday method, which instructs interviewers to talk to the person in the household who has the next birthday (Martin, 1983:697-702).

Becoming a respondent is no longer rare, at least not in the United States. Probably one-third of the U.S. adult population has been surveyed at least once, while one-fifth have been interviewed two or more times (Hartmann, 1968:295-298). Pollsters and others disagree about the consequences of such wide exposure to polling. Some believe that too much interviewing has produced a backlash among prospective respondents. People are now less inclined to cooperate and more cynical about polling. But other observers argue that personal experience with interviewing actually gives respondents new understanding and appreciation for the role of polling in modern society (Gordon, 1969:310). *See also* ENTERPRISERS, MORALISTS, NEW DEALERS, ET AL.; NEXT BIRTHDAY METHOD; TROLDAHL-CARTER METHOD.

RESPONDENT SELECTION TECHNIQUES   *See* NEXT BIRTHDAY METHOD.

RESPONSE RATE   The proportion of eligible respondents actually interviewed during a poll. Response rates are calculated as the (numerator) number of interviews completed over the (denominator) total number of eligible respondents (Mosher and Kalton, 1972:66). An example illustrates the calculation of response rates: a sample of 1,000 is drawn, but during interviewing, 100 of these cannot be reached. Another 100 are designated ineligibles for some reason, such as being too young, not registered to vote, and so on. Before the response rate can be calculated, the original sample of 1,000 must be reduced to 800, because 200 respondents were ineligible or could not be reached. The response rate would then be 600 (number of interviews logged) over 800 (number of eligible respondents)--a 75 percent response rate.

A distinction is drawn between response rates and completion rates.

Response rates exclude respondents who turn out to be ineligible for some reason, but completion rates include all original respondents. Thus the response rate for any given study will always be higher than the completion rate. Comparing response rates among surveys is tricky. Calculation procedures are not consistent among researchers. Knowing how response rates are calculated is probably more important than the rate itself. A high response rate may mask sloppy accounting for missed respondents. On the other hand, a low response rate may reflect rigorous but realistic counting of respondents who should have been interviewed but were not. (Dillman, 1978:49-51; Wilhoit and Weaver, 1980:31). *See also* BLANKS; COMPLETION RATE; NONCONTACT RATE.

RESPONSE SET   Any influence in the interview that motivates respondents toward a particular answer (Isaac and Michael, 1971:62). Response set is also called response bias. The five best-known types are acquiescence bias, social desirability bias, prestige bias, order bias, and auspices bias (Bradburn, 1983:315-318).

1.   Acquiescence bias occurs when respondents give an answer because they believe it is the answer desired by the interviewer or sponsor.

2.   Social desirability bias occurs when respondents give an answer because it is more socially acceptable than the true answer.

3.   Prestige bias occurs when respondents give an answer because doing so enhances their self-esteem.

4.   Order bias occurs when respondents give an answer that is influenced by the sequence or order in which questions are asked--earlier questions suggest answers the respondent would otherwise not give.

5.   Auspices bias occurs when respondents give an answer that is influenced by their attitude or feelings toward the survey sponsor.

Some sources contrast response set bias with instrumentation bias--the former is due to the "predispositions of respondents," while the latter is caused by "questionnaire instructions, questions, scales, or response options" (Alreck and Settle, 1985:112-118). In principle, both forms of bias are subject to control or correction. In practice, however, very few polls are completely free of response bias. *See also* SOCIAL DESIRABILITY BIAS.

ROPER CENTER   A data archive that currently new contains thousands of completed surveys from all over the world. The Roper Center for Public Opinion Research is located in Storrs, Connecticut, and is affiliated with

Williams College and the University of Connecticut. Founded in 1946 by George Gallup and Elmo Roper, the center describes itself in a brochure as "the oldest and largest archive of public opinion data." The Roper Center's holdings go back to the 1930s. The archives currently include data from over 10,000 surveys conducted in more than sixty countries. About 500 new surveys are deposited every year.

Contributors to the Roper Center read like a who's who of international polling: Opinion Research Corporation, NORC, CBS News and the *New York Times*, the Gallup Organization, the Roper Organization, ABC News and the *Washington Post*, NBC News and the *Wall Street Journal*, Canadian Gallup, Brule Ville Associes (France), and Social Survey Ltd. (Britain). Roper Center data is available on a fee basis to public opinion researchers from the academy, business, government, and the press. Roper also offers a much-ballyhooed data base called POLL. POLL includes the surveys of archive contributors back at least ten years--the text of questions, responses, sampling error, and so forth (Turner and Martin, 1984:327-328). *See also* SECONDARY ANALYSIS; SRC:

S

SALIENCE   The importance that a respondent attaches to some issue or problem asked about, or the extent to which an issue is "top of mind" to respondents. Salience is typically described as high or low, as in: "Issue salience was low for those respondents who did not plan to vote, but salience was high for those with a perceived stake in the decision."

A leading textbook on polling gives this definition of salience:

> Salience refers to the level of self-conscious controversy surrounding an issue, social value, event or personality....It refers to the level of individual and public awareness about the matter, the allocation of public attention among many such matters, the degrees and kinds of information about such matters possessed by the public...and the strength of public feelings associated with them. (Nieburg, 1984:150)

Salience can be measured in three ways during a poll. First, respondents' awareness of a problem or issue indicates salience. If they know of it, it is important. Second, knowledge also reveals salience. In general, the more information one has the more salience is the given to the subject of that knowledge. Third, salience reflects intensity of feelings. People with strong feelings about some matter are registering high salience (Sheatsley, 1983:204, 302).

Salience is also related to demographics, time intervals, and issue cycles:

1. Demographics--Upscale, higher income, better educated individuals typically have high salience scores most of the time, while respondents without these demographics tend to have lower scores.

2.   Time Intervals--Some intervals of time record very high salience. Presidential election seasons, for instance, raise levels among likely voters. Other intervals, such as off-year election periods, tend to be low salience.

3.   Issue Cycles--Finally, issues also follow a cycle. Most of the time, issues have low or moderate salience. Some crisis or event increases salience until action is taken or resolution occurs--then a period of lower salience again pushes the issue out of public awareness (Nieburg, 1984:150-154). Polls usually try to measure salience with open-ended questions, since closed questions tend themselves to create salience (Worcester, 1972:105-106).

See also   DEMOGRAPHIC ITEMS; PLURALISTIC IGNORANCE; RESPONDENT; SPIRAL OF SILENCE.

SAMPLE SIZE   The number of respondents interviewed during a poll. Sample size varies.   About 250 is a minimum, while national surveys occasionally interview 3,000 or more. Gallup polls usually sample just over 1,500. Regional, state, and local polls range from 450 to about 1,200 (Roll and Cantril, 1972:71-75).

Sample size is the subject of some prevailing myths. One is that size of the sample is set according to size of the population--small population, small sample; bigger population, bigger sample. This is not so. In fact, the size of the population influences sample size very little. A variant of the sample size myth is the sample fraction myth. This belief holds that samples should be some fraction of the population (one-tenth, one-fifth, one-third, or whatever). Again, not so.   Usually sample size is infinitesimally small compared to population size.

Sample size is not usually influenced by population size, but is influenced by sampling error--defined as the estimated difference between a sample and the population from which it was drawn (Mosher and Kalton, 1972:146-152). The general rule is the larger the sample, the smaller the sampling error; however, the rate of decrease in sampling error falls off sharply after samples get above 500 or so.   The table below illustrates this relationship.   Adding 500 respondents to a sample of 250 reduces sampling error almost by half, but adding the same 500 to a 1,000-person sample brings error down just 15 percent.

RELATIONSHIP BETWEEN SAMPLE SIZE AND
DECREASES IN SAMPLING ERROR

Simple Random Sample Size	Sampling Error	Error Decrease from Next Lowest Size Sample
2,000	2.2%	0.3
1,500	2.5%	0.6
1,000	3.1%	0.5
750	3.6%	0.8
500	4.4%	1.9
250	6.3%	3.7
100	10.0%	5.8
40	15.8%	---

In theory, researchers can specify the exact sample size they need by answering three key questions. First, what type of sampling technique will be employed? Stratified samples permit smaller sizes, while cluster samples require larger samples. Second, how much variability is expected in the poll answers-- specifically, what will be the opinion split on the most important question? Pollsters usually assume a conservative 50-50 split in opinion. Third, what is acceptable sampling error? How will the data be used, and how accurate must the results be (Crespi, 1987:50-54)?

In practice, it is three other questions that are often asked before selecting sample size. First, how much money is available and what will the poll cost? The sample size directly influences polling costs, and so there is almost always tension between "ideal" sample size and the size that can be afforded. Second, what subsamples are needed? When demographic groups are to be broken out for crosstabs--by gender, race, income, age, and so on--it may be necessary to increase sample size. Most pollsters consider about 100 to 150 respondents the minimum needed for meaningful subgroup analysis. Third, how diverse is the population being sampled? Surveys done in small, relatively homogeneous states (for example, Utah, Wyoming, or North Dakota) can use smaller samples than can polls in states like New York, California, or Florida (Weisberg, Krosnick, and Bowen, 1989:56-69).

A few rules of thumb about sample size are also helpful. First, about 40 is the smallest sample size that allows probability theory to operate, while 100 is closer to a practical minimum for probability sampling. Second, a simple random sample is about 50 percent more efficient than a cluster sample. For example, a simple random sample of 1,000 will yield the same sampling error as a cluster sample of 1,500. Third, for very small populations, a 10 percent sample is usually adequate. Thus for a population of 1,500, a sample of 150 might do; and for a population of 5,000, a sample of 500 would suffice. Above 10,000 population, the 10 percent rule of thumb is not useful.

The most important rule of thumb about sample size is that sample size is not that important; by itself it is rarely the cause of a bad poll. Other factors, especially nonsampling error, are usually the culprit when a poll goes wrong. *See also* PROBABILITY SAMPLE; SAMPLING; SAMPLING ERROR.

SAMPLING   The key notion underlying all forms of polling. Sampling is any procedure that collects information from some fraction of a population, and then makes inferences about the entire population from the sample (Survey Research Center, 1976:35-37). Sampling contrasts with a census, which requires that every member of the population be surveyed. Sometimes censuses are referred to as "100 percent samples."

Two broad types of sampling are employed in polling: probability (random sampling), and nonprobability (nonrandom sampling). Each of these is associated with an almost infinite array of techniques (Chein, 1976:512-540). Probability is the sampling version used in so-called scientific polls. Its variants include simple random sampling, stratified sampling, cluster sampling, and multistage sampling (Babbie, 1973:91-102). Nonprobability sampling also has several variations. The three most common nonprobability classifications are convenience samples (also called haphazard samples), purposive samples (also called judgment samples), and quota samples (Warwick and Lininger, 1975:73-74).

The key distinction between probability and nonprobability sampling has to do with choosing respondents. Nonprobability does not use random methods to select respondents. Consequently, there is no statistical way to determine the representativeness of a nonprobability sample. Probability sampling, on the other hand, does use random methods to determine who is interviewed. Thus the findings can legitimately be generalized to the population that provided the sample.

Before 1936, probability sampling was not widely used. The techniques were not well understood, nor was there much demand for them. But the spectacular failure of political polls in 1936 (Roosevelt vs. Landon) and 1948 (Truman vs. Dewey) undermined faith in nonprobability polls. Today probability sampling is the standard against which other sampling methods are measured. Nonprobability sampling, however, still survives. Economics and expediency motivate much of the remaining nonprobability use, but there are also some circumstances in which nonprobability samples can be justified on research grounds alone. *See also* NONPROBABILITY SAMPLE; PROBABILITY SAMPLE.

SAMPLING ERROR   A statistical measure that describes the precision of poll findings. Sampling error is the predicted difference between the sample of people interviewed and the population from which the sample was drawn. It is reported as a numerical range, such as +/3 percent, +/4 percent, and so on. In effect, samples are rough estimates of populations; sampling error indicates how rough the estimate is (Wilhoit and Weaver, 1980:26-29). For example, say a poll with a sampling error of +/-3 percent reports approval ratings for President Bush: 60 percent of Americans approve of him and 40 percent disapprove.   This 60 percent approval means that the actual approval rating among the population as a whole is somewhere between 57 percent and 63 percent. By convention, sampling error is reported at the 95 percent confidence level.   This means that researchers are 95 percent sure (or it is 95 percent probable) that the reported sampling error (+/-3 percent or whatever) will be accurate.

Sampling error is a statistical measure. It depends on two factors more or less under the control of the pollster. One of these is sample size: the larger the sample, the smaller is sampling error-- although decreases in sampling error level off dramatically with larger samples. The other factor influencing the size of sampling error is sampling method. In general, simple random sampling and stratified sampling reduce sampling error, but cluster sampling and multistage sampling increase it (Babbie, 1973:88-102).

Much controversy exists about the use of sampling error. One issue is the great stress put on reporting sampling error. Critics argue that emphasizing sampling error misleads poll consumers into thinking that polls are more accurate than they are. Sampling error may be low, but another type of error, nonsampling error, is often more serious, and it is harder to detect. One respected pollster, Burns Roper, has even suggested that sampling error should not be reported at all. Better not have it Roper says, than to have it imply a precision in poll results that is seldom achieved (Roper, 1985:28-31).

One other controversy about sampling error concerns subsamples--those parts of the sample broken out for special analysis, such as blacks, women, Catholics, labor unions, families, wage earners, and so on. The sampling error for these subsamples is always larger than for the whole sample--sometimes three, four, or even more times the original sampling error. Yet only rarely does the analysis of subsample findings mention the substantial sampling error that afflicts them. This encourages poll users to assume these "breakouts" are more precise than they actually are (Crespi, 1989:52-53).   *See also* NONSAMPLING ERROR; PROBABILITY SAMPLE.

SAMPLING FRAME   The list of prospective respondents from which a sample is drawn. A sampling frame might be a list of registered voters, students enrolled in a school, people listed in a telephone directory, automobile registrations within a state, or members of a particular profession. Sampling frames can be listings of organizations like all cities over one million population or cities, or all Fortune 500 companies. The sampling frame concept also extends to time and space. A frame might be all those people who watch television between 3:00 a.m. and 6:00 a.m., or people who use U.S. Route 99 for the morning commute (Johnson and Joslyn, 1986:137-139).

Researchers stress the difference between the sampling frame and the target population. The target population is the people whom researchers want to study--if they can identify them. The sampling frame, on the other hand, is the list of people actually identified. Gaps between the sampling frame and the target population are referred to as the "frame problem." Four basic frame problems are discussed in the sampling literature (Mosher and Kalton, 1972:154-158):

1. The problem of missing elements--the sampling frame has either excluded people who should be listed or failed to include people who are part of the target population.
2. The problem of clustering elements--the sampling frame has listed elements other than individuals, such as addresses or organizations. Somehow these must be translated into specific respondents.
3. The problem of blanks or foreign elements--blanks are listings that are no longer in the target population, such as a discontinued telephone number or someone who has died. Foreign elements are listings that does not belong in the target population, such as people no longer registered to vote in a sampling frame of likely voters.
4. The problem of duplicate elements--the sampling frame includes individuals listed more than once, introducing bias because the repeat listings are more likely to be picked in the sample.

The most prevalent sampling frame problem today is the incomplete or incorrect listing. Telephone directories are a leading example: people with no phones are excluded from directories, as are those with unlisted numbers; those who have recently moved are now incorrectly listed. The most notorious example of a bad sampling frame is the *Literary Digest* poll of 1936. The *Digest* achieved extinction by predicting Alf Landon over Franklin Roosevelt that year--using a sampling frame of telephone subscribers and automobile owners that egregiously overrepresented the wealthy and Republicans. Few sampling frames miss the target population as badly as did the *Literary Digest*. Many, however, are skewed lesser by lesser deficiencies (Hoinville, 1978:69-71). *See also* BLANKS, ELEMENTS.

SAMPLING INTERVAL   *See* SYSTEMATIC SAMPLING.

SCALE   A measure of public opinion based on answers given to several related questions. Scales are often referred to loosely as indexes, and vice versa, but the two should be distinguished (Johnson and Joslyn, 1986:79-80; Worcester, 1983:112-114).   Indexes use averages of two, three, or more questions. Scales, however, use weighted scores. An example from baseball: the widely followed ERA (earned run average) and the batting average are indexes of pitching and batting, respectively. To convert either to a scale, there would have to be some weighting done. For ERA, one might weight late innings higher than early innings, or "clutch" games higher than other games. Batting averages might be transformed into a scale by weighting more heavily hits made with men on base, or hits which produce runs. Earl Babbie gives a contemporary example of a scale used to measure illegal drug use:

Suppose...that we asked the students whether they had ever tried each of the following: heroin, marijuana, and alcohol...(the) four probable response patterns are shown below.

Simple Index Score	Alcohol	Marijuana	Heroin
3	Yes	Yes	Yes
2	Yes	Yes	No
1	Yes	No	No
0	No	No	No

As indicators of illegal drug use, these three items clearly represent different degrees of severity (as reflected in punishments, for example): heroin highest, marijuana next, and alcohol the mildest. Notice how unlikely it would be for us to find a student who had used heroin and marijuana, but had never used alcohol, for example. These items have the advantage that if we know how many drugs a student used, we know with almost perfect accuracy--which drugs were used. (Babbie, 1982:96)

Both scales and indexes are based on multiple questions asked of one respondent. The key difference between them is how answers to those questions are scored. Indexes average answers, while scales weigh answers. In effect, scales provide much more information about respondents than do indexes. Methodologists think in terms of a rough hierarchy of measurements utility. At the bottom are single questions used to measure an opinion or attitude; next are indexes that average several questions; finally come scales (Selltiz, Wrightsman, and Cook, 1976:400-431). *See also* INDEX.

SCREENERS   Questions used to sort out from a sample, respondents who meet some predetermined characteristic or behavior. A study of meat preference might screen for vegetarians, a study of working people would screen for retirees, and a study of college-educated opinion would screen for people who never attended college. Political polls are heavy users of screeners. There they are designed to sort out likely voters from those unlikely to vote. Political screeners elicit five types of information: (1) evidence of voter registration; (2) knowledge of voting procedures; (3) interest in the election; (4) recent voting experience; and (5) intention to vote on election day. (Backstrom and Hursh-Cesar, 1981:169-171). If respondents do not meet the standards of the screeners, the interview is probably terminated; if it continues, responses will be attributed to an "unlikely voter."

Some screening questions are basic and brief: respondents are simply asked if they are registered to vote. Better screening questions, however, include five or more levels of screening, as in this example:

1. Are you registered to vote at this address?
   Yes __   No __   Don't know __
2. In November of 1988, did you vote in the election for President between George Bush and Michael Dukakis?
   Yes, voted __   No, didn't vote or can't recall __
3. In November of 1986, did you vote in the election for Pennsylvania Governor between Bob Casey and Bill Scranton?
   Yes, voted __   No, didn't vote or can't recall __
4. And in 1988, did you vote in the election for U.S. Senator between John Heinz and Joe Vignolia?
   Yes, voted __   No, didn't vote or can't recall __
5. What would you say are the chances of your voting in the general election in Pennsylvania? Are you almost certain to vote; will you probably vote; are the chances 50-50; or don't you think that you will vote in the general election?

After this series of questions, a decision is made about continuing the interview. If the respondent failed to vote in two or more elections, if the respondent's chances are only 50-50 of voting, or if the respondent will not vote, the interview is probably terminated.

Screening questions influence poll results, because they determine who is "counted." If nonvoters are not identified, their opinions may seriously skew poll findings. Many analysts believe that when polls miscall elections, weak screening is the culprit. Even the highly respected Gallup poll reports that its screening procedures overestimate likely voters by about 15 percent. Few other polls do as well. It is common experience to pass about 80 percent of respondents through screeners as likely voters, while actual voter turnout might be 50 percent or lower (M. L. Young, 1987:103; Perry, 1979:320-324). *See also* LIKELY VOTERS.

SECONDARY ANALYSIS   Using poll data for some research purpose other than the original one. Secondary analysis generally means accessing one of the archives established as depositories for completed surveys, such as the Roper Center of Public Opinion Research, the National Opinion Research Center, the Louis Harris Political Data Center, or the Inter-University Consortium for Political and Social Research. Secondary analysis can accommodate some very sophisticated research designs; but simple or complex, the objective is the same--answering questions by analyzing data collected by someone else (Hyman, 1972:Ch. 1).

Economics--specifically the steep cost of original surveys--explains much of the enthusiasm for secondary analysis. But improved access to data archives also makes secondary analysis very attractive to researchers. Tom W. Smith describes the convenience of the Roper Center's POLL data base:

> Searches can be made for questions by specifying general topic or subject headings of interest, words used in the question text, the date of the survey or the organization that collected the data. For example, on Sept. 25, 1986, I signed onto the system and asked it to find questions with the word "abortion." It found 497 examples. I then further indicated that I also wanted the question to use the word "constitutional." It told me there were 38. Finally, because I wanted only the most recent readings, I asked for points after June 1, 1985. It found two examples. I then told it to type out these examples and it gave me the complete question text, the response distributions and basic documentation such as the data collector, data, sample size and population covered. (T. W. Smith, 1987:3)

The appeal of secondary analysis goes even beyond economics or convenience. Data archives offer historical data in the form of questions asked over and over. This makes it feasible for researchers to construct time series and analyze public opinion trends over a wide range of topics and subjects (Martin, 1983:735). Secondary analysis, of course, has some limits. Data may not be comparable from survey to survey, sampling procedures may vary or lack documentation, codebooks may be absent, and survey quality is variable. Perhaps most serious of all, the secondary analyst is always using someone else's measures rather than their own (Williamson, et al., 1982:156).

The term secondary analysis occasionally has another meaning. In market research, any information collected originally for nonresearch purposes--sales data or financial information, for example--is secondary data, available to supplement primary market research information. *See also* LONGITUDINAL SURVEYS; POLL COSTS; SECONDARY DATA.

SECONDARY DATA   Surveys originally collected for a particular purpose or user, but now archived and available for reuse. Secondary data represents a large and growing resource for public opinion research.

John B. Williamson and his colleagues provide an example of the circumstances that give rise to secondary analysis:

> Suppose you want to isolate factors that predispose people toward racial prejudice and you find an already existing study of factors affecting voting behavior in which a scale of racial prejudice was developed as one of the many variables under investigation. You can obtain the existing data and conduct a reanalysis in which prejudice becomes the most important variable. In this way, you entirely avoid the cost of data collection by producing a new set of findings out of old data. (Williamson, et al., 1982:155)

Herbert Hyman, among others, has been a prominent champion for doing secondary analysis. He lists four main reasons for reusing surveys: first, secondary data allows smaller samples to be built up to large sizes by combining two or more original studies. Second, it permits historical analysis--for example, a researcher may compare recent data with ten years ago, twenty years ago, and so one. Third, secondary data is helpful when designing a new survey: examining earlier questions, response rates and answers gives the researcher clues to what will work and what will not. Fourth, secondary data is relatively inexpensive. Researchers' costs for secondary analysis is only a tiny fraction for the costs of an original survey (Hyman, 1972:Ch. 1).

This last advantage--low cost--is by far the most important spur to reuse of survey data. The costs of original surveys are now prohibitive for scholars without government sponsorship or other funding. Secondary data, on the other hand, is increasingly available. There are now several major archives that store survey data made available by the original researchers. These include the National Opinion Research Center (University of Chicago), the Roper Center for Public Opinion Research (University of Connecticut), the Inter-University Consortium for Political and Social Research (University of Michigan), and the Louis Harris Political Data Center (University of North Carolina).

Secondary data does not come without drawbacks: using someone else's survey means that defects in the sampling or original design must be confronted; differences between question wording makes comparisons difficult; and lack of first-hand familiarity with original survey field conditions can obscure weaknesses in the data. These limitations and some others associated with secondary data are quite real; but they are unlikely to quell the interest in reusing surveys. Secondary data conveniently stored in institutional archives is a resource of immense value--one bound to grow in popularity as the cost of polling continues to rise (Weisberg, Krosnick, and Bowen, 1989:19-20). *See also* LONGITUDINAL SURVEYS; POLL COSTS; ROPER CENTER; SECONDARY DATA.

SECRET BALLOT TECHNIQUE   *See* UNDECIDEDS.

SELF-ADMINISTERED SURVEYS   Any interview that relies on a respondent to complete the questionnaire. Self-administered surveys most often are associated with use of the mail: typically, questionnaires are mailed to a respondent, who then mails them back to the researcher. But at least three nonmail methods are also used for self-administration (Weisberg, Krosnick, and Bowen, 1989:94-101). These are:

1. Self-Administered Group Surveys--the questionnaire is given to an assembled group, such as voters, shoppers, students, or workers. An interviewer may be present, but the questionnaire is filled out by the respondent.

2. Drop Off and Pick Up Surveys--the questionnaire is delivered by an interviewer to each respondent. The interviewer explains the purpose of the study and answers any questions about it. The completed questionnaire is later picked up by the interviewer or mailed in by the respondent.

3. <u>Self-Administered Supplemental Surveys</u>--self-administered interviews that supplement face-to-face or telephone surveys. Typically, supplementals are used to collect sensitive data or ask personal questions. The "secret ballot technique," in which respondents declare voting choices by depositing paper ballots in a mock ballot box, is an example of a supplemental.

Self-administered surveys offer some advantages over other interviewing methods. Since they are private, they can be used to ask sensitive personal questions. Researchers also favor them in situations where respondent answers are likely to be significantly influenced by the presence of an interviewer (Isaac and Michael, 1971:95-99; Dillman, 1978:6-9).

The biggest drawback to self-administered questionnaires is low response rate. When interviewers are absent, fewer respondents complete questionnaires. A related problem is the possibility of contamination--the term used to describe a situation where someone other than the designated respondent answers the questions. These advantages and disadvantages are balanced differently among survey researchers, but cost is frequently the decisive factor in using self-administered interviews. They can often be done for less than half the cost of other interviews (Backstrom and Hursh-Cesar, 1981:22-23; Dillman, 1983:368-373). *See also* CONTAMINATION; FACE-TO-FACE INTERVIEW.

SELF-ANCHORING SCALE   *See* SCALE.

SEMANTIC DIFFERENTIAL (SD)   A popular technique used by survey researchers to measure the meaning respondents have for specific ideas or people. Semantic differentials have been used to gauge "semantic space" for a vast array of "stimuli" ranging from American foreign policy to Pampers diapers (Mosher and Kalton, 1972:323-324; Isaac and Michael, 1971:102-105). SDs measure meaning by asking respondents to rate objects or concepts, typically on a seven-point adjective scale. The following figure illustrates a semantic differential rating business ethics:

SD RATING SCALE
BUSINESS ETHICS

7 6 5 4 3 2 1

GOOD	BAD
TRUE	FALSE
STRONG	WEAK
FAST	SLOW
IMPORTANT	UNIMPORTANT
SUCCESSFUL	UNSUCCESSFUL
WISE	FOOLISH
INTERESTING	BORING
COMPLEX	SIMPLE

SDs are uncomplicated to design and administer, but their simplicity belies the sophisticated theory that underlies them. Claire Selltiz and her colleagues summarize the methodological assumptions involved:

> SDs measure the following three dimensions of attitude: (1) the individual's evaluation of the object or concept being rated, corresponding to the favorable-unfavorable dimension of more traditional attitude scales; (2) the individual's perception of the potency or power of the object or concept; and (3) the individual's perception of the activity of the object or concept (Selltiz, Wrightsman, and Cook, 1976:429)

The evaluation dimension plays a special role in SDs. Researchers believe that 50 percent or more of the meanings respondents give to objects and concepts is rooted in evaluation of some sort. Interpretation and analysis of SDs can be involved. For example, in rating business ethics, the careful researcher would include several adjectives in order to measure all the meanings respondents associate with that issue--wise/foolish, complex/simple, important/unimportant, and so forth.

During analysis, respondent scores (1-7) are summed and mean scores computed so that "semantic profiles" can be drawn. These profiles can then be compared with other populations, or contrasted with SD ratings given to other issues. A business ethics semantic profile might be compared to a semantic profile given to "government ethics." Or demographic groups--men/women, blacks/whites, Northerners/Southerners--might be compared on their business ethics profile.

SDs can also be analyzed using standardized factor scores to weight each adjective. These factor scores illuminate the underlying "dimensions of meaning" represented by individual adjectives on the SD.

The Staple scale is a widely used version of the SD. Respondents are asked to pick a number from, say, one to seven that best describes their attitude toward some object. Staple scale adjectives do not have to be polar opposites as do SD adjectives, so they are even simpler to design and use (Alreck and Settle, 1985:152-154). *See also* LIKERT SCALE; SCALE.

SEMISTRUCTURED INTERVIEW *See* UNSTRUCTURED INTERVIEW.

SHAM POLL *See* PSEUDOSURVEY.

SHOW CARDS A visual aid used in interviewing. Show cards list the response categories respondents need to answer questions. Interviewers hand them to respondents during interviews, usually at the point where a particularly involved series of questions begins. Show cards are used mainly in face-to-face interviews, although versions of them have been adapted to mail questionnaires. Backstrom and Hursh-Cesar (1981:219-221) describe four interviewing situations for which show cards are appropriate. First, discussing sensitive subjects, such as family income, sexual behavior, and voting preference. The respondent is given a card with multiple answer categories, then asked to select the letter or number corresponding to income, behavior, vote choice, or whatever.

Second, clarifying complicated response categories, such as agree-disagree questions, rating scales, or questions requiring complex intellectual tasks. A show card is given to the respondent, then the interviewer begins to read a series of statements or questions. The respondent replies by referring to the show card.

Third, remembering lengthy lists, such as a long series of names or objects. The show card is given to the respondent to facilitate recall of the list. The interviewer then reads the questions and the respondent answers using the show card list.

Fourth, sorting and ordering priorities, as in ranking or other questions that require a physical grouping of answers. The respondent might be asked to rank quality of life factors (good schools, reliable transportation, access to recreation, etc.) by arranging cards representing each in order of importance.

Show cards are the most frequently used interviewing visual aid, but many other techniques are available. Among them are photographs, charts, graphs, audio and video tapes, and even products and services (Alreck and Settle, 1985:175-177). *See also* INTERVIEWING.

SIDEBAR   A methodological note accompanying a news story about a poll. Sidebars describe how the poll was conducted, provide technical information about the methodology, and indicate how results should be interpreted. Most sidebars include the kind of disclosure information that AAPOR and other polling associations call for, such as sample size, sampling error, interviewing times, weighting used, and so on. The text of the questions is not usually included in the sidebar, although the accompanying story does sometimes reprint a few of the questions.

Newspapers follow a wide range of practice with regard to sidebars. Some papers do not have them at all, others use brief sidebars, while a few print extensive sidebars of several hundred words. The *New York Times*' sidebar is a model for many. It runs about forty printed lines. Portions of a typical *New York Times* sidebar are printed below:

HOW THE POLL WAS CONDUCTED

> The latest New York Times/CBS News Poll is based on telephone interviews conducted Saturday and Sunday with 1,174 adults around the United States....The sample of telephone exchanges called was selected by a computer from a computer list of exchange in the county....The results have been weighted to take account of household size...and to adjust for variations in the sample relating to religion, race, sex, age and education. In theory in 19 cases out of 20, the results based on such samples will differ by no more than three percentage points in either direction from...all adult Americans....In addition to sampling error, the practical difficulties of conducting any survey of public opinion may introduce other sources of error into the poll.

Even the longer sidebars do not provide all the information that disclosure advocates recommend. The *New York Times*, for example, does not report response rates, the average length of interviewing, or the full text of the questions asked. The lack of question wording is a particular weakness of sidebars. Polling experts today generally agree that question wording most influences poll findings. Yet even elite publications like the *Times* keep readers from knowing the actual questions that were asked. *See also* DISCLOSURE.

SILENT POLITICS   Making policy according to dictates of the polls. Silent politics is a phrase that connotes rebuke to government officials who allow public opinion polls to dominate policy making (Bogart, 1985). Robinson and Meadow, in *Polls Apart,* discuss the meaning of silent politics:

> The conventional wisdom holds that public opinion polls have played an increasingly decisive role in much of our recent political history. Poll data are said to have hastened the U.S. withdrawal from Vietnam, helped force the resignation of President Richard Nixon in the aftermath of Watergate, and created political support for increased defense budgets in the 1980's. Those who attribute such influence to the polls cite these examples as evidence that the United States has entered an era of "silent politics," a period in which policy makers let public opinion all but dictate their decisions. (Robinson and Meadow, 1983:4)

Conventional wisdom aside, there is no solid evidence otherwise that "policy by poll" is consistent practice in the United States--or anywhere else, for that matter. Robinson and Meadow themselves argue that foreign policy is not much influenced by the polls. And numerous studies have shown that public policy and the polls frequently diverge on major domestic issues (T. W. Smith, 1980:166-173; T. W. Smith, 1985:25-167. 403-404). What anecdotal evidence there is suggests that normally public officials use polls to frame strategy and uncover political opportunity, but not to determine policy goals (Cantril, 1980:133-149).

Just the sheer number of polls makes silent politics an implausible theory. There are so many polls--and their findings often disagree so sharply--that little guidance is available, even if policy makers wanted to use them as referendums. This does not mean that polls never determine policy or dictate decisions. Obviously, polls sometimes perform that role. The Vietnam withdrawal, Nixon's Watergate resignation, the 1980 defense buildup, and the 1989 congressional pay raise cancellation are all plausible examples of policies made in the face of politically compelling polls. But these examples are extreme and unrepresentative. The preponderance of evidence about polls is that most of the time they do not directly determine government policy--nor for that matter, do government policy makers usually pay much attention to what polls say. *See also* POLL USERS; SPIRAL OF SILENCE.

SILLY POLLS   Frivolous, tongue-in-cheek polls whose main purpose is entertainment or satire. Silly polls divide into two main types--popcorn polls and ad hoc polls. Type one sillies, the popcorn polls, use some pseudoscientific measure to forecast election outcomes. Attracting public attention rather than learning public opinion is usually their real purpose. H. L. Nieburg traces the line of the popcorn poll to 1964, when Republican Barry Goldwater challenged Democrat Lyndon Johnson for president. The owner of a cinema put pictures of the rival candidates on adjacent popcorn poppers, and subsequently called the media to report that LBJ popcorn was outselling Goldwater popcorn two to one (Nieburg, 1984:57-60).

Mutations of the popcorn poll have multiplied prodigiously. These now include the following six subtypes:

1. The Jelly Bean Poll--requires strategic placement of two identical bowls of jelly beans, labeled "yes/no," "support/oppose," and so on. The last surviving jelly bean loses.
2. The Toilet Paper Poll--uses sheets of toilet paper embossed with the countenance of a political candidate. This practice has demonstrated uncanny ability to identify unpopular public figures.
3. The Bumper Sticker Poll--counts number of bumper stickers displayed in support of a candidate or issue. The credibility of bumper sticker polls has been undermined by recent studies showing that most people have no idea what is on their bumper.
4. The T-Shirt Poll--measures issue salience or candidate support by monitoring the slogans worn on T-shirts. T-shirt polls are particularly good for measuring strength of support in colder climates.
5. The Magazine Cover Poll--gauges popularity by comparing how well or poorly a magazine sells when it features a candidate on the cover. Politicians as a class do not move magazines well. Exceptions include those under investigation, recently indicted, or otherwise embroiled in scandal.
6. The Toilet Flushing Poll--designed to simultaneously measure support and dramatize mass public opinion in action. Supporters of some cause or candidate are instructed to flush toilets en masse on some prearranged signal. The consequent drop in reservoir water levels tells the tale.

Type two silly polls are the ad hocs. These rely on folklore methods to forecast opinions. Three of the best known ad hocs use: the height of the candidates, the state of the stock market, and the winner of the World Series (Rosenstone, 1983:42-44):

1. The Taller Candidate Wins--this system is not a sure thing. It failed in 1972 (shorter Nixon won) and in 1976 (shorter Carter won). It did work in 1980 and 1984 (taller Reagan won both), and it worked in 1988 (taller Bush beat shorter Dukakis).
2. The World Series--another not quite infallible guide to election outcomes. The rule states that Democrats triumph when the National League wins the series, while Republicans prevail if the American League wins. It did work this way in 1972 and again in 1976, but failed in 1980, 1984, and 1988.

3. The Stock Market--this bellwether employs the Dow Jones averages to predict the election. When the Dow Jones is up the Monday before the election, the incumbent party wins, but if the Dow Jones goes down, the incumbent party loses. This system looks better when read on a roller coaster. It failed in 1972, worked in 1976, failed in 1980, worked in 1984, and worked in 1988. (M. L. Young, 1990:551-552)

The ad hoc polls are widely reported by the press and have some popular following. Unlike popcorn polls, they are accorded some respect. Their accuracy record, however, inspires no confidence and leaves no doubt that they too are silly polls--fun, yes; interesting, perhaps; but nothing to be taken too seriously. *See also* WEIRD SCIENCE.

SIMPLE RANDOM SAMPLING (SRS)   The sampling technique underlying all other probability sampling. Simple random sampling involves three basic steps. First, a researcher pulls together the sampling frame, which must be a complete listing of every member of some target population. Second, each person on that list is identified with a unique number (such as 0001, 0002, 0003, etc.). Finally, a random number procedure is used to designate the actual respondents to be interviewed (Babbie, 1973:88-92).

For example; say a researcher wants to draw a sample of 500 state legislators around the country. A sampling frame of state legislators is available, numbered 0001 to 7800. To draw the sample, the researcher uses a bank of four-digit random numbers (0001 to 7800), drawing 500 of them and matching each drawn to a name on the sampling frame list. If random number 0222 comes up first, legislator number 222 becomes the first designated respondent, followed by, say number 2117, number 0012, number 7002, and so on.

SRS is straightforward and uncomplicated; unfortunately, it is usually also impractical. There are two reasons for this (Weisberg, Krosnick, and Bowen, 1989:35,38-39). First, simple random sampling is not possible unless a complete list of the population is available. And in general, it is not, especially for large populations such as the residents of a particular city, state, or the nation. When a complete list of a population cannot be obtained, researchers must use some other form of sampling. The second reason SRS is infrequently used, is the labor and tedium involved in actually listing and sampling from an entire population. Even when good population lists are available, the more efficient systematic sampling is usually used instead of simple random sampling.

SRS has distinct limits, but it does have its uses. It is the basis for other, more sophisticated forms of sampling, such as cluster sampling and stratified sampling. SRS can also efficiently be used to survey small populations when

good lists are available (Chein, 1976:522-524). *See also* PROBABILITY
SAMPLE; SAMPLING FRAME.

SIMULMATICS   The project name for the first major effort to simulate
public opinion with the computer. The simulmatics project, begun in 1959, was
conducted for the National Democratic Party to provide strategic advice to
national candidates.

It involved four main steps: first, national surveys conducted between 1952
and 1960 were used to create 480 voter types based on gender, religion, sex
status, ethnicity, and residence. For example, a Jewish Democrat male
professional living in the Northeast might be voter type 382. In the second
step, each of the 480 voter types was further subdivided in terms of the answers
given to fifty-two key survey questions. In the third step, opinions within each
state were predicted. This was accomplished by calculating the proportion of
state population represented by each of the 480 types, then weighting the
expected response of each type. Finally, the election itself was predicted. State
simulations were run and turnout was adjusted for voter types believed to be
most motivated to vote (Pool and Abelson, 1961:169-183).

Simulmatics has been faulted on methodological grounds. The two most
frequent criticisms are that turnout variables were not systematically weighted,
and that there was not any allowance made for voter differences in the various
states. Criticisms notwithstanding, simulmatics was close to the mark in both
years it was used--1960 and 1964: the model's average popular vote was off by
3.6% in 1960 and 4.4% in 1964. (Rosenstone, 1983:37-39). *See also* WEIRD
SCIENCE.

SIX-PACKESE   *See* JOE SIX-PACK.

SLEEPER QUESTIONS   *See* METALLIC METALS ACT.

SNOWBALL SAMPLING   *See* STRATEGIC INFORMANT SAMPLING.

SOCIAL DESIRABILITY BIAS   A psychological influence that encourages
respondents to give socially approved answers. Social desirability bias threatens

the accuracy of polling data (Alreck and Settle, 1985:421). When respondents suppress the true answers in favor of socially desirable answers, survey results are biased. In principle, almost any question can be affected by this bias. However, questions about drug use, sexual morality, and voting are believed to be particularly vulnerable.

The Marlowe-Crowne scale is currently the most widely used method of detecting and correcting for social desirability bias (Bradburn, 1983:316-318). Marlowe-Crowne consists of two contrasting sets of items. One set describes behaviors universally seen as socially desirable, but untrue for most people--for example, "I never resent being asked to return a favor." The second set of items describes behaviors that are socially disapproved, but nevertheless true for most people--for example, "I sometimes try to get even rather than forgive and forget." Marlowe-Crowne has been used in a number of surveys to estimate the influence of social desirability bias. A respondent's derived score is supposed to allow researchers to measure and correct for socially desirable answers.

There is some argument in the literature about the nature and extent of social desirability bias. Charles F. Turner and Elizabeth Martin state flatly that it has not been "conclusively demonstrated" to exist; DeMaio's review of the literature on social desirability bias concludes that "much of (that literature) is conceptually flawed and poorly executed" (Turner and Martin, 1984:268; DeMaio, 1984:Ch. 9). *See also* RESPONSE SET; SUCKER BIAS.

SOCIAL EXCHANGE THEORY

An academic perspective used to conceptualize the relationship between poll respondent and interviewer. Social exchange theory emphasizes that respondents incur "costs" during a survey. Interviewers, however, possess the "rewards" necessary to defray those costs (Dillman, 1978:12-14).

Costs for the respondent include competing time demands, threats to the ego, "chronological confusion," and forgetting. To offset these costs, interviewers offer rewards such as sympathetic understanding, giving recognition, fulfilling expectations, and providing opportunity for catharsis. Gordon puts it this way:

> The essential fact that the interviewer must take stock of (is) the social psychological rewards he can offer in exchange for the information he seeks from the respondent. (Gordon, 1969:134)

Thinking about interviewing as social exchange is useful. In the real world, respondents usually must be motivated to participate in a survey. Even altruists need recognition of their contribution. But providing only a social exchange may no longer be enough to induce cooperation--especially in an era of declining response rates. Already focus groups and some mail surveys are using money incentives to gain interviews. Polling, too, may eventually have to provide some extrinsic financial rewards where intrinsic social exchange no longer works. *See also* INCENTIVES; INTERVIEWERS; INTERVIEWING.

SOFT SUPPORTERS People whose voting intentions are not firm. Soft supporters are prospective voters who favor a candidate or issue, but express some reservations or qualifications about that choice. They are not committed. Pollsters use this term without great precision. A soft supporter might be someone who has deep misgivings about their indicated choice, but it might also be someone who is all but certain how they will vote.

As many as one-third of a given candidate's supporters can be classified as soft. The weak commitment of these voters, however, has several different causes (M. L. Young, 1987:104). Sometimes soft support is caused by so-called cross pressures: voters feel attracted to a candidate or position for certain reasons, but repelled for other reasons. Cross-pressured soft supporters are considerably less likely to vote than other voters. Soft support also occurs because information about the favored candidate or position is meager. A respondent might claim to support a particular candidate, but then acknowledge knowing very little about the candidate.

Soft supporter is just one of about a dozen standard ways pollsters classify respondents for political campaigns. Some other categories commonly used are: likely voters, swing voter, shifters, and undecideds. Soft supporter and other designations facilitate analysis of survey data and help predict how specific groups of respondents will behave. *See also* CROSSTABS; LIKELY VOTERS; RESPONDENT; UNDECIDEDS.

SPECIFICATION *See* ELABORATION PARADIGM.

SPIRAL OF SILENCE A widely discussed theory about public opinion and the social dynamics that influence it. The spiral of silence was proposed by German social scientist Elizabeth Noelle-Neumann in 1974. Noelle-Neumann argued that public opinion is greatly influenced by social pressures on people to conform to prevailing views: people who think their own opinions to be those of the majority are more ready to express those opinions vigorously, but people who think their opinions to be those of the minority are likely to express them weakly or not at all (Noelle-Neumann, 1974:43-51; Noelle-Neumann, 1984).

Over time, according to Noelle-Neumann, majority opinion holders grow more bold and vocal, while minority opinion holders grow more reticent and quiet. This is the spiral of silence. The result is that the most confidently held opinion appears to have more support than it actually does, while the opinion most diffidently held appears to have less support than is really the case. Ultimately, opinion thought to be the majority view virtually smothers opinion thought to be the minority view.

The spiral of silence theory rests on the assumption that social pressures such as the desire to belong push people toward conformity and away from views that have little community support. Perception is a key factor in the spiral of silence. If the public perceives opinion X to be in the minority, opinion X will eventually lose ground--even if opinion X is actually the majority opinion (Sheatsley, 1983:204).

Polls play a role in the spiral of silence, but not a direct role. In fact, there is no evidence of any direct effect of polls on public opinion. That is, people do not read a poll and then make up or change their minds based on poll findings. But there is reason to believe that polls have some indirect effects on public opinion, because journalists and other opinion makers themselves heed the polls (Gallup, 1972:222-226). If polls do influence opinion--even indirectly-- they play a critical role in the spiral of silence. The good news is that accurate polls will push the spiral toward "true" public opinion. The bad news, however, is that poll respondents themselves may not be reporting "true" public opinion: their opinions may also be caught in the spiral of silence. *See also* PLURALISTIC IGNORANCE.

SPLIT BALLOT TECHNIQUE   A methodological procedure used by survey researchers to improve the quality of question wording. The split ballot technique tests alternate wording by trying different versions of a question with two or more groups of respondents (Nieburg, 1984:142). Pollsters now generally recognize that it is poor question phrasing that most often produces unsatisfactory survey results. In no other phase of the polling enterprise is there greater chance for bias. Even a small difference in the form of questions can result in substantial variations in answers given. The split ballot technique detects these differences and controls for them:

> With this method, sample respondents are randomly divided into two groups. One half is asked one version of each question and the other half a second version. If 60 percent of the first random group gives a pro response, while only 10% of the second group gives a pro response, one has a...basis for concluding that the question framing used for the two groups is responsible for the difference. (Robinson and Meadow, 1983:103)

One variant of the split ballot technique is used in connection with so-called secret ballots, which allow respondents to mark answers on a slip of paper and deposit it in a "ballot box." Pollsters employ secret ballots to reduce the number of respondents who claim to be undecided about candidate preference. The split ballot procedure compares the differences between those who voted on a secret ballot and those who did not. Typically, undecideds go down by 50 percent or more when respondents are polled via secret ballot (Perry, 1979:315-318). *See also* BLAB WORDS; GOOD WORDS.

SPONSOR   The person, organization, or institution that commissions a poll and pays for it. Polls have many different sorts of sponsors: political polls are usually paid for by candidates, so-called media polls are conducted for print and electronic outlets, and private polls are done for organizational and institutional clients. University research institutes also sponsor some polls; and pollsters themselves sometimes produce polls for syndication or other purposes (M. L. Young, 1990:113-114).

Poll sponsorship raises an ethical question linked to a methodological issue. The ethical question concerns the disclosure of sponsor identity; the methodological issue concerns the bias that may occur when respondents are told who is paying for the poll (Fowler, 1984:135-144). The ethical codes of the major professional polling associations call for sponsors to be identified when results are released. The rationale is that the public can evaluate the objectivity of a poll by knowing who paid for it. Or as Catherine Marsh puts it:

> Who decides the broad topic, the selection of issues...the presentation of those issues and the fundamental of question wording....The fact of the matter is that different sponsors do pay for rather different questions to be asked. (Marsh, 1982:143, 144)

There is very little debate within the polling profession about identifying sponsors when polls are released. There is controversy, however, about telling prospective respondents who is behind a poll. Some believe that respondents have a right to know--and should be told--the sponsor before giving their "informed consent" to be interviewed. But others disagree with this view. They argue that disclosing poll sponsorship to respondents produces bias and distorts findings, and that respondents answer questions differently when they know the identity of the sponsor. Prevailing practice among pollsters is to disclose sponsorship when releasing a poll, but to withhold or gloss quickly over that sponsor when interviewing respondents. Thus poll consumers usually know who paid for the poll, but poll respondents usually do not (Fowler, 1984:141-

144; Nieburg, 1984:Ch. 12). *See also* DISCLOSURE; INFORMED
CONSENT.

SRC The Survey Research Center, located at the University of Michigan.
SRC was founded in 1946 by former staffers of the U.S. Department of
Agriculture (USDA) program survey unit. Congress forbade the Department of
Agriculture to continue survey work--apparently because the USDA program
survey unit had done surveys that depicted the oppression of Southern blacks.
Angus Campbell, Rensis Likert, Leslie Kish, and some others moved to
Michigan and established the SRC (Rossi, Wright, and Anderson, 1983:7-8;
12).
    SRC is now one of the two or three best-known academic survey centers.
It carries on a wide range of survey operations, runs training programs each
summer, and publishes books and monographs about survey research. The
Interviewer's Manual, produced by SRC, is a popular reference tool found in
virtually every researcher's library (Survey Research Center, 1976). SRC also
operates the annual Detroit Area Study. SRC is probably best known for its
continuing series on political behavior and voting studies. In each presidential
election year beginning in 1948, SRC has surveyed the electorate. The off-year
congressional elections have been similarly charted since 1952. And since 1980,
SRC has carried on primary election research as early as February of presidential
election years (Hennessey, 1985:69). For over forty years, SRC voting studies
have produced a rich stream of books and articles about American voting and
political behavior. Indeed, a substantial amount of current theory and
knowledge about elections has come from SRC surveys. *See also* ROPER
CENTER; SECONDARY ANALYSIS.

STANDARDIZED QUESTION Any question asked regularly in polls.
Standardized questions include questions like the most important problem
question, the presidential approval question, and trial heat questions asked about
upcoming elections (T. W. Smith, 1985). Any standardized question provides
opportunity for a time series. This is an analysis that tracks answers to the same
question asked over and over. Time series data permits researchers to monitor
trends revealed by shifting opinion.
    Standardization--using the same question in poll after poll--is accepted
practice in survey research. Pollsters borrow each other's phrasing so regularly
that common sets of questions and question types have grown up in each polling
specialization (Crespi, 1989:97-98). There is a kind of "survival of the fittest"
competition among questions, with better questions surviving and lesser

questions perishing. Few pollsters object to this imitation, and most agree that the field advances through the liberal purloining of questions.

The term standardized question has a couple of alternative meanings. One of these refers to a question (or questionnaire) that has been methodologically tested and refined. These standardized questions usually come with reported validity and reliability scores. Validity is a technical notion that refers to how well a particular question actually measures some attitude or opinion. Reliability refers to consistency of that measurement with different respondents-- or with the same respondent on different occasions (Raj, 1972:118-120).

Another sense in which the term standardized question is used refers to interviewing practice: a standardized question (or interview) is one that must be asked exactly the same for each respondent in a survey. This standardization is intended to insure comparability of responses (Sheatsley, 1983:196-198). A better term for the practice of asking each respondent the same question is structured question. An unstructured question would then be one whose exact wording differs from respondent to respondent. *See also* INSTRUMENT; MOST IMPORTANT PROBLEM QUESTION; UNSTRUCTURED INTERVIEW.

STATISTICAL SIGNIFICANCE   A statistical measure used to analyze poll results.   Statistical significance "tests" whether given poll findings are statistically important--that is, not just flukes in the sample. For example, a particular question reveals differences between male voters and female voters in the sample; say 40 percent of the men favor some policy, compared to only 30 percent of the women. The appropriate statistical significance test would show whether the 10 percent differences found in the sample would probably also be found among voters generally. A statistically significant difference in the sample means there is a high probability that there is a real difference that would be discovered had the entire population been surveyed (Nieburg, 1984:210-212).

Statistical significance is probably the second most overrated aspect of polling; sampling error is the first. One reason for this is that significance tests are very much influenced by sample size. Even very small numerical differences--say 1 or 2 percent--are statistically significant if the sample is large enough, while even large numerical differences may not be statistically significant with very small samples. The rule of thumb is that the larger the sample, the more likely it is that even small sample differences are statistically significant. Statistical significance, then, is really a probability statement-- given the size of my sample and the results I have seen, what are the odds the same results exist in the larger population?

The other serious misunderstanding about statistical significance is semantic. The term is often misconstrued to mean that the findings are also meaningful beyond the statistical sense (Weisberg, Krosnick, and Bowen, 1989:237-238).

But not every statistically significant finding is also meaningful or of practical significance. A popular methodology text puts it this way:

> In the researcher's zeal to obtain statistically significant findings, he often overlooks the more relevant question:...is the difference large enough to be practical? Are the gains important enough to be worth the cost and effort to obtain them? (Isaac and Michael, 1971:144)

There are a number of significance tests that can be applied to poll data. In theory, they differ according to assumptions about the level of statistical sophistication poll questions allow. In practice, the chi-square significance test is used with a wide range of survey questions. This is the test most likely to have been employed when a pollster reports that findings are statistically significant (M. L. Young, 1987:105). Chi-square calculates the probability that a statistic (e.g., 40 percent of men, 30 percent of women) could have occurred in the sample if such difference didn't also occur in the population from which the sample was drawn. If that probability is very low, (typically 5 percent) the observed difference in the sample is said to be statistically significant. *See also* CONTROL VARIABLE; CROSSTABS; SAMPLING ERROR.

STRATEGIC INFORMANT SAMPLING   A type of nonprobability, purposive sampling used in circumstances in which the appropriate respondents are hard to identify. Strategic informant sampling first locates individuals with special knowledge about some population of interest. These "strategic informants" are asked to name prospective respondents, who are then sought out for interviews (Chein, 1976:321).

Two versions of strategic informant sampling are typically used: expert choice sampling and snowball sampling. Expert choice sampling uses well-informed contacts to provide the sampling frame from some population. The judgment of these experts determines who is interviewed. For example, a researcher studying the sources of public opinion in a community might use an expert choice sample to locate the "movers and shakers" who mold opinion.

The other main version of strategic sampling is the snowball sample. As with expert choice, these samples are based on an informant's notion of who is or is not a member of some population. Snowball samples differ, however, in that each identified respondent is asked to refer other prospective respondents. An informant might refer three respondents, who each refer three others, who, in turn, refer three more, and so on. In this way, the snowball sample unfolds until it reaches a specified size. Snowball sampling is probably most appropriate for esoteric or hard to locate populations, such as elites or people on the fringes of social behavior (Babbie, 1982:125-126; H. W. Smith, 1975:117-118). *See also* NONPROBABILITY SAMPLE; PURPOSIVE SAMPLING.

STRATIFIED SAMPLING   A technique that divides the population into layers or strata, then samples from those strata, such as male/female, Republican/Democrat, urban/suburban, rural, and so on. Stratified sampling improves the representativeness of a sample, thus reducing sampling error. Virtually any population characteristic can be used to form strata. The most common are race, political party, geography, religion, income, education, age, and ethnic background (Williamson et al., 1982:110; Babbie, 1973:94-95).

The underlying logic of stratified sampling is not complicated: stratification makes populations more homogeneous, and homogeneous populations produce less sampling error for any given size sample. The key to selecting strata is knowing what population characteristics are important to the survey at hand. Political polls, for example, often stratify by race, geography, and political party, because these variables historically predict real differences in the political opinions people hold (Roll and Cantril, 1972:82-89).

An example illustrates the steps in drawing a stratified sample. A researcher wants to sample 500 state legislators around the country. A sampling frame of state legislators is available, numbered 0001 to 7800. The sample will be stratified by region of the country: North, South, Midwest, and West. To draw the sample, the researcher first assigns each of the 7800 legislators to one of the four strata, after calculating what proportion of the 7800 are in each stratum. Then the researcher draws four separate samples, one for each stratum (the four samples can be systematic random). The table below shows the mathematics necessary to determine sample size for each stratum:

STRATIFIED SAMPLE MATHEMATICS

Stratum	% of Population	X Sample Size	Stratum Sample
North	35%	X 500	= 175
South	20%	X 500	= 100
Midwest	15%	X 500	= 75
West	30%	X 500	= 150

The main advantage of stratified sampling is reduction of sampling error. Stratification can bring about a sampling error reduction of 20 percent or more. This means that a researcher stratifying can have smaller sampling error--or, alternatively, can accept the same sampling error but reduce sample size (Mosher and Kalton, 1972:85-88).

Stratified sampling is sometimes confused with quota sampling. They are very different. Quota sampling does employ strata, but interviewers nonrandomly choose who to interview. In sharp contrast, stratified sampling selects respondents strictly by random selection. *See also* CLUSTER SAMPLING; QUOTA SAMPLE; SIMPLE RANDOM SAMPLING (SRS); SYSTEMATIC SAMPLING.

STRAW POLL   The king of nonprobability surveys, used mainly by newspaper and broadcast outlets. Straw polls carry on an enduring tradition in American politics, dating back to 1824, when the first was published by the *Harrisburg Pennsylvanian* (Roll and Cantril, 1972:7, 8). Since then, newspaper straw polls have been regular features of campaign coverage. Today, the *New York Daily News* presidential straw poll is probably the best known of these. It has conducted on since 1928, with an average error rate of about 5 percent (Parten, 1966:23-26).

Most newspaper straw polls employ the mails to collect responses. Some print ballots in the paper to be clipped and returned by readers. Others mail out questionnaires to be completed and mailed back (Hennessey, 1985:62-63). There are at least four other versions of straw polling in current use. One is the so-called congressional mail poll, a survey in which members of Congress (using their franking privilege) send questionnaires to their constituents, sounding out opinions on issues of the day. Methodologically, congressional mail polls have some serious problems: questions are often poorly written, the sample is usually unrepresentative, and return rates are minuscule (typically under 5%).

Another type of straw poll is the street corner poll conducted by reporters for newspapers or television stories. These "man in the street" interviews are usually lacking in any rigor or sophistication. In fact, the street corner poll is done only to illustrate a news story or provide "visuals" for a television report (M. L. Young, 1987:106).

An electronic version of straw polling is the QUBE system. QUBE is an interactive cable video that allows subscribers to record their opinions by activating a computer terminal attached to their TV. Still another twist on straw polling are the call-in polls run by some radio and television outlets. Listeners are invited to call a designated number (often for a fee) and record their opinion on some issue or question.

The common drawback to all these versions of straw polling is sampling technique. None of them use probability methods to select respondents; consequently, no confident generalizations can be made about how well the sample represents the target population (Nieburg, 1984:62-69). Nevertheless, straw polls can be useful and have their place--especially if their limitations are recognized. They are comparatively easy to design and inexpensive to carry out. Moreover, they can be accurate. The real problem with them is that there is no way to tell statistically how good or bad they are. *See also* *HARRISBURG PENNSYLVANIAN*; *LITERARY DIGEST*; NONPROBABILITY SAMPLE.

STREET TALK   The informal conversations, gossip, rumors, and chitchat that spontaneously takes place in any community or neighborhood. Street talk occurs any place people congregate: churches, bars, stores, beauty shops, athletic events, civic occasions, parties, and (of course) on the street (Hennessey, 1985:55-60).

> The term street talk is political lingo from an earlier era. Before modern polling developed, street talk was a main way to measure public opinion. Politicians would talk and listen to their constituents as a way to gauge opinion and forecast trends. Even today many politicians armed with polls still pay attention to street talk. Many believe the street provides early signals to opinion change. (M. L. Young, 1990:540-541)

Another argument made for street talk is that it gives texture and dimension to polls--embellishing them with real people instead of relying only on cold numbers and abstract generalizations. Focus groups, which are so popular today, provide more evidence that street talk is still useful even in the polling era (Sabato, 1981:77, 90). What are focus groups after all, stripped of their formal trappings, other than a sanitized version of street talk--the talk sans the street. *See also* FOCUS GROUPS; NATURAL STRAW POLLS; WEIRD SCIENCE.

SUBJECTIVE DATA   Any survey information that reports opinions and attitudes. Subjective data measures subjective phenomena--personal knowledge that can be validated only by the respondent who is reporting it.
    Objective data, by contrast, measures objective phenomena--factual knowledge that can be validated by external records or other independent corroboration.

> Thus if an individual is asked to name a favorite author, to state whether the draft system is fair, to indicate how many

children she wants to have (or) to identify an area in which she or he is afraid to walk at night...the information sought is subjective. But if an individual is asked whether she or he has served in the armed forces, how many children she has ever borne, how far she or he lives from the place of work, or to state his or her sex, the information is objective. (Bohrnstedt, 1983:81)

The distinction between subjective and objective data raises some knotty epistemological issues about facts versus values; and some practical questions, too. For example, there are many quasi-factual questions that do not clearly qualify as either subjective or objective--such as political party identification or ethnic group membership. Moreover, most surveys collect both kinds of information. Respondents are asked subjective opinion questions and objective demographic questions in the same poll (Turner and Martin, 1984:8-10, 407-410).

Nevertheless, there are real differences between the two kinds of information. In the United States, there are also differences in who collects them. Subjective data is normally the domain of the private sector--political pollsters, statisticians, and market researchers. Objective data, on the other hand, is more often collected by the public sector--local, state, and federal governments. In part, this division of labor reflects fundamental differences between what government does and what private enterprise does. But it also expresses a prevailing distrust about government "snooping" into the lives of its citizens. *See also* COOPER SNOOPERS.

SUCKER BIAS   Survey answers given because a respondent wants to trick or deceive. Sucker bias involves respondents giving false answers as part of a hoax--rather than to conceal information (Warwick and Lininger, 1975:202). Respondents, for example, might "sucker" interviewers by reporting shocking behavior that never occurred, or by expressing extreme opinions that they do not really hold. This sort of respondent behavior has been found among several survey populations, although it may be more common among some elites.

Sucker bias is only one version of a large category of survey errors rooted in respondents' unwillingness or inability to give accurate answers. The best known of these is probably social desirability bias. This occurs when respondents slant answers to conform to prevailing norms and values (Bradburn, 1983:315-318). *See also* RESPONDENT; RESPONSE SET; SOCIAL DESIRABILITY BIAS.

SUGGING   The acronym for selling under the guise of a poll or survey. Sugging involves duping people to participate in interviews when the real purpose is to sell something. Sugging has two major forms. In one, telephone solicitors sell services or merchandise by enticing a prospect's interest with mention of a survey. Typical is this pitch from a telephone sales organization selling cosmetics:

> Hello, Mrs. Brown. My name is Cindy and I'm conducting
> a survey of your friends and neighbors to find out what they
> think about various beauty products.   Would you mind
> answering a few brief questions for me?

After Cindy gains the prospect's cooperation, she leads her through a sales solicitation that asks Mrs. Brown to help her with her survey--by ordering from the line of cosmetics.

Magazine solicitors seem particularly heavy users of sugging tactics. Generally, they begin with a telephone call from a group called "Advertisers' Research Bureau," or something very similar. The caller claims to be surveying local consumers on their tastes and preferences in television, radio, or reading. People who agree to be "interviewed" are then asked several questions before getting down to the specifics of which magazines they like. Only at this point does the caller get around to the real point of it all: a sales pitch to buy a subscription magazine (Frey, 1983:174-176).

The other main form of sugging uses the mail to solicit contributions to some political organization. Typically, a questionnaire is enclosed with an appeal for money. Almost always the questionnaire is blatantly biased for or against some cause. The solicitation letter accompanying the questionnaire is likely to be a passionate plea for contributions to stem the tide, save the world, put John Smith in Congress, or whatever. Tieing fund-raising to phoney polls has become so common that a new term has been coined for it. The word "frugging" has been suggested to denote fund-raising under the guise of a survey (Gilfeather, 1985:1).

Sugging is very common. More than twenty-five years ago, one researcher found that about one quarter (27%) of respondents had been sugged (Baxter, 1964:124-127). Today 60 percent or more of adults may have been exposed to phoney interviews selling something.   Sugging concerns many survey researchers, who worry that legitimate opinion research is harmed by phoney interviews. They fear that sugged victims, once fooled by a fraudulent survey, will refuse to be interviewed for any survey. No one knows for sure what proportion of refusals in legitimate interviews are due to bad experiences with sugging, but some researchers believe it is very high (Turner and Martin, 1984:73,268). *See also* REFUSALS.

SURVEY RESEARCH   The now almost universally accepted method for scientifically studying public opinion. Survey research has five separate phases:

1. Developing questions to be used in measuring attitudes and opinions.
2. Drawing probability samples that accurately represent a defined population.
3. Interviewing respondents and faithfully reporting their answers.
4. Performing statistical analysis using standard principles and procedures.
5. Interpreting results and reporting the findings.(Backstrom and Hursh-Cesar, 1981; Weisberg and Bowen, 1977:Ch. 1)

In his book, *The Structure of Scientific Revolution*, Thomas Kuhn explains how fad and fashion follow each other in science: one set of ideas is introduced, resisted for awhile, gradually adopted by a few, then finally accepted by almost everyone. These unchallenged ideas became the "dominant paradigm" (Kuhn, 1962).

Today, in social science, survey research is the dominant paradigm, that is, the almost unchallenged belief about how public opinion should be measured. This has happened only after some rough beginnings, such as the *Literary Digest* fiasco in 1932 and the Truman-Dewey embarrassment in 1948--not to mention a host of less celebrated but more egregious errors made by pollsters at state and local levels.

Through it all, polling has gained wide acceptance. Today, there are an estimated 350 polling firms operating in the United States alone. Virtually every major political candidate now hires a pollster, and most large newspapers regularly sponsor polls (Ismach, 1984:106-118). So do all the broadcast networks, and an increasing number of local TV and radio stations. Polls are also heavily used in the private sector--where they are more often called market research. Government, too, is becoming both a producer and a consumer of polls and surveys. Even the academic community has gotten into the spirit of things. Major polling centers at the University of Michigan and the University of Chicago have been joined by dozens of other colleges and universities carrying on polls around the country (Rossi, Wright, and Anderson, 1983:9-15). *See also*   PUBLIC OPINION RESEARCH; SURVEY VS. POLL; WEIRD SCIENCE.

SURVEY VS. POLL   A distinction that is probably of little significance. Defining surveys as separate from polls seems labored and contrived. Common usage, in fact, mixes the two terms interchangeably--many writers endorse that practice--and contemptuously dismiss efforts to contrast surveys from polls:

> There is no objective basis to the distinction between polls and surveys other than the snob value of Latin root words as opposed to Anglo-Saxon ones. Poll is to survey as cow is to beef. (Marsh, 1982:171)

Some writers, however, do distinguish polls from surveys.   Donald P. Warwick and Charles A. Lininger, in *The Sample Survey*, define a survey as "information gathered from a representative fraction of the population," a poll as a survey dealing with "issues of public opinion or elections" (1972:2). And Catherine Marsh insists there are substantial differences between the two forms of research.   According to her, polls and surveys differ on such things as "orientation to the audience," "orientation to policy," and "orientation to action" (Marsh, 1982:125-128).

But efforts in the academic literature to separate polls and surveys seem a little silly, and a touch arrogant.   Many of these definitions come close to describing a survey as well-designed, carefully executed, high-quality research done by some academic--and a poll as everything else.

Probably the most useful distinction between polls and surveys classifies polls as a category of survey research.   The University of Michigan's *Interviewer's Manual*, for example, lists the "public opinion poll" as one of four basic types of survey.   The other three are market research, descriptive statistical surveys, and social research surveys (Survey Research Center, 1976:1-2).

Census is another term often discussed in the context of surveys and polls, but it is not a synonym.   In the United States, the frame of reference is the Decennial Census conducted by the U.S. Census Bureau.   It differs from polls and surveys in two fundamental ways.   First, the census is a population count designed to enumerate everyone, rather than only a sample of people.   Second, census questions are mostly limited to so-called objective data: age, gender, income, housing conditions, employment status, and so forth.   Opinion and attitude questions--so-called subjective data--are common in polls and surveys, but rare in a census. *See also* SUBJECTIVE DATA; SURVEY RESEARCH.

SWITCHERS   One of the numerous categories used by pollsters to classify voters. Switchers are voters who support political party A in one election, but political party B in the next.   Switchers may vote Republican in 1988, but Democratic in 1992.   The term floater is a synonym--switchers float back and forth between the two parties (Asher, 1988:117-118).   Swing voters are often confused with switchers, but the two terms are very different. Swing voters are simply those who are undecided or leaners. They may swing the election one way or another depending on which candidate they finally choose (Salmore and Salmore, 1989:204-205).

Another way to distinguish switchers from swing voters is whether they vote straight ticket, that is for all the candidates of one party, or are ticket-splitters. Ticket-splitters split their ballots--voting for a Republican for one office and a Democrat for another (M. L. Young, 1987:207; Sabato, 1981:284). Switchers usually vote straight tickets. *See also* LIKELY VOTERS; UNDECIDEDS.

SYNDICATED RESEARCH   *See* OMNIBUS POLL.

SYSTEMATIC SAMPLING   A sampling technique that builds on the basic idea of simple random sampling. Systematic sampling, like simple random, begins with a list of everyone in the target population. To this, it adds two embellishments: a systematic random start to choose the initial respondent; and a sampling interval to select the remaining respondents (Babbie, 1973:92-93,95-96).

Four phases are involved in doing systematic sampling: (1) a sampling frame listing everyone in the population is assembled; (2) the sampling interval is calculated to determine how many names to skip over between respondents; (3) a systematic random start is used to select the first respondent; and (4) the balance of the sample is drawn using the sampling interval to choose respondents (Backstrom and Hursh-Cesar, 1981:59-60).

An example illustrates these steps. Say a researcher wants to draw a sample of 500 newspaper editors around the country. A sampling frame of 5,000 editors is available, numbered 0001 to 5000. To draw the sample, the researcher first calculates the sampling interval (I) by dividing the sample size (S) into the population (P):

$$I = \frac{P \ \text{(population)}}{S \ \text{(sample)}}$$

$$I = \frac{5000}{500} = 10$$

A sampling interval of ten means that every ten editors on the list will be selected for interviewing. First, however, the initial editor/respondent must be identified. This is done with a systematic random start, which means that a random number procedure is used to select a number between one and ten (the range of the sampling interval). If that random start were five, the fifth editor on the list would become the first respondent. The second respondent would be five plus ten (the sampling interval), or editor number fifteen. Thus the completed sample would consist of respondents number 5, 15, 25, 35, and so on ending with 4965, 4975, 4985, and 4995.

Systematic samples are generally preferred to simple random ones, and for good reason. They are much more efficient in time and money (Wilhoit and Weaver, 1980:22-23). Systematic samples, however, have their drawbacks, the most serious of which is the threat of periodicity. Periodicity is bias in the population list because of some recurring pattern or cycle. The classic example of periodicity is drawing a systematic sample that hits every corner lot (corner lot houses tend to have more affluent owners). Any ordering of the population listing can cause bias and should be examined. Periodicity, however, is not a fatal flaw. Once detected, it can easily be corrected simply by reordering or renumbering the population list (Sudman, 1983:169-173). *See also* PROBABILITY SAMPLE; SIMPLE RANDOM SAMPLING (SRS).

T

TANDEM SURVEYS Two identical surveys. Tandem surveys are taken at the same time, from the same population, but by separate polling organizations. Tandems resemble controlled experiments because they allow the two surveys to be directly compared. And like experiments, tandems control for most extraneous factors that can influence poll results. They do not control, however, for house effects--the term used to describe the idiosyncrasies that distinguish one survey organization from another (T. W. Smith, 1978:443-463).

Researchers prize tandem surveys because they provide replication--the sine qua non of scientific proof. Replicated surveys produce the strongest evidence and inspire the greatest confidence in the scientific accuracy of a study. If the results obtained are comparable, then reliance on both studies is increased. Unfortunately, tandem surveys are uncommon. Turner and Martin report only five "instances in which two survey organizations cooperated in the fielding of a survey." These range from the Stouffer study on civil liberties conducted in 1954 by Gallup and NORC to the National Health Care Expenditures Survey conducted in 1977 by NORC and the Research Triangle Institute. Interestingly, most of the differences observed in these tandems were attributed to house effects. Otherwise, differences between the compared surveys were small (Turner and Martin, 1984:149-154). *See also* HOUSE EFFECTS.

TDM Popular acronym for Total Design Method, a widely known set of procedures for carrying out mail surveys. TDM was described by Don Dillman in *Mail and Telephone Surveys: The Total Design Method* (1978). Dillman's book, which has been influential, argues that mail surveys need not be the black sheep of polling methods. Mail's generally notorious reputation may have been deserved, but nothing inherent in the method itself made this inevitable.

According to Dillman, response rates of 90 percent or better are possible using TDM. The key to the TDM method is, first, careful planning of the questionnaire, using tested techniques to maximize response rates. Second, survey implementation must be continuously monitored to insure these plans are faithfully carried out. "The TDM can be viewed as the completed architectural plan and building schedule, showing how a successful mail survey project is to be completed" (Dillman, 1983:361).

An elaborate conceptual framework known as social exchange theory provides TDM's theoretical foundation. Social exchange theory assumes that social transactions occur in ways analogous to economic transactions, with people responding to expectations about the costs versus the rewards of doing something. According to Dillman, social exchange provides three rules to follow in designing mail surveys:

1. Minimize respondent's costs for responding;
2. Maximize respondent's reasons for responding;
3. Establish trust between respondent and researcher. (Dillman, 1978:12)

TDM has influenced many survey researchers to reconsider their prejudice against using mail. Economic incentives have always made mail an attractive alternative to telephone or face-to-face interviewing. But methodological weaknesses, particularly dismal response rates, have traditionally hobbled the case for "going mail." Now Dillman and TDM have made mail surveys respectable. *See also* SELF-ADMINISTERED SURVEYS; SOCIAL EXCHANGE THEORY.

TELEPHONE BANK *See* BOILER ROOM OPERATION.

TELESCOPING A memory problem encountered in polling--respondents remember something that happened, but incorrectly recall when it happened. Telescoping involves the compression of time: an individual thinks an event or incident occurred more recently than it actually did. For instance, a respondent might remember three trips to a store in the past week, but in fact, two of them occurred ten days ago (Tull and Hawkins, 1980:259; Raj, 1972:211). Telescoping is one of two types of survey errors caused by faulty memory. The other is omission, which occurs when a respondent is unable to recall at all some past event--he has simply forgotten about it (Mosher and Kalton, 1972:340).

Several studies have concluded that both telescoping and omission are widespread. Consequently, researchers have developed procedures that rely less on individual memory, or else verify memory with independent records. One popular technique is bounded recall, used in panel studies where respondents are interviewed over and over. During second (or subsequent) interviews, respondents are reminded what they reported earlier about some behavior. Then they are asked to report similar behavior occurring since that earlier time. Ideally, bounded recall is checked against independent information, such as voting or purchase records. Bounded recall techniques reduce telescoping, but cannot correct for error due to omission. Nevertheless, the effort seems worthwhile. Some studies have shown that unbounded recall results in as much as 55 percent overreporting of some kinds of behavior (Bradburn, 1983:308-310). *See also* AIDED RECALL; MISREPORTING; OVERREPORTING.

THERMOMETER SCALE   *See* IMAGE QUESTIONS.

THIRD-PARTY QUESTION   *See* PROJECTIVE TECHNIQUES.

THE THREE M'S   Money, media and morale. The three Ms represent the three areas in which campaigners feel that polls influence the outcome of elections. George Gallup, Sr., attributes the phrase to *Los Angeles Times* writer David Shaw. According to Shaw, campaigners believe that money, media, and morale are often adversely affected by the publication of polls (Gallup, 1972:222-227).

1. Money--Campaigners charge that "bad polls"--polls showing them dropping behind or trailing badly--sharply reduce campaign contributions. Most contributors want to back winners, the reasoning goes, so polls tend to eliminate from competition candidates who do not show well.
2. Media--Campaigners charge that poor poll showings limit the amount of media coverage given to a candidate. The mass media allocate news coverage according to the credibility a candidate has, and polls confer credibility. Polls that reveal low support encourage reporters and editors to ignore a candidate.
3. Morale--Campaigners charge that polls showing a candidate slipping discourage campaign workers and reduce the supply of volunteers. The argument here is that staffers, volunteers, and others who work in campaigns pour enormous physical energy and emotional involvement

into them. These "troops" need to believe they will win to sustain their grueling pace.

Evidence of the view that polls somehow influence elections is not strong. Most researchers flatly reject the notion that polls directly influence voters (Roll and Cantril, 1972:23-29; Field, 1983:208-216).

But indirect effects are a separate, and less settled, issue. The three Ms do describe indirect effects. Do bad polls dry up campaign contributions, reduce media coverage and wreck campaign morale? No one knows for sure, but most campaigners and many pollsters believe that they do. *See also* BANDWAGON EFFECT.

THROWAWAYS   Poll questions used to warm up respondents and make them comfortable before proceeding to more difficult or embarrassing questions (Backstrom and Hursh-Cesar, 1981:158). Throwaways are often used for the first question in a survey. The *Handbook of Survey Research* explains why:

> The first question is crucial...if respondents find the first question difficult or beyond their knowledge and expertise or embarrassing or threatening in some way, they are likely to break off immediately....Researchers sometimes use throwaway questions as openers, simply to warm up respondents and accustom them to their role before proceeding to the more difficult or sensitive items. (Sheatsley, 1983:221-222)

Throwaways should not be confused with either screening or filter questions. All three question types do share a common purpose--to move the interview along. Screening questions, however, identify respondents with specific traits or characteristics (such as age, income, voting history, and so forth). Filter questions, on the other hand, filter out respondents who lack certain knowledge or understanding, such as familiarity with a particular issue, information about some problem, or awareness of some public figure. *See also* INTRODUCTION; SCREENERS.

TIME REFERENCE   *See* REFERENCE PERIOD.

TRACKING POLLS   Short polls, using small samples, that are conducted continuously for several days or weeks. Tracking polls are typically run during the closing stages of a political campaign. They monitor trends and detect last minute shifts of opinion among voters (Sabato, 1981:76-77).

The 1980 presidential campaign marked the first widespread use of tracking. Richard Wirthlin was Ronald Reagan's pollster. Mark Levy describes Wirthlin's system:

> To track the election, 500 randomly selected voters were telephoned throughout the nation every night starting in mid-October. Interviewees were asked a small number of questions about the latest campaign developments as well as their vote intentions. After five nights of polling, more than enough interviews have been completed for Wirthlin to have substantial statistical confidence in the results....500 fresh interviews (were) added to the pot each night...(and)...the six-day-old interviews were dropped from the (sample totals). Thus, rolling or moving averages could be calculated, averages that gave a statistically stable trend line...but that also reflected the bumps and blips in voter sentiment. (Levy, 1984:90)

Wirthlin's sample of 500 is larger than necessary. Daily samples as small as 50 are often used. About 1,000 is the maximum--and that would be used only in national surveys. Tracking polls have two distinctive methodological features. One is the system of moving averages, which builds up a large sample over several days. The other methodological feature is the systematic jettisoning of old data. Interviews completed more than six or seven days earlier are dropped from the overall sample.

Tracking polls are currently popular, and this is understandable. They monitor opinion trends reliably and they capture electorate shifts promptly. Moreover, tracking polls are also simple to conduct--and relatively cheap (Salmore and Salmore, 1989:115-116; 168-169). *See also* BENCHMARK POLL.

TREND STUDIES   Repeat surveys of the same population taken over a relatively long period of time--typically months or years. Trend studies are sometimes called successive samples. They use separate samples for each survey, but each sample draws from the same population (Babbie, 1982:61-62). Gallup and Harris polls are often cited as trend studies because they ask many of the same questions in poll after poll. Actually, many regional and local polls also constitute trend studies, since they use the same questions over and over.

The great appeal of trend studies is that they allow public opinion to be tracked over long intervals. Base periods can be established, trend lines measured, and changes in opinion indexed to earlier and later periods (T. W. Smith, 1985:264-267). Trend studies are conventionally grouped with cohort studies and panels. All three produce longitudinal data--information that has been collected in repeat polls scheduled over an extended period. *See also* COHORT STUDIES; LONGITUDINAL SURVEYS; PANELS.

TRIAL HEATS   Poll questions that match prospective political opponents against one another. Trial heats ask the so-called horse race question: "Which candidate will you support on election day?"

Trial heats are much maligned by pollsters and others, who argue they are notoriously misleading in predicting candidate performance. They tend to measure name recognition and are influenced by the party affiliation of the respondent answering questions. These defects notwithstanding, candidates and campaigns remain avid consumers of trial heat "numbers," and virtually all election polls include a horse race question (Sabato, 1981:83-84).

One popular form of the horse race question goes beyond trial heat matchups to identify leaners:

> If the election for governor was held today, and the candidates were Barbara Hafer, the Republican, and Bob Casey, the Democrat, for whom would you vote? Barbara Hafer__ Bob Casey__ Not sure__
>
> (If not sure) Well, which candidate do you lean a little more towards--Hafer the Republican or Casey the Democrat?
>
> Now, how do you feel about (the choice you made)? Would you say you totally support (him or her), support (him or her) with reservations, support (him or her) only slightly, or not sure?

In nonelection years, pollsters now use a battery of questions that "even when there is no election in the immediate offing...purport to measure political strength as if there were one to be held." These include, along with trial heat question, party identification questions, and most capable party questions (Crespi, 1989:16-18). *See also*   APPROVAL RATING; MR. SMITH QUESTION; NAME RECOGNITION QUESTION.

TROLDAHL-CARTER METHOD   A widely used respondent selection technique. The Troldahl-Carter method employs a random procedure that gives everyone living in a household an equal chance of being interviewed (Troldahl and Carter, 1964:71-76). Respondents are selected after interviewers ask two questions: (1) How many adults live in this household? and (2) How many men live in this household? A matrix provided to interviewers lists various combinations of age and sex, such as oldest man, youngest woman, oldest adult, and so on. The interviewer then selects one of these combinations to be interviewed based on the number of men living in the household.

The Troldahl-Carter method is sometimes loosely referred to as the Kish grid. But there are important differences between these two respondent selection techniques. Kish requires the interviewer to list all adults living in the household by sex, age, and relationship to head of household. Each adult is then assigned a serial number--1, 2, 3, 4, and so on. Eventually, respondent selection is made by matching these serial numbers to a preprinted random number listed on the questionnaire (Kish, 1949:338-387).

The Kish grid is considered unwieldy because of the demands it places on both interviewer and respondent. It is time-consuming and may raise respondent suspicions about the survey; and this lowers the response rate. But most other selection respondent procedures also have flaws. Troldahl-Carter, for example, is faulted for asking personal questions early in the interview--and for arbitrarily excluding those adults who happen to be neither the oldest in or the youngest living in a household (Salmon and Nichols, 1983:270-276; Martin, 1983:697-702). *See also* NEXT BIRTHDAY METHOD; NOT AT HOMES.

TRUSTEES AND DELEGATES Popular allusion to an old scholarly debate about public opinion--and how much attention public officials should give to it. Trustees and delegates are often cast as extreme opposites. Trustees follow principles attributed to the eighteenth-century Englishman Edmund Burke, who argued that legislators should follow their own judgment, even when they conflict with constituent views. The delegate role is associated with eighteenth-century French philosopher Jean-Jacques Rousseau, who argued that legislators should champion constituent opinions rather than their own (Stephenson et al., 1988:358).

The ancient debate about trustees and delegates is relevant to modern polling: what influence should polls have on public officials? Should officials simply be delegates and follow the polls--or should they be trustees and follow their own counsel regardless of polls? Framing the question this starkly, however, is misleading. Very few contemporary public officials feel they are always delegates or always trustees. In fact, most public officials seem to identify with the "politico" role--someone who consults constituents but also weighs personal views (Erikson, Luttbeg, and Tedin, 1988:287-297). Former Senator John Culver of Iowa, in a 1987 speech at Harvard described the dilemma facing elected officials today:

> The duty of the elected representative, in my judgment, is not
> only to represent and reflect public opinion, but also to lead
> and educate in the public interest.   Such an approach
> represents far greater respect for the electorate, as well as faith
> in democracy, then to think it one's responsibility merely to
> mimic, assuming it can every be known, the popular will of
> the moment. (Culver, 1987:24)

Congress and state legislatures are often studied to see which role, the
trustee or the delegate, is actually followed by policy makers. Sometimes the
delegate model does prevail--especially on highly visible issues that attract wide
attention or stir deep emotions.   The outcome of the notorious 51 percent
congressional pay raise in 1989 is an example.   Other probably examples are
Vietnam and Watergate.   But other times legislators do not follow public
opinion on many issues, and look much more like trustees. Even on such high-
profile issues as the ERA, abortion, and gun control, public opinion and
legislative policy keep separate company. *See also* PHANTOM PUBLIC;
PLURALISTIC IGNORANCE.

TRUTH IN POLLING BILL   The popular name for polling legislation
introduced into Congress during the late 1960s by Lucien N. Nedzi. The truth
in polling bill (or Nedzi) would have required pollsters to file a report with the
Library of Congress for any published poll.   Within seventy-two hours of
completion, the particulars on the poll would be available to anyone who wanted
to examine them (M. L. Young, 1990: 494-495).   The Library of Congress
filing required eight items of information: (1) the name of the sponsor; (2)
sampling methodology; (3) sample size; (4) time of interviewing; (5) method of
interviewing; (6) questions asked; (7) response and completion rates; and (8) the
results of the poll.
    The truth in polling bill was never enacted, in fact never emerged from
committee. Nevertheless, it sparked intense debate about government regulation
of polling--and furnished both advocates and opponents of regulation with most
of the arguments still heard today (Hollander, 1971:335-349). Nedzi supporters
argued that polls are powerful: they influence elections and drive public policy.
Yet there is no way to verify their bona fides. If pollsters were required to file
with the Library of Congress, the public would have the information necessary
to use polls intelligently.
    Nedzi opponents sidestepped some of the poll criticisms and emphasized
instead that government regulation was not the best way to deal with problems.
Four persistent points were made by regulation opponents: first, pollsters have
professional trade secrets--such as weighting procedures, screening techniques,
and the locations of sampling points. Government regulation would compromise

poll confidentiality. Second, all polls, not just political polls, would fall under the regulations. Market research studies, for example, would also have to be reported, because it is not possible to precisely distinguish opinion polls from other kinds of surveys. Third, demand for polls would fall precipitously with regulation. Clients would hesitate to commission a poll that would be free within 72 hours to anyone who wanted it. Fourth, government regulation of polls is not constitutional. First amendment free speech rights specifically are violated by Nedzi-type regulations (Bogart, 1985:xx-xxii).

This last point, the constitutional issue, may pose a fatal defect for poll regulation. Testimony given during NEDZI hearings continually raised free speech questions. Most constitutional law specialists who testified expressed doubt that government can regulate polls without substantial violation of first amendment rights. But what cannot be compelled can still be done voluntarily. And that has happened. Debate over truth in polling has provoked the professional polling associations to promulgate their own ethical standards. AAPOR, NCPP, and CASRO now all have disclosure standards not greatly different from the provisions in the original truth in polling bill. *See also* AAPOR; DISCLOSURE; POLL REGULATION.

TURNOUT *See* LIKELY VOTERS.

TURNOVER TABLE Used to analyze data from respondents interviewed again and again as part of an ongoing panel study. Turnover tables track respondent answers from survey to survey. Doing so allows an analyst to measure change between interviews; more important, it identifies individual shifters or turnovers (Babbie, 1973:65; H.W. Smith, 1975:338-339). Here's an example from a political poll: wave one of a panel study shows candidate A with a 48 percent voting preference; candidate B has 52 percent. Wave two, four months later, reveals Candidate A has picked up to a 54 percent vote, while candidate B has dropped to 46 percent.

Thus, candidate A has gained 6 percent between studies. Net change alone, however, can obscure enormous shifting (gross changes) that has occurred among respondents. Some important groups who supported A may now support B, while some of B's supporters may now support A. A turnover table like the one below can illuminate these changes.

TURNOVER TABLE

2nd Wave Interviews

		Vote for A	Vote for B	Total Vote
1st Wave Interviews}	Vote for A	20%	28%	A 48% 1st Wave
	Vote for B	34%	18%	B 52% 1st Wave
		A 54% 2nd Wave	B 46% 2nd Wave	

The turnover table shows the vote totals for both panel waves: the first wave reads across; the second wave reads down. Candidate A got a total of 48 percent (across) in the first wave, then 54 percent (down) in the second wave. Candidate B got 52 percent (across) in the first wave, then 46 percent (down) in the second wave.

But the turnover table tells much more than these totals. It also shows the breakdown of voting in each wave of interviews. After the second round of interviews, A has 54 percent of the vote, but only 20 percent of this total comes from respondents who supported A in the first wave; the other 34 percent comes from B defectors. Similarly, B's support has shifted sharply. After the second round of interviews, B has 46 percent of the vote; 18 percent of that is from first wave B supporters, but 28% is from A defectors--that is, those who preferred A in the first round (Mosher and Kalton, 1972:139).

With this information, analysts know much more than that candidate A has gained 6 percent and candidate B lost 6 percent. They know, more importantly, that 28 percent now support B who originally supported A, and 34 percent who supported B now support A. What seemed to be a modest 6 percent gain for one candidate turns out to mask a substantial and undoubtedly significant shift involving almost two-thirds of the electorate. *See also* PANELS.

U

UNAIDED RECALL   *See* AIDED RECALL.

UNDECIDEDS   Respondents in a political poll who have not made a candidate choice. Undecideds are unsure who they will vote for. Pollsters use three techniques to reduce the number of undecideds. One of these involves follow-up questions to identify "leaners."   If respondents say they are undecided, the interviewer then asks which candidate they are "leaning to as of now" (M. L. Young, 1987:91). A second technique for reducing undecideds is the "secret ballot." Respondents are handed a sample ballot, which they use to "vote" for their preferred candidate. The ballot is then folded and deposited in a cardboard ballot box provided by the interviewer (Sabato, 1981:99).

The third technique used to reduce undecideds is phrasing the voting choice question in terms of "if the election were held today"--instead of asking voters about their future intentions. Using pollster techniques like leaner questions and secret ballots, can reduce undecided by 50 percent or more (Welch and Comer, 1975:370-372).

There are three useful rules of thumb about the undecided vote. First, people tend to go through an undecided phase when switching from one candidate to another. Fluctuations in undecideds from one poll to the next may forecast shifting loyalties among voters.

Second, the undecided vote tends to be higher in primary elections than in general elections. In general elections, there are party cues to influence voter choice, so undecided voters tend to come from among independents and ticket splitters. Third, pollsters consider undecideds of more than about 20 percent to be the mark of a flawed poll. Three to five percent undecided is in the comfort zone. Even competent polls, however, sometimes show high undecideds very early in a campaign (Roll and Cantril, 1972:130-135). *See also* LEANERS; TRIAL HEATS.

UNDERDOG EFFECT   *See* BANDWAGON EFFECT.

UNDERREPORTING   *See* OVERREPORTING.

UNDERSAMPLING   *See* OVERSAMPLING.

UNIT OF ANALYSIS   *See* CASE.

UNIVERSE   *See* ELEMENTS.

UNOBTRUSIVE MEASURES   Research techniques that avoid contact between researcher and subject.   Instead, public opinion or other topics are studied by unobtrusively observing everyday events that occur in public life: overheard conversations, changes in styles, shifts in behavior, or other evidence that may proxy public opinion. The term unobtrusive measures comes from the title of a now classic book, *Unobtrusive Measures: Non-Reactive Research in the Social Sciences* (Webb et al., 1966).

The book argues that traditional measuring tools, such as surveys, are inadequate used alone. First, most social phenomena cannot be captured with a single measurement; hence several points of observation are necessary. Second, reactivity--respondent bias caused by the measuring process--is a serious drawback in surveys. *Unobtrusive Measures* describes four main nonreactive ways to measure opinion and attitudes:

1.   Erosion Measures--Unobtrusive measures that rely on the degree of physical wear to measure some past behavior.   One example is measurement of the wear on vinyl tiles in a museum to evaluate an exhibit's population.
2.   Accretion Measures--Unobtrusive measures that rely on the traces of

some deposit of material. Checking the dial settings of radios or TVs to determine audience size is an accretion measure.

3. Archives--Unobtrusive measures that use older records to study public opinion. Archival measures that have been used to study opinion include government budgets, party platforms, and voting records.

4. Simple Observation--Unobtrusive measures that allow an observe to record behavior while isolated from the observed person. Examples include "conversation sampling" of people walking down the street, waiting for a bus, and so on; observing body language; and measuring external symbols such as hair style and clothes. (Webb et al., 1966:35-141)

Unobtrusive measures are just one type of a large collection of nonpoll research sometimes called "weird science." Other examples of the category are Delphi forecasts and epistolary opinion research. All these, including unobtrusive measures, are designed to measure public opinion without conducting a poll (M. L. Young, 1990:540-563). *See also* EPISTOLARY OPINION RESEARCH (EOR); LAS VEGAS POLLS; WEIRD SCIENCE.

UNSTRUCTURED INTERVIEW An interview in which question wording and question order have not been planned in advance. The unstructured interview contrasts with the structured interview, in which everyone asks the same questions in the same order (Williamson et al., 1982:137,173). Interviewing is frequently discussed in terms of these two extreme categories, structured and unstructured (or standardized and nonstandardized). But it is more useful to think of structure as a continuum, ranging from tightly structured interview schedules that detail every interviewer action, to loosely structured lists of "target topics" that give wide latitude to the interviewer (Selltiz, Wrightsman, and Cook, 1976:309-321).

One interesting hybrid is the semistructured interview. These include some structured questions asked of all respondents, such as demographic items, and then other questions that differ among respondents, depending on background, experience, and so forth. A semistructured interview provides some data that is comparable for all respondents and other data that is tailored to the unique characteristics of individual respondents. *See also* INTERVIEWING.

UPS *See* EPSEM.

W

WAKSBURG TECHNIQUE *See* RANDOM DIGIT DIALING (RDD).

WAPOR The World Association of Public Opinion Research. WAPOR was established in 1947 in Williamstown, Massachusetts. Linking university scholars with commercial researchers was a major reason for forming this international group. That objective is expressed clearly in the WAPOR Code of Professional Ethics and Practices:

> The purpose of the World Association for Public Opinion Research (WAPOR) is to establish a world wide meeting ground for those working in the area of survey research. Through its activities, WAPOR unites the world of survey research within the universities and the world of survey research within private institutes--two worlds which far too often are still strictly separated. It is the express goal of WAPOR to bridge the gap existing between practitioners...and theoreticians of the academe. (Worcester, 1983:229)

WAPOR is governed by an executive council elected by the membership in an international mail ballot. The two-year presidency generally alternates between Europe and North America. The last five presidents (1978-1988) have come from West Germany, Canada, the United Kingdom, the United States, and Sweden. WAPOR's annual conference rotates between Europe and North America. In even years, the meeting is held with the American Association for Public Opinion Research (AAPOR) in Canada or the United States; in odd years WAPOR meets jointly with the European Society for Opinion and Market Research (ESOMAR) in Europe.

Membership in WAPOR is open to all who subscribe to the purposes of the association and have been directly associated with the conduct, use, or teaching of opinion research. WAPOR's several hundred members come from some fifty-five countries around the world. Association offices are managed by the Secretariat, located in the United States at the University of Connecticut's Roper Center. *See also* AAPOR; ROPER CENTER.

WEIGHTING   A statistical procedure used after the sample has been drawn and respondents interviewed. Weighting adjusts the sample to make it more faithfully represent the population polled. For example, if some group is underrepresented in the sample--say men, or westerners--that group is "weighted up." Or if a group was overrepresented--say women, or southerners--that group is "weighted down" (Nieburg, 1984:226-232).

Two main circumstances justify weighting. One is people who are hard to interview because they are often away from home. Roll and Cantril describe the "times at home" weighting technique designed to correct for this problem:

> All respondents who are interviewed are asked how many of the three previous days they were at home at the very same time the interview on the fourth day was taking place. Thus, people who were home only once--the day of the interview-- are given a weight of four; those at home two out of the four days possible--including the day the interview took place--are given a weight of two; those at home three times are given a weight of one and one-third (1 1/3); and those at home all four days are given a weight of one. (Roll and Cantril, 1972:90)

The other time weighting is employed involves respondent demographics. Most pollsters weight if one or more key demographic groups--women, blacks, Catholics, union members, and so on--have been under- or overrepresented in the sample. The method of demographic weighting is uncomplicated:

> Samples are compared to census data or other demographic information. If a population group is under-represented in the sample, it is weighted up by multiplying those persons in the sample by a factor that will bring them into balance. For example, if a survey of 1,000 produced 50 blacks or 5% of the sample, but blacks actually constituted 10% of the population, the answers of the 50 black respondents would be weighted by two. (M. L. Young, 1987:108)

Weighting is routine in both private and public polls. Disclosure codes require that published polls describe their weighting procedures. Most print media do this in the sidebars accompanying poll stories. Nevertheless, weighting is sometimes challenged as a questionable procedure. Critics charge that pollsters use it to "cook the data"--that is, manipulate poll answers to ensure the desired results (Wheeler, 1976:115-117, 273-275). Political pollsters in particular hear this criticism when weighting for "likely voters"--an admittedly slippery objective. But most weighting is necessary and legitimate. Today's polling climate, with response rates declining, leaves little choice. The pollster who fails to weight runs a high risk of reporting misleading results (Sabato, 1981:97-98). *See also* DEMOGRAPHIC ITEMS; DISCLOSURE; NOT AT HOMES; SIDEBAR.

WEIRD SCIENCE   A loose collection of unusual procedures and techniques designed to measure public opinion. Weird science is performing public opinion research without polling (M. L. Young, 1990:540-563). It includes such things as Delphi forecasting, unobtrusive measures, and Las Vegas polls (Childs, 1965:66-67; Hennessey, 1985:50-66; Nieburg, 1984:57-66; Webb et al., 1966:1-34).

Weird science rests on two premises about opinion research. The first is that a survey is only one way to measure public opinion. The second premise of weird science is that nonpolling methods are sometimes as effective as traditional survey methods; and that sometimes the alternative methods are more appropriate. Weird science includes eight major categories of nonpoll opinion research (M. L. Young, 1990:540-561):

1. The Informal Methods--such as canvassing and listening to "street talk."
2. The Unobtrusive Methods--such as simple observation and using archives.
3. The Indirect Methods--such as monitoring news reports and interpreting election results.
4. The Exotic Methods--such as studying body language and betting odds.
5. The Government Methods--such as public hearings and solicitation of comments.
6. The Economic Methods--such as complex modeling and simple economic rules of thumb.
7. The Expert Methods--such as Delphi and other types of "prophecy" polls that rely on expert forecasts to predict public opinion.
8. The Simulation Methods--such as computer simulation and operational gaming.

Weird science methods range from the loose informality of techniques like street talk, to the rigor of procedures like economic modeling and computer simulation. Most methods have specialized uses and significant limitations--especially used alone. In fact, virtually all weird techniques are more powerful when combined with polling or another weird technique.

Weird science methods are serious and more or less systematic. As a category, they should be distinguished from the "silly polls"--popcorn polls, toilet paper polls, and the like--which are neither serious nor systematic. *See also* SILLY POLLS; UNOBTRUSIVE MEASURES.

Y

YEASAYER   A respondent who habitually answers questions with "yes" or in the affirmative--regardless of the question asked or their real feelings. Some yeasayers are motivated by hostility or indifference. They simply want to get the interview over quickly. But other yeasayers are so deferential that they try to please interviewers by being agreeable. They may, for example, respond to a series of "agree/disagree" questions by agreeing with all of them, even if some contradict others (Alreck and Settle, 1985:423).

Naysayers, in contrast, are respondents who constantly answer questions in the negative. Of the two, researchers have been more concerned with yeasayers and their effects.   Some studies show that the "social distance" between interviewer and respondent increases yeasaying. It is particularly more common among those with less formal education, and is more frequent among blacks than whites.   Researchers consider yeasaying as a form of social desirability bias-- defined as any psychological influence that encourages respondents to answer questions consistent with social expectations   (Bradburn, 1983:316-318). Interviewer reactivity is responsible for most yea saying, so attention to interview dynamics is emphasized in its prevention (Turner and Martin, 1984:267).   *See also*   AGREE-DISAGREE; INTERVIEWERS; INTER- VIEWING; RESPONDENT.

Bibliography

Abercrombie, N. *Penguin Directory of Sociology*. New York: Penguin, 1988.

Adams, W. C. "Media Coverage of Campaign 84: A Preliminary Report." *Public Opinion* (April/May 1984): 9-10.

Adler, K. "Polling the Attentive Public." *Annals of the American Academy of Political and Social Science* 472 (March 1984): 143-154.

Agranoff, R. *The Management of Election Campaigns*. Boston: Holbrook Press, 1976.

Aldrich, J. *Before the Convention*. Chicago: University of Chicago Press, 1980.

Almond, G. *The American People and Foreign Policy*. New York: Praeger, 1960.

Alreck, P. L., and R. P. Settle. *The Survey Research Handbook*. Homewood, Ill.: Irwin, 1985.

Altschuler, B. *Keeping a Finger on the Public Pulse*. Westport, Conn.: Greenwood, 1982.

American Association for Public Opinion Research. *Code of Professional Ethics and Practices*. New York: AAPOR Directory of Members, 1988.

Anderson, A., A. Basilevsky, and D. Hum. "Measurement Theory and Techniques." In P. H. Rossi et al., eds.; *Handbook of Survey Research*, 231-287. New York: Academic Press, 1983.

Asher, H. *Polling And The Public: What Every Citizen Should Know*. Washington, D.C.: Congressional Quarterly Press, 1988.

Asher, H. B. *Presidential Elections and American Politics*. Chicago: Dorsey Press, 1988.

Atkin, C. K., and J. Gaudino. "The Impact of Polling on the Mass Media." *Annals of the American Academy of Political and Social Science* 472 (March 1984): 119-128.

Babbie, E. R. *Survey Research Methods*. Belmont, Calif.: Wadsworth, 1973.

Babbie, E. R. *Social Research for Consumers*. Belmont, Calif.: Wadsworth, 1982.

Backstrom, C. H., and G. Hursh-Cesar. *Survey Research*. 2nd ed. New York: John Wiley and Sons, 1981.

Bailar, B. A., and C. M. Lamphier. *Development of Survey Methods to Assess Survey Practices*. Washington, D.C.: American Statistical Association, 1978.

Baxter, R. "An Inquiry into the Misuse of the Survey Technique by Sales Solicitors." *Public Opinion Quarterly* 28 (1964): 124-134.

Beville, H. M. *Audience Ratings: Radio, Television, and Cable*. New York, N.Y.: Lerbaum Associates, 1988.

Berelson, B., and M. Janowitz, eds. *Reader in Public Opinion and Communication*. New York: Free Press, 1966.

Berk, R., M. Hennessy, and J. Swan. "The Vagaries and Vulgarities of Scientific Jury Selection: A Methodological Evaluation." *Evaluation Quarterly* (1977); 143-158.

Blakenship, K. *Professional Telephone Surveys*. New York: McGraw-Hill, 1977.

Bogart, B. "Polls Shape Politicians and Campaigns." *Advertising Age* (Feb. 28, 1984); 30-31.

Bogart, L. *Silent Politics: Polls and the Awareness of Public Opinion*. New Brunswick, N.J.: Transaction Books, 1985.

Bohrnstedt, G. W. "Measurement." In P. H. Rossi et al., eds., *Handbook of Survey Research*, 69-121. New York: Academic Press, 1983.

Boyd, Deborah. Unpublished working paper. Boyd Associates, August, 1989.

Bradburn, N. M. "Response Effects." In P. H. Rossi et al., eds.; *Handbook of Survey Research*, 289-328. New York: Academic Press, 1983.

Bradburn, N. M., and W. Mason. "The Effect of Question Order on Responses." *Journal of Marketing Research* 7 Vol. I, No. 4 (Nov. 1964): 57-61.

Bradburn, N. M., and S. Sudman. *Improving Interview Methods and Questionnaire Design*. San Francisco: Jossey-Bass, 1979.

Bradburn, N. M., and S. Sudman. *Polls and Surveys: Understanding What They Tell Us*. San Francisco: Jossey-Bass, 1988.

Campbell, D. J. and J. C. Stanley *Experimental and Quasi Experimental Designs For Research*. Chicago: Rand-McNally, 1963.

Cantril, A. H. ed. *Polling on the Issues*. Cabin John, Md.: Seven Locks Press, 1980.

Cantril, A. H., and C. W. Roll. *Hopes and Fears of the American People*. Washington, D.C.: Potomac Associates, 1971.

Chein, I. "An Introduction to Sampling." Appendix A in C. Selltiz, L. S. Wrightsman, and S. W. Cook, eds., *Research Methods in Social Relations*, 3rd ed.: New York: Holt, Rinehart and Winston, 1976.

Childs, H. L. *Public Opinion: Nature, Formation and Role.* New York: Van Nostrand, 1965.

Clark, L. P. *Introduction to Surveys and Interviews.* Croton-on-Hudson, N.Y.: Policy Studies Associates, 1976.

Cochran, W. G. *Sampling Techniques.* New York: John Wiley and Sons, 1963.

Connors, T. D. *Longman Dictionary of Mass Media and Communications.* New York: Longman, 1982.

Converse, J. M. *Survey Research in the United States, Roots and Emergence.* Berkeley: University of California Press, 1987.

Converse, J. M., and H. Schuman. *Conversations at Random: Survey Research as Interviewers See It.* New York: John Wiley and Sons, 1974.

Converse, P. E. "The Nature of Belief Systems in Mass Publics." In D. E. Apter, ed. *Ideology and Discontent*, 206-261. New York: Free Press, 1964.

Conway, M. M. "The Use of Polls in Congressional, State, and Local Elections." *Annals of the American Academy of Political and Social Science* 472 (March 1984): 97-105.

Council of American Survey Research Organizations. *Code of Standards for Survey Research.* Port Jefferson, N. Y.: CASRO, 1982.

Crespi, I. "Modern Marketing Techniques: They Could Work in Washington Too." *Public Opinion* (June/July 1979): 15-19, 58-59.

Crespi, I. *Public Opinion, Polls and Democracy.* Boulder, Colo.: Westview Press, 1989.

Culver, J. C. "Mr. Smith Goes to Charm School." *Washington Post Weekly* June 29, 1987); 24-25.

Davis, J. A. *Elementary Survey Analysis.* Englewood Cliffs, N.J.: Prentice-Hall, 1971.

DeMaio, T. J. "Social Desirability and Survey Measurement: A Review." In C. F. Turner and E. Martin, eds., *Surveying Subjective Phenomena*, 2: 257-281. New York: Russell Sage Foundation, 1984.

Devine, D. J. *The Attentive Public; Polyarchial Democracy.* Chicago: Rand-McNally, 1970.

Dexter, L. A. *Elite and Specialized Interviewing.* Evanston, Ill.: Northwestern University Press, 1970.

Dillman, D. A. *Mail and Telephone Surveys: The Total Design Method.* New York: John Wiley and Sons, 1978.

Dillman, D. A. "Mail and Other Self-Administered Questionnaires." In P. H. Rossi et al., eds., *Handbook of Survey Research*, 359-377. New York: Academic Press, 1983.

Duncan, M. G., ed. *A Dictionary of Sociology.* Chicago, Ill.: Aldine, 1968.

Ehrenholt, A. "Poll Fever Infects 1986 Campaign Coverage." *Congressional Quarterly* (April 5, 1986); 779.

Erickson, R. S., N. R. Luttbeg, and K. L. Tedin. *American Public Opinion*. New York: Macmillan, 1988.

Farah, B. G. "Delegate Polls: 1944 to 1988." *Public Opinion* (Aug./Sept. 1984); 43-45.

Field, M. D. "Political Opinion Polling in the USA." In R. Worcester, ed. *Political Opinion Polling*, 198-216. New York: St. Martin's Press, 1983.

Fields, J. M., and H. Schuman. "Public Beliefs About the Beliefs of the Public." *Public Opinion Quarterly* 43 (1977): 429-446.

Fowler, F. J. *Survey Research Methods*. Beverly Hills, Calif.: Sage, 1984.

Frankel, M. "Sampling Theory." In P. H. Rossi et al., eds., *Handbook of Survey Research*; 21-67. New York: Academic Press, 1983.

Frankovic, K. "Sex and Politics--New Alignments, Old Issues." *Political Science* 3 (1982): 439-448.

Free, L., and H. Cantril. *The Political Beliefs of Americans*. New Brunswick, N.J.: Rutgers University Press, 1967.

Frey, J. H. *Survey Research by Telephone*. Beverly Hills, Calif.: Sage, 1983.

Gallup, G. "The Quintamensional Plan of Question Design." *Public Opinion Quarterly* 11 (1947); 385-931.

Gallup, G. *The Sophisticated Poll Watcher's Guide*. Princeton, N.J.: Princeton Opinion Press, 1972.

Gallup, G., and S. Rae. *The Pulse of Democracy*. Westport, Conn.: Greenwood Press, 1968.

Gergen, D., and W. Schambra. "Polls and Polling." *Wilson Quarterly* 3, 2 (Spring 1979): 66-78.

Gilfeather, J. "Fund Raising Under the Guise of a Survey." *CASRO Newsletter* 9.5 (1985); 7.

Glasser, G. J., and G. D. Metzger. "Random Digit Dialing as a Method of Telephone Sampling." *Journal of Marketing Research* 9 (1972): 59-64.

Glock, C. Y. *Survey Research in the Social Sciences*. New York: Russell Sage Foundation, 1967.

Gordon, R. L. *Interviewing: Strategy, Techniques, and Tactics*. Homewood, Ill.: Dorsey Press, 1969.

Gould, J., and W. L. Kolb. *A Dictionary of the Social Sciences*. New York: Free Press, 1964.

Graber, D. A. *Mass Media and American Politics*. Washington, D.C.: Congressional Quarterly Press, 1980.

Groves, R. M., and R. L. Kahn. *Surveys by Telephone*. New York: Academic Press, 1979.

Groves, R. M., and L. J. Magilavy. "Increasing Response Rates to Telephone Surveys: A Door in the Face for a Foot in the Door." *Public Opinion Quarterly* 45 (1981): 346-358.

Groves, R. M., and L. J. Magilavy. "Measuring and Explaining Interviewer Effects in Centralized Telephone Interviews." *Public Opinion Quarterly* 50 (1986): 251-266.

Hansen, H., N. Hurwitz, and G. Madow. *Sample Survey Methods and Theory.* New York: John Wiley and Sons, 1953.

Harris, L. "Polls and Politics in the United States." *Public Opinion Quarterly* 27 (1963): 3-8.

Harris, L. *The Anguish of Change.* New York: W. W. Norton, 1973.

Hartmann, E. "Public Reaction to Public Opinion Surveying." *Public Opinion Quarterly* 32 (1968): 295-298.

Hastings, E. H., and P. K. Hastings. *Index to International Public Opinion 1988-1989.* Westport, Conn.: Greenwood Press, 1990.

Heidepriem, N., and C. C. Lake. "The Winning Edge." *Polling Report* 3.7 (1987) 1, 6-7.

Hennessey, B. *Public Opinion.* 5th ed. Monterey, Calif.: Brooks/Cole Publishing, 1985.

Hill, D. "Letter Opinion on ERA: A Test of the Newspaper Bias Hypothesis." *Public Opinion Quarterly* 45 (1981): 384-392.

Hirsch, T., and H. Selvin. *Principles of Survey Research.* New York: Free Press, 1973.

Hoinville, G. W., and R. M. Jowell. *Survey Research Practice.* London: Heinemann, 1978.

Hollander, S. "Toward Responsibility in Reporting Opinion Surveys." *Public Opinion Quarterly* 35 (1971): 335-349.

Hyman, H. H. *Survey Design and Analysis.* New York: Free Press, 1955.

Hyman, H. H. *Secondary Analysis of Sample Surveys: Principals, Procedures, and Potentialities.* New York: John Wiley and Sons, 1972.

Isaac, S., and W. B. Michael. *Handbook in Research and Evaluation.* San Diego, Calif.: Edits Publishers, 1971.

Ismach, A. H. "Polling as a News Gathering Tool." *Annals of the American Academy of Political and Social Science* 472 (March 1984): 106-118.

Johnson, J. B., and R. Joslyn. *Political Science Research Methods.* Washington, D.C.: Congressional Quarterly Press, 1986.

Kahn, R. L., and C. F. Cannell. *The Dynamics of Interviewing.* New York: John Wiley and Sons, 1967.

Kalton, G. *Introduction to Survey Sampling.* Beverly Hills, Calif.: Sage, 1983.

Kaplan, A. *The Conduct of Inquiry.* San Francisco: Chandler, 1964.

Karweit, N., and E. D. Myers, Jr. "Computers in Survey Research." In P. H. Rossi et al., eds. *Handbook Of Survey Research, 379-414. New York: Academic Press, 1983.*

Kendall, M. G., and W. R. Buckland. A Dictionary of Statistical Terms. 4th ed. New York: John Wiley and Sons, 1983.

Key, V. O. Jr. *Public Opinion And American Democracy.* New York: Knopf, 1967.

King, R., and M. Schnitzer. "Contemporary Use of Private Political Polling." *Public Opinion Quarterly* 32 (1968): 431-436.

Kirkpatrick, J. J. *The New Presidential Elite*. New York: Russell Sage Foundation, 1976.

Kish, L. "A Procedure for Objective Respondent Selection Within the Household." *Journal of the American Statistical Association* 44 (1949): 338-387.

Kish, L. *Survey Sampling*. New York: John Wiley and Sons, 1965.

Kornhauser, A., and P. B. Sheatsley. "Questionnaire Construction and Interview Procedure." Appendix B in C. Selltiz, L. S. Wrightsman, and S. W. Cook, eds., *Research Methods in Social Relations*. 3rd ed. New York: Holt, Reinhart and Winston, 1976.

Krewski, D., R. Platex, and J. N. K. Rao. *Current Topics in Survey Sampling*. New York: Academic Press, 1981.

Kuhn, T. S., *The Structure of Scientific Revolution*. Chicago: University of Chicago Press, 1962.

Labaw, P. *Advanced Questionnaire Design*. Boston: Abt Books, 1981.

Lake, C. C. *Public Opinion Polling: A Handbook for Public Interest and Citizen Advocacy Groups*. Washington, D.C. Island Press, 1987.

Landon, E. L., Jr., and S. K. Banks. "Relative Efficiency and Bias of Plus-One Telephone Sampling," *Journal of Marketing Research* 14 (1977): 294-299.

Lazarsfeld, P. "The Art of Asking Why: Three Principles Underlying the Formulation of Questionnaires." In D. Katz, ed., *Public Opinion and Propaganda*, 675-686. New York: Dryden, 1954.

Lazarsfeld, P. F., and M. Rosenberg eds. *The Language of Social Research*. New York: The Free Press, 1955.

Levy, M. "The Methodology and Performance of Election Day Polls." *Public Opinion Quarterly* 47 (1983): 54-67.

Levy, M. "Polling and the Presidential Election." *The Annals of the American Academy of Political and Social Science*, 472 (March 1984): 86-96.

Lewis, T. A., and W. Schneider. "Is the Public Lying to the Pollsters?" *Public Opinion* (April/May 1982): 42-47.

Link, R. "The Literary Digest Poll: Appearances Can Be Deceiving." *Public Opinion* (Feb./March 1980): 16-19.

Lippman, W. *The Phantom Publics!* New York: Harcourt Brace, 1925.

Lippman, W. *The Public Philosophy*. Boston: Little, Brown, 1960.

Lippman, W. *Public Opinion*. New York: Free Press, 1965.

Lipset, S. M. "The Wavering Polls." *Public Interest* 7 (1976): 70-89.

Lucy, W. H. "Polls Primaries and Presidential Nominations." *Journal of Politics* 35 (1973): 830-848.

Marsh, C. *The Survey Method*. London: George Allen and Unwin, 1982.

Martin, E. "Surveys As Social Indicators." In P. H. Rossi et al., eds. *Handbook of Survey Research*, 677-743. New York: Academic Press, 1983.

Martin, L. J. "The Genealogy of Public Opinion Polling." *Annals of the American Academy of Political and Social Science* 472 (March 1984): 12-23.

Mauser, G. A. *Political Marketing: An Approach to Campaign Strategy.* New York: Praeger, 1983.

Mendelsohn, H. A., and I. Crespi. *Polls, Television and the New Politics.* Scranton, Pa.: Chandler, 1970.

Meyer, P. *Precision Journalism: A Reporter's Introduction to Social Science Methods.* Bloomington: Indiana University Press, 1973.

Miller, M. M., and R. Hurd. "Conformity to AAPOR Standards in Newspaper Reporting of Public Opinion Polls." *Public Opinion Quarterly* 46 (1982): 243-249.

Mitofsky, W. J., and M. Plissner. "A Reporter's Guide to Published Polls." *Public Opinion* (June/July 1980): 16-19.

Mitofsky, W. J., and M. Plissner. "The Making of the Delegates, 1968-1980." *Public Opinion* (Oct./Nov. 1980): 37-43.

Morin, R. "The Quick and Dirty Polls on the Iran Hearings Are Just That." *Washington Post Weekly* (Aug. 3, 1987): 37.

Morin, R. "Wanted: Experienced, Older Male Candidate Without a Lot of Money." *Washington Post Weekly* (Aug. 10, 1987): 37.

Morin, R. "An Early Lead in the Polls Is a Mixed Blessing." *Washington Post Weekly* (Sept. 7, 1987): 37.

Mosher, C. A., and G. Kalton. *Survey Methods in Social Investigation.* 2nd ed. New York: Basic Books, 1972.

National Council on Public Polls. *Principles of Disclosure.* Washington, D.C.: NCPP, 1979.

Nederhof, A. J. "The Effects of Material Incentives in Mail Surveys: Two Studies." *Public Opinion Quarterly* 47 (1983): 103-111.

Nieburg, H. L. *Public Opinion: Tracking and Targeting.* New York: Praeger, 1984.

Niemi, R. G., J. Mueller, and T. W. Smith. *Trends in Public Opinion: A Compendium of Survey Data.* Westport, Conn.: Greenwood Press, 1989.

Noelle-Neumann, E. "The Spiral of Silence: A Theory of Public Opinion." *Journal of Communication* 24 (1974): 43-51.

Noelle-Neumann, E. *The Spiral of Silence.* Chicago: University of Chicago Press, 1984.

O'Gorman, H. J. "White and Black Perceptions of Racial Values." *Public Opinion Quarterly* 43 (1979): 48-59.

Oppenheim, A. N. *Questionnaire Design and Attitude Measurement.* New York: Basic Books, 1966.

Paletz, D. "Polls in the Media: Content, Credibility and Consequences." *Public Opinion Quarterly* 44 (1980): 495-513.

Paletz, D., J. Short, H. Baler, B. Campbell, R. Cooper, and R. Oeslander. "Polls in the Media: Content, Credibility, and Consequences." *Public Opinion Quarterly* 44 (1980): 495-513.

Parten, M. *Surveys, Polls, and Samples: Practical Procedures.* New York: Cooper Square Publishers, 1966.

Payne, S. L. *The Art of Asking Questions.* Princeton, N.J.: Princeton University Press, 1951.

Perry, P. "Certain Problems in Election Survey Methodology." *Public Opinion Quarterly* 43 (1979): 312-324.

Plano, J. L., R. E. Riggs, and H. S. Robin. *The Dictionary of Political Analysis.* Santa Barbara, Calif.: ABC-CLIO, 1982.

Pool, I. de Sola, and R. Abelson. "The Simulmatics Project." *Public Opinion Quarterly* 25 (1961): 167-183.

Raj, D. *The Design of Sample Surveys.* New York: McGraw-Hill, 1972.

Roberts, G. K. *A Dictionary of Political Analysis.* New York: St. Martin's Press, 1971.

Robinson, C. *Straw Votes.* New York: Columbia University Press, 1932.

Robinson, J. P., and R. G. Meadow. *Polls Apart.* Cabin John, Md.: Seven Locks Press, 1982.

Rogers, L. *The Pollsters.* New York: Knopf, 1949.

Roll, C. W. Jr., and A. H. Cantril. *Polls: Their Use and Misuse in Politics.* New York: Basic Books, 1972.

Roper, B. W. "The Media and the Polls: A Boxscore." *Public Opinion* (Feb./March 1980): 46-49.

Roper, B. W. "Are Polls Accurate" *The Annals of the American Academy of Political and Social Science* 472 (March 1984): 24-34.

Roper, B. W. "Early Election Calls: The Larger Dangers." *Public Opinion Quarterly* 49 (1985): 5-9.

Roper, B. W. "Political Polls." *Society* (May/June 1985): 28-31.

Rosenberg, L., ed. *The Roots of Marketing Strategy: A Collection of Pre 1958 Readings.* New York: Arno Press, 1978.

Rosenberg, M. *The Logic of Survey Analysis.* New York: Basic Books, 1968.

Rosenstone, S. J. *Forecasting Presidential Elections.* New Haven: Yale University Press, 1983.

Rossi, P. H., J. D. Wright, and A. B. Anderson. "Sample Surveys: History, Current Practice, and Future Prospects." In P. H. Rossi, et al., eds., *Handbook of Survey Research,* 1-20. New York: Academic Press, 1983.

Sabato, L. *The Rise of the Political Consultant.* New York: Basic Books, 1981.

Salant, R. "Projections and Exit Polls." *Public Opinion Quarterly* 49 (1985): 9-15.

Salmon, C. T., and J. S. Nichols. "The Next Birthday Method of Respondent Selection." *Public Opinion Quarterly* 47 (1983): 270-276.

Salmore, B. G., and S. A. Salmore. *Candidates, Parties and Campaigns*. 2nd ed. Washington D.C.: C.Q. Press, 1989.

Schuman, H. "Editorial Statement: 1987." *Public Opinion Quarterly* 51 (1987): 1-2.

Schuman, H., and S. Presser. *Questions and Answers in Attitude Surveys*. New York: Academic Press, 1981.

Schwartzman, E. *Political Campaign Craftsmanship*. New York: Transaction Books, 1988.

Selltiz, C., L. S. Wrightsman, and S. W. Cook. *Research Methods in Social Relations*. New York: Holt, Rinehart and Winston, 1976.

Sheatsley, P. B. "Questionnaire Construction and Item Writing." In P. H. Rossi et al., eds. *Handbook of Survey Research*, 195-231. New York: Academic Press, 1983.

Smith, H. W. *Strategies of Social Research*. Englewood Cliffs, N.J.: Prentice-Hall, 1975.

Smith, T. W. "In Search of House Effect: A Comparison of Responses to Various Questions by Different Survey Organizations." *Public Opinion Quarterly* 42 (1978): 443-463.

Smith, T. W. "America's Most Important Problem--A Trend Analysis, 1946-1976." *Public Opinion Quarterly* 44 (1980): 164-180.

Smith, T. W. "The Polls: "America's Most Important Problems." *Public Opinion Quarterly* 49 (1985): 264-274, 403-410.

Smith, T. W. "System Masters the Datamaster." *AAPOR Newsletter* (Spring 1987): 2.

Stephenson, D. G., Jr., R. J. Bresler, R. J. Friedrich and J.J. Karlesky. *American Government*. New York: Harper and Row, 1988.

Sudman, S. "The Uses of Telephone Directories for Survey Sampling." *Journal of Marketing Research* 10 (1973): 204-207.

Sudman, S. *Applied Sampling*. New York: Academic Press, 1978.

Sudman, S. "Applied Sampling." In P. H. Rossi et al., eds. *Handbook of Survey Research*, 145-193. New York: Academic Press, 1983a.

Sudman, S. "The Network Polls: A Critical Review." *Public Opinion Quarterly* 47 (1983b): 490-496.

Sudman, S. "Do Exit Polls Influence Voting Behavior?" *Public Opinion Quarterly* 50 (1986): 331-339.

Sudman, S., and N. M. Bradburn. *Response Effects in Surveys*. Chicago: Aldine, 1974.

Survey Research Center. *Interviewer's Manual*. Ann Arbor: Institute for Social Research, University of Michigan, 1976.

Sussman, B. "His Approval Rating and 50 Cents Will Get Reagan a Cup of Coffee." *Washington Post Weekly* (Nov. 23, 1985): 37.

Sussman, B. "Do Blacks Approve of Reagan? It Depends Who's Asking." *Washington Post Weekly* (Feb. 10, 1986): 37.

Times Mirror. *The People, The Press, and Politics.* A Times Mirror Study of the American Electorate. Conducted by the Gallup Organization. September 1987.

Troldahl, V., and R. Carter. "Random Selection of Respondents Within Households in Phone Surveys." *Journal of Marketing Research* 1 (1964): 71-76.

Tufte, E. R., and R. A. Sun. "Are There Bellwether Electoral Districts?" *Public Opinion Quarterly* 39 (1975): 1-18.

Tull, R. S., and D. I. Hawkins. *Marketing Research.* New York: Macmillan, 1980.

Turner, C. F., and E. Martin, eds. *Surveying Subjective Phenomena*, Vol. 1. New York: Russell Sage Foundation, 1984.

Waksberg, J. "Sampling Methods for Random Digit Dialing." *Journal of the American Statistical Association* 73 (March 1978): 40-46.

Warwick, D. P., and C. A. Lininger. *The Sample Survey: Theory and Practice.* New York: McGraw-Hill, 1975.

Webb, E. J., D. T. Campbell, R. D. Schwartz, and L. Sechrest. *Unobstrusive Measures: Non-Reactive Research in the Social Sciences.* Chicago: Rand-McNally, 1966.

Weinberg, E. "Data Collection: Planning and Management." In P. H. Rossi et al. eds. *Handbook of Survey Research*, 329-358. New York: Academic Press, 1983.

Weisberg, H. F., and B. Bowen. *Introduction to Survey Research and Data Analysis.* San Francisco: W. H. Freeman, 1977.

Weisberg, H. F., J. A. Krosnick, and B. D. Bowen. *An Introduction To Survey Research And Data Analysis.* New York: W. H. Freeman, 1989.

Weiss, C. H., and H. Hatry. *An Introduction to Sample Surveys for Government Managers.* Washington, D.C.: Urban Institute, 1971.

Welch, S., and J. C. Comer eds. *Public Opinion: Its Formation, Measurement and Impact.* Palo Alto, Calif.: Mayfield Publishing, 1975.

Welch, S., and J. C. Comer. *Quantitative Methods for Public Administration.* Homewood, Ill.: Dorsey Press, 1983.

Wheeler, M. "Primaries and Opinion Polls." *The Atlantic Monthly* 229 (1972): 6-8.

Wheeler, M. *Lies, Damn Lies and Statistics: The Manipulation of Public Opinion in America.* New York: W. W. Norton, 1976.

Wilhoit, G. C., and D. H. Weaver. *Newsroom Guide to Polls and Surveys.* Washington, D.C.: American Newspaper Publishers Association, 1980.

Williams, W. H. *A Sampler on Sampling.* New York: John Wiley and Sons, 1978.

Williamson, J., D. Karp, J. Dalphin, and P. Gray. *The Research Craft.* 2nd ed. Boston: Little, Brown, 1982.

Wilson, T. E. *Researchers Guide to Statistics.* Lanham, Md.: University Press of America, 1980.

Winfrey, L. "Nielsen Is Giving TV Ratings Game A New Set of Rules." July 12, 1987: 1G, 12G.

Wolman, B. *Dictionary of Behavioral Science.* New York: Van Nostdrand Reinhold, 1973.

Worcester, R. M. ed. *Consumer Market Research Handbook.* New York: McGraw-Hill, 1972.

Worcester, R. M. *Political Opinion Polling.* New York: St. Martin's Press, 1983.

Young, M. L. "Distribution of Exit Poll Questions by Type." Unpublished working paper; Institute of State and Regional Affairs, Penn State at Harrisburg, 1986.

Young, M. L.   "Alternate Scenarios for Gubernatorial Revote Question." Working papers, 1989.

Young, M. L. *American Dictionary of Campaigns and Elections.* Lanham, Md.: Hamilton Books, 1987.

Young, M. L. *The Classics of Polling.* Metuchen, N. J.: Scarecrow Press, 1990.

Young, P. V. *Scientific Social Surveys and Research.* Englewood Cliffs, N. J.: Prentice-Hall, 1966.

Zdep, S. M., and I. N. Rhodes.   "Making the Randomized Response Techniques Work." *Public Opinion Quarterly* 40 (1976): 531-537.

Index

Page numbers in bold refer to main entries.

About the Author

MICHAEL L. YOUNG is Professor of Politics and Public Affairs at Pennsylvania State University in Harrisburg. He is the author of *The American Dictionary of Campaigns and Elections* (1987) and *The Classics of Polling* (1989) and is active as a pollster, media analyst on radio and TV, and consultant to the private and public sectors. Currently he is also Associate Director of the Institute of State and Regional Affairs on the Penn State/Harrisburg campus.